Praise for *The Enterprise Big Data Lake*

Alex is a visionary in the data industry. He has encapsulated his practical insights into a thorough treatise examining the technical considerations, firm-wide implications, and leveraged business impact of transitioning to a data-driven enterprise. This is a book for any business or technical professional who wishes to succeed with data.

—*Keyur Desai, Chief Data Officer, TD Ameritrade*

Data lakes are essential in achieving many of the benefits of decision- and analytics-driven solutions. This book does a great job clarifying the architecture of data lakes, what value they provide, what challenges they pose, and how to address those challenges.

—*Jari Koister, VP of Product and Technology, FICO, and professor in the data science program at UC Berkeley, California*

Big Data is one of the most confusing terms in the industry today. This book breaks down the components into easy, understandable terms and explains the best ways to approach such projects. I found the sections that articulate the interconnectedness of data streams, data ponds, and data lakes especially helpful. The book is a must-read for any executive looking to understand and educate themselves on contemporary methods of analytics.

—*Opinder Bawa, Vice President and Chief Information Officer, University of San Francisco*

I can't wait to share this book with managers I know who have joined data lake teams and need an introduction to the tools and terms they will need to converse and understand their new teams. They will also get a great idea for the direction they should try and steer their teams. This book is a great place to start, whether you are building a data lake or have inherited one.

—*Nicole Schwartz, Agile and Technical Product Management consultant*

The Enterprise Big Data Lake

*Delivering the Promise of Big Data
and Data Science*

Alex Gorelik

Beijing · Boston · Farnham · Sebastopol · Tokyo

The Enterprise Big Data Lake

by Alex Gorelik

Published by O'Reilly Media, Inc., 1005 Gravenstein Highway North, Sebastopol, CA 95472.

O'Reilly books may be purchased for educational, business, or sales promotional use. Online editions are also available for most titles (*http://oreilly.com*). For more information, contact our corporate/institutional sales department: 800-998-9938 or *corporate@oreilly.com*.

Editor: Andy Oram
Production Editor: Kristen Brown
Copyeditor: Rachel Head
Proofreader: Rachel Monaghan

Indexer: Ellen Troutman Zaig
Interior Designer: David Futato
Cover Designer: Karen Montgomery
Illustrator: Rebecca Demarest

March 2019:   First Edition

Revision History for the First Edition
2019-02-19:   First Release

See *http://oreilly.com/catalog/errata.csp?isbn=9781491931554* for release details.

978-1-491-93155-4

[LSI]

Table of Contents

Preface. ix

1. Introduction to Data Lakes. 1
    Data Lake Maturity   3
      Data Puddles   5
      Data Ponds   6
    Creating a Successful Data Lake   7
      The Right Platform   7
      The Right Data   8
      The Right Interface   9
      The Data Swamp   11
    Roadmap to Data Lake Success   12
      Standing Up a Data Lake   13
      Organizing the Data Lake   14
      Setting Up the Data Lake for Self-Service   15
    Data Lake Architectures   20
      Data Lakes in the Public Cloud   20
      Logical Data Lakes   21
    Conclusion   24

2. Historical Perspective. 25
    The Drive for Self-Service Data—The Birth of Databases   25
    The Analytics Imperative—The Birth of Data Warehousing   28
    The Data Warehouse Ecosystem   29
      Storing and Querying the Data   31
      Loading the Data—Data Integration Tools   37
      Organizing and Managing the Data   41
      Consuming the Data   46

    Conclusion   47

3. Introduction to Big Data and Data Science. **49**
    Hadoop Leads the Historic Shift to Big Data   50
      The Hadoop File System   50
      How Processing and Storage Interact in a MapReduce Job   51
      Schema on Read   53
      Hadoop Projects   53
    Data Science   55
    What Should Your Analytics Organization Focus On?   56
    Machine Learning   59
      Explainability   60
      Change Management   61
    Conclusion   62

4. Starting a Data Lake. **63**
    The What and Why of Hadoop   63
    Preventing Proliferation of Data Puddles   66
    Taking Advantage of Big Data   67
      Leading with Data Science   67
      Strategy 1: Offload Existing Functionality   70
      Strategy 2: Data Lakes for New Projects   71
      Strategy 3: Establish a Central Point of Governance   72
      Which Way Is Right for You?   73
    Conclusion   74

5. From Data Ponds/Big Data Warehouses to Data Lakes. **75**
    Essential Functions of a Data Warehouse   76
      Dimensional Modeling for Analytics   77
      Integrating Data from Disparate Sources   78
      Preserving History Using Slowly Changing Dimensions   78
      Limitations of the Data Warehouse as a Historical Repository   78
    Moving to a Data Pond   79
      Keeping History in a Data Pond   79
      Implementing Slowly Changing Dimensions in a Data Pond   81
    Growing Data Ponds into a Data Lake—Loading Data That's Not in the Data
      Warehouse   83
      Raw Data   83
      External Data   84
      Internet of Things (IoT) and Other Streaming Data   86
    Real-Time Data Lakes   87
    The Lambda Architecture   89

Data Transformations   90
Target Systems   92
    Data Warehouses   93
    Operational Data Stores   93
    Real-Time Applications and Data Products   93
Conclusion   95

6. Optimizing for Self-Service. 97
The Beginnings of Self-Service   98
Business Analysts   100
    Finding and Understanding Data—Documenting the Enterprise   101
    Establishing Trust   103
    Provisioning   110
    Preparing Data for Analysis   112
Data Wrangling in the Data Lake   113
    Situating Data Preparation in Hadoop   113
    Common Use Cases for Data Preparation   114
Analyzing and Visualizing   116
The New World of Self-Service Business Intelligence   116
    The New Analytic Workflow   117
    Gatekeepers to Shopkeepers   118
    Governing Self-Service   119
Conclusion   120

7. Architecting the Data Lake. 121
Organizing the Data Lake   121
    Landing or Raw Zone   123
    Gold Zone   123
    Work Zone   125
    Sensitive Zone   125
Multiple Data Lakes   127
    Advantages of Keeping Data Lakes Separate   127
    Advantages of Merging the Data Lakes   128
Cloud Data Lakes   129
Virtual Data Lakes   131
    Data Federation   131
    Big Data Virtualization   132
    Eliminating Redundancy   134
Conclusion   136

8. Cataloging the Data Lake. 137
Organizing the Data   137

Technical Metadata	138
Business Metadata	143
Tagging	145
Automated Cataloging	146
Logical Data Management	147
Sensitive Data Management and Access Control	147
Data Quality	149
Relating Disparate Data	151
Establishing Lineage	152
Data Provisioning	153
Tools for Building a Catalog	154
Tool Comparison	155
The Data Ocean	156
Conclusion	156

9. Governing Data Access. **157**

Authorization or Access Control	158
Tag-Based Data Access Policies	159
Deidentifying Sensitive Data	162
Data Sovereignty and Regulatory Compliance	165
Self-Service Access Management	167
Provisioning Data	171
Conclusion	177

10. Industry-Specific Perspectives. **179**

Big Data in Financial Services	180
Consumers, Digitization, and Data Are Changing Finance as We Know It	180
Saving the Bank	182
New Opportunities Offered by New Data	185
Key Processes in Making Use of the Data Lake	188
Value Added by Data Lakes in Financial Services	190
Data Lakes in the Insurance Industry	192
Smart Cities	193
Big Data in Medicine	195

Index. **197**

Preface

In recent years many enterprises have begun experimenting with using big data and cloud technologies to build data lakes and support data-driven culture and decision making—but the projects often stall or fail because the approaches that worked at internet companies have to be adapted for the enterprise, and there is no comprehensive practical guide on how to successfully do that. I wrote this book with the hope of providing such a guide.

In my roles as executive at IBM and Informatica (major data technology vendors), Entrepreneur in Residence at Menlo Ventures (a leading VC firm), and founder and CTO of Waterline (a big data startup), I've been fortunate to have had the opportunity to speak with hundreds of experts, visionaries, industry analysts, and hands-on practitioners about the challenges of building successful data lakes and creating a data-driven culture. This book is a synthesis of the themes and best practices that I've encountered across industries (from social media to banking and government agencies) and roles (from chief data officers and other IT executives to data architects, data scientists, and business analysts).

Big data, data science, and analytics supporting data-driven decision making promise to bring unprecedented levels of insight and efficiency to everything from how we work with data to how we work with customers to the search for a cure for cancer—but data science and analytics depend on having access to historical data. In recognition of this, companies are deploying big data lakes to bring all their data together in one place and start saving history, so data scientists and analysts have access to the information they need to enable data-driven decision making. Enterprise big data lakes bridge the gap between the freewheeling culture of modern internet companies, where data is core to all practices, everyone is an analyst, and most people can code and roll their own data sets, and enterprise data warehouses, where data is a precious commodity, carefully tended to by professional IT personnel and provisioned in the form of carefully prepared reports and analytic data sets.

To be successful, enterprise data lakes must provide three new capabilities:

- Cost-effective, scalable storage and computing, so large amounts of data can be stored and analyzed without incurring prohibitive computational costs
- Cost-effective data access and governance, so everyone can find and use the right data without incurring expensive human costs associated with programming and manual ad hoc data acquisition
- Tiered, governed access, so different levels of data can be available to different users based on their needs and skill levels and applicable data governance policies

Hadoop, Spark, NoSQL databases, and elastic cloud–based systems are exciting new technologies that deliver on the first promise of cost-effective, scalable storage and computing. While they are still maturing and face some of the challenges inherent to any new technology, they are rapidly stabilizing and becoming mainstream. However, these powerful enabling technologies do not deliver on the other two promises of cost-effective and tiered data access. So, as enterprises create large clusters and ingest vast amounts of data, they find that instead of a data lake, they end up with a data swamp—a large repository of unusable data sets that are impossible to navigate or make sense of, and too dangerous to rely on for any decisions.

This book guides readers through the considerations and best practices of delivering on all the promises of the big data lake. It discusses various approaches to starting and growing a data lake, including data puddles (analytical sandboxes) and data ponds (big data warehouses), as well as building data lakes from scratch. It explores the pros and cons of different data lake architectures—on premises, cloud-based, and virtual—and covers setting up different zones to house everything from raw, untreated data to carefully managed and summarized data, and governing access to those zones. It explains how to enable self-service so that users can find, understand, and provision data themselves; how to provide different interfaces to users with different skill levels; and how to do all of that in compliance with enterprise data governance policies.

Who Should Read This Book?

This book is intended for the following audiences at large traditional enterprises:

- Data services and governance teams: chief data officers and data stewards
- IT executives and architects: chief technology officers and big data architects
- Analytics teams: data scientists, data engineers, data analysts, and heads of analytics

- Compliance teams: chief information security officers, data protection officers, information security analysts, and regulatory compliance heads

The book leverages my 30-year career developing leading-edge data technology and working with some of the world's largest enterprises on their thorniest data problems. It draws on best practices from the world's leading big data companies and enterprises, with essays and success stories from hands-on practitioners and industry experts to provide a comprehensive guide to architecting and deploying a successful big data lake. If you're interested in taking advantage of what these exciting new big data technologies and approaches offer to the enterprise, this book is an excellent place to start. Management may want to read it once and refer to it periodically as big data issues come up in the workplace, while for hands-on practitioners it can serve as a useful reference as they are planning and executing big data lake projects.

Conventions Used in This Book

The following typographical conventions are used in this book:

Italic
: Indicates new terms, URLs, email addresses, filenames, and file extensions.

`Constant width`
: Used for program listings, as well as within paragraphs to refer to program elements such as variable or function names, databases, data types, environment variables, statements, and keywords.

`Constant width italic`
: Shows text that should be replaced with user-supplied values or by values determined by context.

O'Reilly Online Learning

 For almost 40 years, *O'Reilly Media* has provided technology and business training, knowledge, and insight to help companies succeed.

Our unique network of experts and innovators share their knowledge and expertise through books, articles, conferences, and our online learning platform. O'Reilly's online learning platform gives you on-demand access to live training courses, in-depth learning paths, interactive coding environments, and a vast collection of text and video from O'Reilly and 200+ other publishers. For more information, please visit *http://oreilly.com*.

How to Contact Us

Please address comments and questions concerning this book to the publisher:

O'Reilly Media, Inc.
1005 Gravenstein Highway North
Sebastopol, CA 95472
800-998-9938 (in the United States or Canada)
707-829-0515 (international or local)
707-829-0104 (fax)

We have a web page for this book, where we list errata, examples, and any additional information. You can access this page at *http://bit.ly/Enterprise-Big-Data-Lake*.

To comment or ask technical questions about this book, send email to *bookquestions@oreilly.com*.

For more information about our books, courses, conferences, and news, see our website at *http://www.oreilly.com*.

Find us on Facebook: *http://facebook.com/oreilly*

Follow us on Twitter: *http://twitter.com/oreillymedia*

Watch us on YouTube: *http://www.youtube.com/oreillymedia*

Acknowledgments

First and foremost, I want to express my deep gratitude to all the experts and practitioners who shared their stories, expertise, and best practices with me—this book is for and about you!

A great thank you also to all the people who helped me work on this project. This is my first book, and I truly would not have been able to do it without their help. Thanks to:

- The O'Reilly team: Andy Oram, my O'Reilly editor, who breathed new life into this book as I was running out of steam and helped bring it from a stream of consciousness to some level of coherency; Tim McGovern, the original editor who helped get this book off the ground; and Rachel Head, the copyeditor who shocked me with how many more improvements could still be made to the book after over two years of writing, editing, rewriting, reviewing, more rewriting, more editing, more rewriting...; and Kristen Brown, who shepherded the book through the production process.

- The industry contributors who shared their thoughts and best practices in essays and whose names and bios you will find next to their essays inside the book

- The reviewers who made huge improvements with their fresh perspective, critical eye, and industry expertise: Sanjeev Mohan, Opinder Bawa, and Nicole Schwartz

Finally, this book would not have happened without the support and love of my wonderful family—my wife, Irina; my kids, Hannah, Jane, Lisa, and John; and my mom, Regina—my friends, and my wonderful Waterline family.

CHAPTER 1

Introduction to Data Lakes

Data-driven decision making is changing how we work and live. From data science, machine learning, and advanced analytics to real-time dashboards, decision makers are demanding data to help make decisions. Companies like Google, Amazon, and Facebook are data-driven juggernauts that are taking over traditional businesses by leveraging data. Financial services organizations and insurance companies have always been data driven, with quants and automated trading leading the way. The Internet of Things (IoT) is changing manufacturing, transportation, agriculture, and healthcare. From governments and corporations in every vertical to non-profits and educational institutions, data is being seen as a game changer. Artificial intelligence and machine learning are permeating all aspects of our lives. The world is bingeing on data because of the potential it represents. We even have a term for this binge: *big data*, defined by Doug Laney of Gartner in terms of the three Vs (volume, variety, and velocity), to which he later added a fourth and, in my opinion, the most important V—veracity.

With so much variety, volume, and velocity, the old systems and processes are no longer able to support the data needs of the enterprise. Veracity is an even bigger problem for advanced analytics and artificial intelligence, where the principle of "GIGO" (garbage in = garbage out) is even more critical because it is virtually impossible to tell whether the data was bad and caused bad decisions in statistical and machine learning models or the model was bad.

To support these endeavors and address these challenges, a revolution is occurring in data management around how data is stored, processed, managed, and provided to the decision makers. Big data technology is enabling scalability and cost efficiency orders of magnitude greater than what's possible with traditional data management infrastructure. Self-service is taking over from the carefully crafted and labor-intensive approaches of the past, where armies of IT professionals created well-governed data warehouses and data marts, but took months to make any changes.

The *data lake* is a daring new approach that harnesses the power of big data technology and marries it with agility of self-service. Most large enterprises today either have deployed or are in the process of deploying data lakes.

This book is based on discussions with over a hundred organizations, ranging from the new data-driven companies like Google, LinkedIn, and Facebook to governments and traditional corporate enterprises, about their data lake initiatives, analytic projects, experiences, and best practices. The book is intended for IT executives and practitioners who are considering building a data lake, are in the process of building one, or have one already but are struggling to make it productive and widely adopted.

What's a data lake? Why do we need it? How is it different from what we already have? This chapter gives a brief overview that will get expanded in detail in the following chapters. In an attempt to keep the summary succinct, I am not going to explain and explore each term and concept in detail here, but will save the in-depth discussion for subsequent chapters.

Data-driven decision making is all the rage. From data science, machine learning, and advanced analytics to real-time dashboards, decision makers are demanding data to help make decisions. This data needs a home, and the data lake is the preferred solution for creating that home. The term was invented and first described by James Dixon, CTO of Pentaho, who wrote in his blog (*https://jamesdixon.wordpress.com/ 2010/10/14/pentaho-hadoop-and-data-lakes/*): "If you think of a datamart as a store of bottled water—cleansed and packaged and structured for easy consumption—the data lake is a large body of water in a more *natural* state. The contents of the data lake stream in from a source to fill the lake, and *various users* of the lake can come to examine, dive in, or take samples." I italicized the critical points, which are:

- The data is in its original form and format (*natural* or raw data).
- The data is used by *various users* (i.e., accessed and accessible by a large user community).

This book is all about how to build a data lake that brings raw (as well as processed) data to a large user community of business analysts rather than just using it for IT-driven projects. The reason to make raw data available to analysts is so they can perform self-service analytics. Self-service has been an important mega-trend toward democratization of data. It started at the point of usage with self-service visualization tools like Tableau and Qlik (sometimes called *data discovery* tools) that let analysts analyze data without having to get help from IT. The self-service trend continues with data preparation tools that help analysts shape the data for analytics, and catalog tools that help analysts find the data that they need and data science tools that help perform advanced analytics. For even more advanced analytics generally referred to as data science, a new class of users called data scientists also usually make a data lake their primary data source.

Of course, a big challenge with self-service is governance and data security. Everyone agrees that data has to be kept safe, but in many regulated industries, there are prescribed data security policies that have to be implemented and it is illegal to give analysts access to all data. Even in some non-regulated industries, it is considered a bad idea. The question becomes, how do we make data available to the analysts without violating internal and external data compliance regulations? This is sometimes called data democratization and will be discussed in detail in subsequent chapters.

Data Lake Maturity

The data lake is a relatively new concept, so it is useful to define some of the stages of maturity you might observe and to clearly articulate the differences between these stages:

- A *data puddle* is basically a single-purpose or single-project data mart built using big data technology. It is typically the first step in the adoption of big data technology. The data in a data puddle is loaded for the purpose of a single project or team. It is usually well known and well understood, and the reason that big data technology is used instead of traditional data warehousing is to lower cost and provide better performance.

- A *data pond* is a collection of data puddles. It may be like a poorly designed data warehouse, which is effectively a collection of colocated data marts, or it may be an offload of an existing data warehouse. While lower technology costs and better scalability are clear and attractive benefits, these constructs still require a high level of IT participation. Furthermore, data ponds limit data to only that needed by the project, and use that data only for the project that requires it. Given the high IT costs and limited data availability, data ponds do not really help us with the goals of democratizing data usage or driving self-service and data-driven decision making for business users.

- A *data lake* is different from a data pond in two important ways. First, it supports self-service, where business users are able to find and use data sets that they want to use without having to rely on help from the IT department. Second, it aims to contain data that business users might possibly want even if there is no project requiring it at the time.

- A *data ocean* expands self-service data and data-driven decision making to all enterprise data, wherever it may be, regardless of whether it was loaded into the data lake or not.

Figure 1-1 illustrates the differences between these concepts. As maturity grows from a puddle to a pond to a lake to an ocean, the amount of data and the number of users grow—sometimes quite dramatically. The usage pattern moves from one of high-touch IT involvement to self-service, and the data expands beyond what's needed for immediate projects.

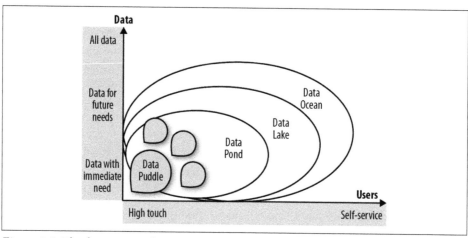

Figure 1-1. The four stages of maturity

The key difference between the data pond and the data lake is the focus. Data ponds provide a less expensive and more scalable technology alternative to existing relational data warehouses and data marts. Whereas the latter are focused on running routine, production-ready queries, data lakes enable business users to leverage data to make their own decisions by doing ad hoc analysis and experimentation with a variety of new types of data and tools, as illustrated in Figure 1-2.

Before we get into what it takes to create a successful data lake, let's take a closer look at the two maturity stages that lead up to it.

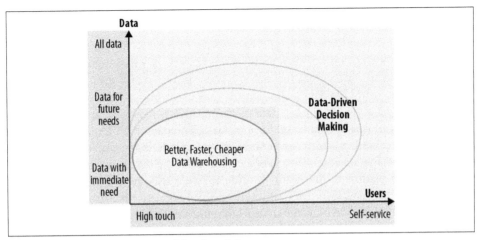

Figure 1-2. Value proposition of the data lake

Data Puddles

Data puddles are usually built for a small focused team or specialized use case. These "puddles" are modest-sized collections of data owned by a single team, frequently built in the cloud by business units using shadow IT. In the age of data warehousing, each team was used to building a relational data mart for each of its projects. The process of building a data puddle is very similar, except it uses big data technology. Typically, data puddles are built for projects that require the power and scale of big data. Many advanced analytics projects, such as those focusing on customer churn or predictive maintenance, fall in this category.

Sometimes, data puddles are built to help IT with automated compute-intensive and data-intensive processes, such as extract, transform, load (ETL) offloading, which will be covered in detail in later chapters, where all the transformation work is moved from the data warehouse or expensive ETL tools to a big data platform. Another common use is to serve a single team by providing a work area, called a *sandbox*, in which data scientists can experiment.

Data puddles usually have a small scope and a limited variety of data; they're populated by small, dedicated data streams, and constructing and maintaining them requires a highly technical team or heavy involvement from IT.

Data Ponds

A data pond is a collection of data puddles. Just as you can think of data puddles as data marts built using big data technology, you can think of a data pond as a data warehouse built using big data technology. It may come into existence organically, as more puddles get added to the big data platform. Another popular approach for creating a data pond is as a data warehouse offload. Unlike with ETL offloading, which uses big data technology to perform some of the processing required to populate a data warehouse, the idea here is to take all the data in the data warehouse and load it into a big data platform. The vision is often to eventually get rid of the data warehouse to save costs and improve performance, since big data platforms are much less expensive and much more scalable than relational databases. However, just offloading the data warehouse does not give the analysts access to the raw data. Because the rigorous architecture and governance applied to the data warehouse are still maintained, the organization cannot address all the challenges of the data warehouse, such as long and expensive change cycles, complex transformations, and manual coding as the basis for all reports. Finally, the analysts often do not like moving from a finely tuned data warehouse with lightning-fast queries to a much less predictable big data platform, where huge batch queries may run faster than in a data warehouse but more typical smaller queries may take minutes. Figure 1-3 illustrates some of the typical limitations of data ponds: lack of predictability, agility, and access to the original untreated data.

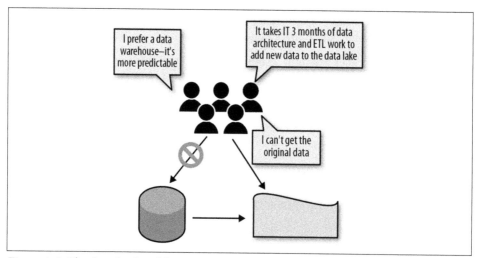

Figure 1-3. The drawbacks of data warehouse offloading

Creating a Successful Data Lake

So what does it take to have a successful data lake? As with any project, aligning it with the company's business strategy and having executive sponsorship and broad buy-in are a must. In addition, based on discussions with dozens of companies deploying data lakes with varying levels of success, three key prerequisites can be identified:

- The right platform
- The right data
- The right interfaces

The Right Platform

Big data technologies like Hadoop and cloud solutions like Amazon Web Services (AWS), Microsoft Azure, and Google Cloud Platform are the most popular platforms for a data lake. These technologies share several important advantages:

Volume

These platforms were designed to scale out—in other words, to scale indefinitely without any significant degradation in performance.

Cost

We have always had the capacity to store a lot of data on fairly inexpensive storage, like tapes, WORM disks, and hard drives. But not until big data technologies did we have the ability to both store and process huge volumes of data so inexpensively—usually at one-tenth to one-hundredth the cost of a commercial relational database.

Variety

These platforms use filesystems or object stores that allow them to store all sorts of files: Hadoop HDFS, MapR FS, AWS's Simple Storage Service (S3), and so on. Unlike a relational database that requires the data structure to be predefined (*schema on write*), a filesystem or an object store does not really care what you write. Of course, to meaningfully process the data you need to know its schema, but that's only when you use the data. This approach is called *schema on read* and it's one of the important advantages of big data platforms, enabling what's called "frictionless ingestion." In other words, data can be loaded with absolutely no processing, unlike in a relational database, where data cannot be loaded until it is converted to the schema and format expected by the database.

Future-proofing

Because our requirements and the world we live in are in flux, it is critical to make sure that the data we have can be used to help with our future needs. Today, if data is stored in a relational database, it can be accessed only by that relational database. Hadoop and other big data platforms, on the other hand, are very modular. The same file can be used by various processing engines and programs—from Hive queries (Hive provides a SQL interface to Hadoop files) to Pig scripts to Spark and custom MapReduce jobs, all sorts of different tools and systems can access and use the same files. Because big data technology is evolving rapidly, this gives people confidence that any future projects will still be able to access the data in the data lake.

The Right Data

Most data collected by enterprises today is thrown away. Some small percentage is aggregated and kept in a data warehouse for a few years, but most detailed operational data, machine-generated data, and old historical data is either aggregated or thrown away altogether. That makes it difficult to do analytics. For example, if an analyst recognizes the value of some data that was traditionally thrown away, it may take months or even years to accumulate enough history of that data to do meaningful analytics. The promise of the data lake, therefore, is to be able to store as much data as possible for future use.

So, the data lake is sort of like a piggy bank (Figure 1-4)—you often don't know what you are saving the data for, but you want it in case you need it one day. Moreover, because you don't know how you will use the data, it doesn't make sense to convert or treat it prematurely. You can think of it like traveling with your piggy bank through different countries, adding money in the currency of the country you happen to be in at the time and keeping the contents in their native currencies until you decide what country you want to spend the money in; you can then convert it all to that currency, instead of needlessly converting your funds (and paying conversion fees) every time you cross a border. To summarize, the goal is to *save as much data as possible in its native format*.

Figure 1-4. A data lake is like a piggy bank, allowing you to keep the data in its native or raw format

Another challenge with getting the right data is *data silos*. Different departments might hoard their data, both because it is difficult and expensive to provide and because there is often a political and organizational reluctance to share. In a typical enterprise, if one group needs data from another group, it has to explain what data it needs and then the group that owns the data has to implement ETL jobs that extract and package the required data. This is expensive, difficult, and time-consuming, so teams may push back on data requests as much as possible and then take as long as they can get away with to provide the data. This extra work is often used as an excuse to not share data.

With a data lake, because the lake consumes raw data through frictionless ingestion (basically, it's ingested as is without any processing), that challenge (and excuse) goes away. A well-governed data lake is also centralized and offers a transparent process to people throughout the organization about how to obtain data, so ownership becomes much less of a barrier.

The Right Interface

Once we have the right platform and we've loaded the data, we get to the more difficult aspects of the data lake, where most companies fail—choosing the right interface. To gain wide adoption and reap the benefits of helping business users make data-driven decisions, the solutions companies provide must be self-service, so their users can find, understand, and use the data without needing help from IT. IT will simply not be able to scale to support such a large user community and such a large variety of data.

There are two aspects to enabling self-service: providing data at the right level of expertise for the users, and ensuring the users are able to find the right data.

Providing data at the right level of expertise

To get broad adoption for the data lake, we want everyone from data scientists to business analysts to use it. However, when considering such divergent audiences with different needs and skill levels, we have to be careful to make the right data available to the right user populations.

For example, analysts often don't have the skills to use raw data. Raw data usually has too much detail, is too granular, and frequently has too many quality issues to be easily used. For instance, if we collect sales data from different countries that use different applications, that data will come in different formats with different fields (e.g., one country may have sales tax whereas another doesn't) and different units of measure (e.g., lb versus kg, $ versus €).

In order for the analysts to use this data, it has to be *harmonized*—put into the same schema with the same field names and units of measure—and frequently also aggregated to daily sales per product or per customer. In other words, analysts want "cooked" prepared meals, not raw data.

Data scientists, on the other hand, are the complete opposite. For them, cooked data often loses the golden nuggets that they are looking for. For example, if they want to see how often two products are bought together, but the only information they can get is daily totals by product, data scientists will be stuck. They are like chefs who need raw ingredients to create their culinary or analytic masterpieces.

We'll see in this book how to satisfy divergent needs by setting up multiple *zones*, or areas that contain data that meets particular requirements. For example, the raw or landing zone contains the original data ingested into the lake, whereas the production or gold zone contains high-quality, governed data. We'll take a quick look at zones in "Organizing the Data Lake" on page 14; a more detailed discussion can be found in Chapter 7.

Getting to the data

Most companies that I have spoken with are settling on the "shopping for data" paradigm, where analysts use an Amazon.com-style interface to find, understand, rate, annotate, and consume data. The advantages of this approach are manifold, including:

A familiar interface
Most people are familiar with online shopping and feel comfortable searching with keywords and using facets, ratings, and comments, so they require no or minimal training.

Faceted search

Search engines are optimized for faceted search. Faceted search is very helpful when the number of possible search results is large and the user is trying to zero in on the right result. For example, if you were to search Amazon for toasters (Figure 1-5), facets would list manufacturers, whether the toaster should accept bagels, how many slices it needs to toast, and so forth. Similarly, when users are searching for the right data sets, facets can help them specify what attributes they would like in the data set, the type and format of the data set, the system that holds it, the size and freshness of the data set, the department that owns it, what entitlements it has, and any number of other useful characteristics.

Ranking and sorting

The ability to present and sort data assets, widely supported by search engines, is important for choosing the right asset based on specific criteria.

Contextual search

As catalogs get smarter, the ability to find data assets using a semantic under-standing of what analysts are looking for will become more important. For example, a salesperson looking for customers may really be looking for prospects, while a technical support person looking for customers may really be looking for existing customers.

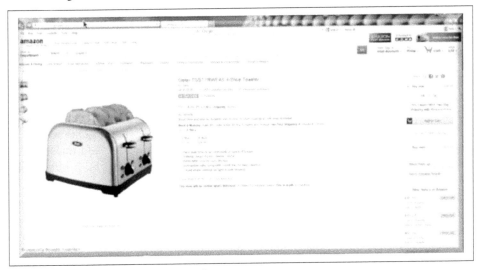

Figure 1-5. An online shopping interface

The Data Swamp

While data lakes always start out with good intentions, sometimes they take a wrong turn and end up as *data swamps*. A data swamp is a data pond that has grown to the size of a data lake but failed to attract a wide analyst community, usually due to a lack of self-service and governance facilities. At best, the data swamp is used like a data pond, and at worst it is not used at all. Often, while various teams use small areas of the lake for their projects (the white data pond area in Figure 1-6), the majority of the data is dark, undocumented, and unusable.

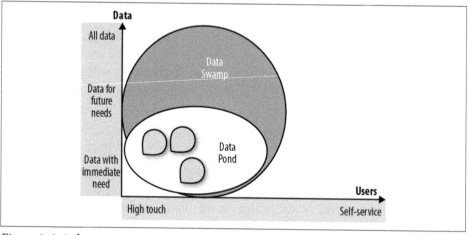

Figure 1-6. A data swamp

When data lakes first came onto the scene, a lot of companies rushed out to buy Hadoop clusters and fill them with raw data, without a clear understanding of how it would be utilized. This led to the creation of massive data swamps with millions of files containing petabytes of data and no way to make sense of that data.

Only the most sophisticated users were able to navigate the swamps, usually by carving out small puddles that they and their teams could make use of. Furthermore, governance regulations precluded opening up the swamps to a broad audience without protecting sensitive data. Since no one could tell where the sensitive data was, users could not be given access and the data largely remained unusable and unused. One data scientist shared with me his experience of how his company built a data lake, encrypted all the data in the lake to protect it, and required data scientists to prove that the data they wanted was not sensitive before it would unencrypt it and let them use it. This proved to be a catch-22: because everything was encrypted, the data scientist I talked to couldn't find anything, much less prove that it was not sensitive. As a result, no one was using the data lake (or, as he called it, the swamp).

Roadmap to Data Lake Success

Now that we know what it takes for a data lake to be successful and what pitfalls to look out for, how do we go about building one? Usually, companies follow this process:

1. Stand up the infrastructure (get the Hadoop cluster up and running).

2. Organize the data lake (create zones for use by various user communities and ingest the data).

3. Set the data lake up for self-service (create a catalog of data assets, set up permissions, and provide tools for the analysts to use).

4. Open the data lake up to the users.

Standing Up a Data Lake

When I started writing this book back in 2015, most enterprises were building on-premises data lakes using either open source or commercial Hadoop distributions. By 2018, at least half of enterprises were either building their data lakes entirely in the cloud or building hybrid data lakes that are both on premises and in the cloud. Many companies have multiple data lakes, as well. All this variety is leading companies to redefine what a data lake is. We're now seeing the concept of a *logical data lake*: a virtual data lake layer across multiple heterogeneous systems. The underlying systems can be Hadoop, relational, or NoSQL databases, on premises or in the cloud.

Figure 1-7 compares the three approaches. All of them offer a catalog that the users consult to find the data assets they need. These data assets either are already in the Hadoop data lake or get provisioned to it, where the analysts can use them.

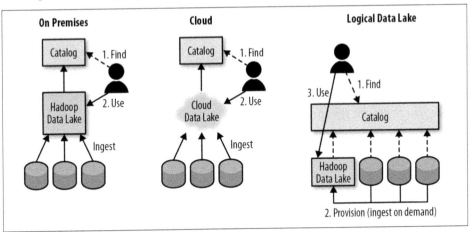

Figure 1-7. Different data lake architectures

Organizing the Data Lake

Most data lakes that I have encountered are organized roughly the same way, into various zones:

- A *raw* or *landing* zone where data is ingested and kept as close as possible to its original state.
- A *gold* or *production* zone where clean, processed data is kept.
- A *dev* or *work* zone where the more technical users such as data scientists and data engineers do their work. This zone can be organized by user, by project, by subject, or in a variety of other ways. Once the analytics work performed in the work zone gets productized, it is moved into the gold zone.
- A *sensitive* zone that contains sensitive data.

Figure 1-8 illustrates this organization.

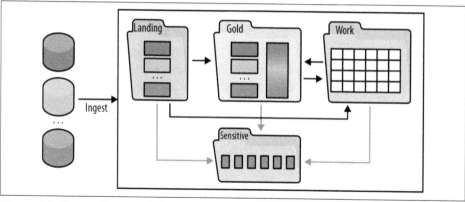

Figure 1-8. Zones of a typical data lake

For many years, the prevailing wisdom for data governance teams was that data should be subject to the same governance regardless of its location or purpose. In the last few years, however, industry analysts from Gartner have been promoting the concept of *multi-modal IT*—basically, the idea that governance should reflect data usage and user community requirements. This approach has been widely adopted by data lake teams, with different zones having different levels of governance and service-level agreements (SLAs). For example, data in the gold zone is usually strongly governed, is well curated and documented, and carries quality and freshness SLAs, whereas data in the work area has minimal governance (mostly making sure there is no sensitive data) and SLAs that may vary from project to project.

Different user communities naturally gravitate to different zones. Business analysts use data mostly in the gold zone, data engineers work on data in the raw zone (converting it into production data destined for the gold zone), and data scientists run their experiments in the work zone. While some governance is required for every zone to make sure that sensitive data is detected and secured, data stewards mostly focus on data in the sensitive and gold zones, to make sure it complies with company and government regulations. Figure 1-9 illustrates the different levels of governance and different user communities for different zones.

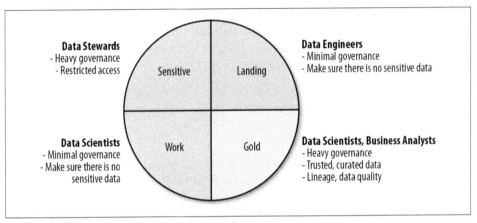

Figure 1-9. Governance expectations, zone by zone

Setting Up the Data Lake for Self-Service

Analysts, be they business analysts or data analysts or data scientists, typically go through four steps to do their job. These steps are illustrated in Figure 1-10.

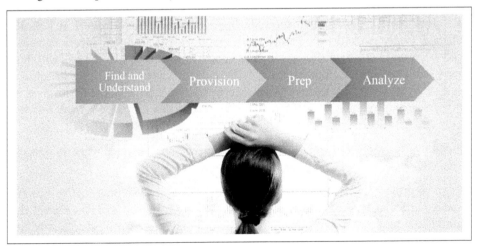

Figure 1-10. The four stages of analysis

The first step is to *find and understand* the data. Once they find the right data sets, they need to *provision* the data—that is, get access to it. Once they have the data, they often need to *prep* it—that is, clean it and convert it to a format appropriate for analysis. Finally, they need to use the data to answer questions or create visualizations and reports.

The first three steps theoretically are optional: if the data is well known and understood by the analyst, the analyst already has access to it, and it is already in the right shape for analytics, the analyst can do just the final step. In reality, a lot of studies have shown that the first three steps take up to 80% of a typical analyst's time, with the biggest expenditure (60%) in the first step of finding and understanding the data (see, for example, "Boost Your Business Insights by Converging Big Data and BI" by Boris Evelson, Forrester Research, March 25, 2015).

Let's break these down, to give you a better idea of what happens in each of the four stages.

Finding and understanding the data

Why is it so difficult to find data in the enterprise? Because the variety and complexity of the available data far exceeds human ability to remember it. Imagine a very small database, with only a hundred tables (some databases have thousands or even tens of thousands of tables, so this is truly a very small real-life database). Now imagine that each table has a hundred fields—a reasonable assumption for most databases, especially the analytical ones where data tends to be denormalized. That gives us 10,000 fields. How realistic is it for anyone to remember what 10,000 fields mean and which tables these fields are in, and then to keep track of them whenever using the data for something new?

Now imagine an enterprise that has several thousand (or several hundred thousand) databases, most an order of magnitude bigger than our hypothetical 10,000-field database. I once worked with a small bank that only had 5,000 employees, but managed to create 13,000 databases. I can only imagine how many a large bank with hundreds of thousands of employees might have. The reason I say "only imagine" is because none of the hundreds of large enterprises that I have worked with over my 30-year career were able to tell me how many databases they had—much less how many tables or fields.

Hopefully, this gives you some idea of the challenge analysts face when looking for data.

A typical project involves analysts "asking around" to see whether anyone has ever used a particular type of data. They get pointed from person to person until they stumble onto a data set that someone has used in one of their projects. Usually, they have no idea whether this is the best data set to use, how the data set was generated, or even whether the data is trustworthy. They are then faced with the awful choice of using this data set or asking around some more and perhaps not finding anything better.

Once they decide to use a data set, they spend a lot of time trying to decipher what the data it contains means. Some data is quite obvious (e.g., customer names or account numbers), while other data is cryptic (e.g., what does a customer code of 1126 mean?). So, the analysts spend still more time looking for people who can help them understand the data. We call this information "tribal knowledge." In other words, the knowledge usually exists, but it is spread throughout the tribe and has to be reassembled through a painful, long, and error-prone discovery process.

Fortunately, there are new *analyst crowdsourcing* tools that are tackling this problem by collecting tribal knowledge through a process that allows analysts to document data sets using simple descriptions composed of business terms, and builds a search index to help them find what they are looking for. Tools like these have been custom-developed at modern data-driven companies such as Google and LinkedIn. Because data is so important at those companies and "everyone is an analyst," the awareness of the problem and willingness to contribute to the solution is much higher than in traditional enterprises. It is also much easier to document data sets when they are first created, because the information is fresh. Nevertheless, even at Google, while some popular data sets are well documented, there is still a vast amount of dark or undocumented data.

In traditional enterprises, the situation is much worse. There are millions of existing data sets (files and tables) that will never get documented by analysts unless they are used—but they will never be found and used unless they are documented. The only practical solution is to combine crowdsourcing with automation. Waterline Data is a tool that my team and I have developed to provide such a solution. It takes the information crowdsourced from analysts working with their data sets and applies it to all the other dark data sets. The process is called *fingerprinting*: the tool crawls through all the structured data in the enterprise, adding a unique identifier to each field, and as fields get annotated or tagged by analysts, it looks for similar fields and suggests tags for them. When analysts search for data sets, they see both data sets tagged by analysts and data sets tagged by the tool automatically, and have a chance to either accept or reject these suggested tags. The tool then applies machine learning (ML) to improve its automated tagging based on the user feedback.

The core idea is that human annotation by itself is not enough, given the scope and complexity of the data, while purely automated annotation is undependable given the unique and unpredictable characteristics of the data—so, the two have to be brought together to achieve the best results. Figure 1-11 illustrates the virtuous cycle.

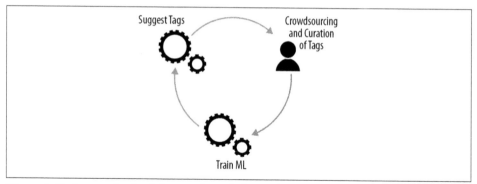

Figure 1-11. Leveraging both human knowledge and machine learning

Accessing and provisioning the data

Once the right data sets have been identified, analysts need to be able to use them. Traditionally, access is granted to analysts as they start or join a project. It is then rarely taken away, so old-timers end up with access to practically all the data in the enterprise that may be even remotely useful, while newbies have virtually no access and therefore can't find or use anything. To solve the data access problem for the data lake, enterprises typically go for one of the two extremes: they either grant everyone full access to all the data or restrict all access unless an analyst can demonstrate a need. Granting full access works in some cases, but not in regulated industries. To make it more acceptable, enterprises sometimes deidentify sensitive data—but that means they have to do work ingesting data that no one may need. Also, as regulations change, more and more data may need to be deidentified (this topic will be covered in depth in later chapters).

A more practical approach is to publish information about all the data sets in a metadata catalog, so analysts can find useful data sets and then request access as needed. The requests usually include the justification for access, the project that requires the data, and the duration of access required. These requests are routed to the data stewards for the requested data. If they approve access, it is granted for a period of time. This period may be extended, but it is not indefinite, eliminating the legacy access problem. An incoming request may also trigger the work to deidentify sensitive data, but now it is done only if and when needed.

Provisioning or physical access can be granted to the data in a number of ways:

- Users can be granted read access to the entire data set.
- If only partial access should be granted, a copy of the file containing just the data appropriate to the user can be created (and kept up to date), or a Hive table or view can be created that contains only the fields and rows that the analyst should see.

- If needed, a deidentified version of the data set can be generated that replaces sensitive information with randomly generated equivalent information, so all the applications still work, but no sensitive data is leaked.

Preparing the data

Occasionally, data comes in perfectly clean and ready for analytics. Unfortunately, most of the time, the data needs work to render it appropriate for the analysts. Data preparation generally involves the following operations:

Shaping
Selecting a subset of fields and rows to work on, combining multiple files and tables into one (joining), transforming and aggregating, bucketizing (for instance, going from discrete values to ranges or buckets—e.g., putting 0- to 18-year-olds into the "juvenile" bucket, 19- to 25-year-olds into the "young adult" bucket, etc.), converting variables into features (for instance, converting age into a feature that has a value of 0 if a person is over 65 and 1 if not), and many other possible steps.

Cleaning
Filling in missing values (for instance, guessing a missing gender from the first name or looking up the address in an address database), correcting bad values, resolving conflicting data, normalizing units of measure and codes to common units, and the like.

Blending
Harmonizing different data sets to the same schema, same units of measure, same codes, and so on.

As you can tell from these few examples, a lot of sophisticated work and thinking goes into data preparation. Automation is crucial, to take advantage of lessons learned by transformations and to avoid repeating the same tedious steps over thousands of tables and data sets.

The most common data preparation tool is Excel. Unfortunately, Excel doesn't scale to data lake sizes, but a plethora of new tools provide Excel-like capabilities for large-scale data sets. Some, like Trifacta, apply sophisticated machine learning techniques to suggest transformations and help analysts prep the data. Many large vendors have also debuted data prep tools, and analytics vendors like Tableau and Qlik are enhancing data prep capabilities in their tools as well.

Analysis and visualization

Once data is prepared, it can be analyzed. Analysis ranges from creation of simple reports and visualizations to sophisticated advanced analytics and machine learning.

This is a very mature space, with hundreds of vendors providing solutions for every type of analytics. Specifically for Hadoop data lakes, Arcadia Data, AtScale, and others provide analysis and visualization tools designed to run natively and take advantage of Hadoop's processing power.

Data Lake Architectures

Originally, most companies I talked to thought that they would have one huge, on-premises data lake that would contain all their data. As their understanding and best practices evolved, most enterprises realized that a single go-to point was not ideal. Between data sovereignty regulations (e.g., you are not allowed to take data out of Germany) and organizational pressures, multiple data lakes typically proved to be a better solution. Furthermore, as companies realized the complexity of supporting a massively parallel cluster and experienced the frustration at their inability to find and hire experienced administrators for Hadoop and other big data platforms, they started opting for cloud-based data lakes where most hardware and platform components are managed by the experts that work for Amazon, Microsoft, Google, and others.

Data Lakes in the Public Cloud

Aside from the benefits of access to big data technology expertise and short deployment times, the low cost of storage and the elastic nature of cloud computing make this an extremely attractive option for implementing a data lake. Since a lot of data is being stored for future use, it makes sense to store it as inexpensively as possible. This works well with the cost optimization possibilities supported through various storage tiers provided by Amazon and others: access ranges from high-speed to glacial, with slower-access media being significantly cheaper.

In addition, the elasticity of cloud computing allows a very large cluster to be spun up on demand, when needed. Compare this to an on-premises cluster, which has a fixed size and stores its data in attached storage (although new architectures with network-attached storage are being explored). That means that as nodes fill up with data, new nodes need to be added just for storage. Furthermore, if analytic loads are CPU-heavy and need more compute power, you need to add nodes even though you may only use them for a short time.

In the cloud, you pay only for the storage that you need (i.e., you don't have to buy extra compute nodes just to get more storage) and can spin up huge clusters for short periods of time. For example, if you have a 100-node on-premises cluster and a job that takes 50 hours, it is not practical to buy and install 1,000 nodes just to make this one job run faster. In the cloud, however, you would pay about the same for the compute power of 100 nodes for 50 hours as you would for 1,000 nodes for 5 hours. This is the huge advantage of elastic compute.

Logical Data Lakes

Once enterprises realized that having one centralized data lake wasn't a good solution, the idea of the *logical data lake* took hold. With this approach, instead of loading all the data into the data lake just in case someone may eventually need it, it is made available to analysts through a central catalog or through data virtualization software.

Logical data lakes address the issues of completeness and redundancy, as illustrated in Figure 1-12.

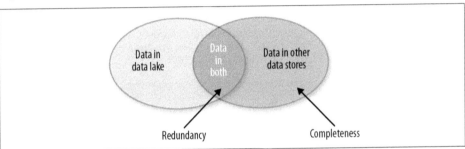

Figure 1-12. Completeness and redundancy issues

These issues can be summarized as follows:

Completeness
> How do analysts find the best data set? If the analysts can find only data that is already in the data lake, other data that has not been ingested into the data lake won't be found or used (the crescent area on the right in Figure 1-12).

Redundancy
> If we ingest all the data into the data lake, we will have redundancy between the sources of data and the data lake (illustrated as the area of overlap between the two circles in Figure 1-12). With multiple data lakes, to achieve completeness we would need to ingest the same data into each data lake.

> To make matters worse, there is already a lot of redundancy in the enterprise. Traditionally, when a new project is started, the most expedient and politically simple approach is for the project team to spin up a new data mart, copy data from other sources or the data warehouse, and add its own unique data. This is much easier than studying existing data marts and negotiating shared usage with current owners and users. As a result, there is a proliferation of data marts that are mostly the same. If we blindly load all the data from these data marts into the data lake, we will have extremely high levels of redundancy in our lake.

The best approach to the completeness and redundancy challenges that I have seen involves a couple of simple rules:

- To solve the completeness problem, create a catalog of all the data assets, so the analysts can find and request any data set that is available in the enterprise.
- To solve the redundancy problem, follow the process shown in Figure 1-13:
  - Store data that is not stored anywhere else in the data lake.
  - Bring data that is stored in other systems into the data lake if and when it is needed, and keep it in sync while it is needed.
  - Bring each data set in only once for all users.

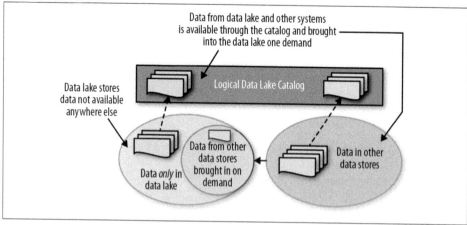

Figure 1-13. Managing data in the logical data lake

Virtualization versus a catalog-based logical data lake

Virtualization (sometimes also called *federation* or EII, for *enterprise information integration*) is a technology developed in 1980s and improved through several generations into the 2010s. It basically creates a virtual view or table that hides the location and implementation of the physical tables. In Figure 1-14, a view is created by joining two tables from different databases. The query would then query that view and leave it up to the data virtualization system to figure out how to access and join the data in the two databases.

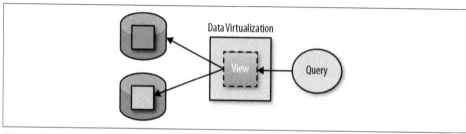

Figure 1-14. Creating a custom data set through a view

Although this technology works well for some use cases, in a logical data lake, to achieve completeness, it would require every data set to be published as a virtual table and kept up to date as underlying table schemas change.

Even if the initial problem of publishing every data asset were solved, views still present significant problems:

- Creating a virtual view does not make data any easier to find.

- Joining data from multiple heterogeneous systems is complex and compute-intensive, often causing massive loads on the systems and long execution cycles. These so-called *distributed joins* of tables that don't fit into memory are notoriously eresource intensive.

By contrast, in the catalog-driven approach, only metadata about each data set is published, in order to make it findable. Data sets are then provisioned to the same system (e.g., Hadoop cluster) to be processed locally, as demonstrated in Figure 1-15.

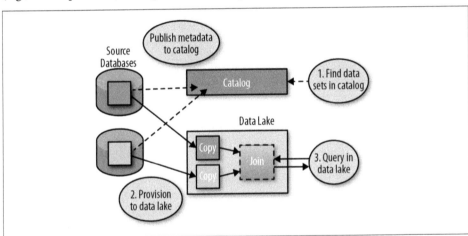

Figure 1-15. Providing metadata through a catalog

In addition to making all the data findable and accessible to analysts, an enterprise catalog can serve as a single point of access, governance, and auditing, as shown in Figure 1-16. On the top, without a centralized catalog, access to data assets is all over the place and difficult to manage and track. On the bottom, with the centralized catalog, all requests for access go through the catalog. Access is granted on demand for a specific period of time and is audited by the system.

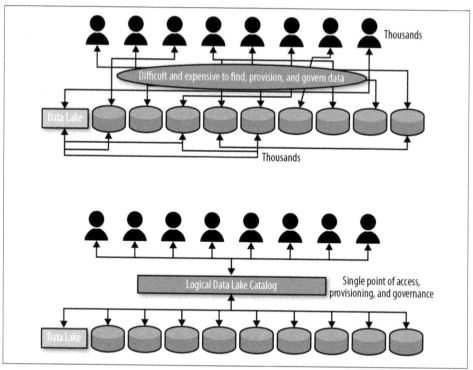

Figure 1-16. Data provisioning and governance through the catalog

Conclusion

In summary, getting the right platform, loading it with the right data, and organizing and setting it up for self-service with a skills- and needs-appropriate interface are the keys to creating a successful data lake. In the rest of this book, we'll explore how to accomplish these tasks.

CHAPTER 2

Historical Perspective

Data has been around for a very long time. First, it was visual: paintings on cave walls, mounds arranged a certain way. Once humans developed systems of writing, they used these to keep track of things: many ancient clay tablets and manuscripts seem to contain inventories, ledgers, and bills of sale and debt. Later, more general data was collected and published in almanacs and encyclopedias: records of the longest rivers, tallest mountains, deepest lakes, most populous countries, average rainfall, highest and lowest temperatures, and so on. We seem to have an endless fascination with measuring and counting, comparing and tracking. Traditionally, this measuring and counting process was laborious and manual, so we invented machines to help us with it. Eventually, those machines evolved into modern computers.

Very early on, it became obvious that computers had a capacity to count, measure, and store information that far exceeded a human's. However, computers were also great at other things, like applying logic and executing business processes. Most of the focus in the early days of computers was on programs and logic. Data was considered an artifact of programs, something that could be accessed and made sense of only by the programs that had originally stored it.

To make data humanly accessible, programmers developed *reports* that packaged data into a human-readable form. If an analyst wanted to look at data in a different way, they had to make a request and wait for developers to create a new report.

The Drive for Self-Service Data—The Birth of Databases

The first step in the self-service data revolution was the spreadsheet. It allowed non-developers to work with data directly. For the first time, the analysts were able to work with the data themselves and manipulate it into the shapes they desired. Once that genie was out of the bottle, there was no putting it back. But while spreadsheets quickly became the most common decision support tool, they did not scale beyond small amounts of data and could address only a small subset of the problems that analysts wanted to address.

Meanwhile, companies began to realize that the data, not the applications, was the crown jewel. Losing data meant the business would come to a grinding halt. Data had to be carefully managed, checked for consistency, and backed up. Instead of each program having to develop these capabilities itself, they were extracted and provided by a new class of systems called *database management systems* (DBMSs). These systems did not contain programming logic and existed purely to manage the data.

Early systems were still tied very closely to applications and required application logic to make sense of the data, but eventually, the separation between data and application became more institutionalized—especially with the advent of relational databases.

Relational database management systems (RDBMSs) allow the users to describe the data explicitly to the database. Users create a *schema*—a human-readable collection of tables and fields. Instead of having to always go through the programs to get to the data, the users of RDBMSs were able to query data directly. Eventually, a somewhat standard language called Structured Query Language (SQL) emerged and became the *lingua franca* of databases. Using this language, the users could write their own queries and do their own analysis of data.

Even though it was now possible to analyze the data used by applications directly, most database schemas were still designed to support applications. Because writing or reading data to and from disk was orders of magnitude slower than processing it in memory, a schema design technique called *normalization* broke data into the smallest possible chunks to ensure that each database update could write as little data as possible. This worked well for updates and queries that retrieved specific pieces of data, such as information about a single customer, but was extremely inefficient for doing large-scale analytics, such as looking at all the activity of a customer, that required a number of tables to be joined together.

Many books have been written on both relational database theory and schema design, so I will just cover the key concepts of relations, primary and foreign keys, and normalization here. Relational databases contain tables that have columns and rows. Imagine trying to store all the information you have about your customers in a table —you would have columns for different customer attributes like name, address, age, gender, and so on. Now imagine that you also want to keep track of the orders that each customer places. You could add new columns for order number, date, amount, and other order attributes. If you only had one order per customer, you would have one row for each customer and their order. But what if customers placed multiple orders? Would you now have a row for each order? That would mean that all the customer data would be replicated for each order, as illustrated in Table 2-1. If a customer had a thousand orders, their data would be replicated a thousand times. Worse, if their information were to change—if a customer were to move or change their name after getting married, for example—you would have to update each of those thousand records. Clearly, this is not a very efficient approach.

Table 2-1. The Customer_Orders table

Name	Gender	Marital_ Status	Zip_Code	Order_ Number	Amount	Date
Mary Ng	F	Married	94301	2123123	987.19	7/12/18
Mary Ng	F	Married	94301	2221212	12.20	9/2/18
Mary Ng	F	Married	94301	2899821	5680.19	10/15/18
Tom Jones	M	Single	93443	2344332	1500.00	9/12/18

The solution to this problem applied in relational databases is called *normalization*. It is a way to break tables into smaller tables in order to avoid repeating information. For example, we would store customer information in one table and all the orders for all the customers in another table. Then, in order to identify which orders belong to which customers, we would generate a *key*—for example, Customer_ID—and have it as part of both the Customers and Orders tables, such that each order will contain the Customer_ID value that corresponds to the Customer_ID value in the record of the customer that placed the order. The Customer_ID column in the Customers table (Table 2-2) will be called the *primary key* because it uniquely identifies the customer, and the Customer_ID column in the Orders table (Table 2-3) will be called the *foreign key* because it refers to the Customer_ID column in the Customers table. Primary keys are expected to be unique, so, for example, the customer IDs in the Customers table would uniquely identify each customer, while foreign keys are expected to be a proper subset of primary keys. If we have a Customer_ID value in the Orders table that does not correspond to any Customer_ID value in the Customers table, we have what is called an *orphaned* foreign key and will not be able to tell which customer placed that order. This correspondence between primary and foreign keys is called *referential integrity*. Note that by breaking the data into separate Customers and Orders tables, we store customer information exactly once in the Customers table regardless of how many orders each customer places.

Table 2-2. Customers table

Customer_ID	Name	Gender	Marital_Status	Zip_Code
112211	Mary Ng	F	Married	94301
299821	Tom Jones	M	Single	93443

Table 2-3. Orders table

Customer_ID	Order_Number	Amount	Date
112211	2123123	987.19	7/12/18
112211	2221212	12.20	9/2/18
112211	2899821	56.80.19	10/15/18
299821	2344332	1500.00	9/12/18
299821	2554322	11.99	9/13/18

In order to determine, say, how many orders are placed by married customers compared to unmarried customers, the query would have to combine data from the Orders and Customers tables by performing a SQL operation called a *join*. It would look something like this:

```
select customers.marital_status, sum(orders.total) as total_sales from customers
join orders on
customers.customer_id = orders.customer_id group by customers.marital_status
```

This query would return the total of orders for each marital status by joining the two tables together, as illustrated in Table 2-4.

Table 2-4. Total orders for married and single customers

Marital_Status	Total_Sales
Married	2,221,222.12
Single	102,221,222.18

While joins are very powerful and flexible, they are also computationally expensive. For larger systems that normalize data into dozens or even hundreds of tables, doing all the joins required for every query can bring a highly normalized operational database to its knees. To help with that problem, a new solution was developed. The idea was to completely separate data from applications and, in fact, to combine data from multiple applications in one system and use that system for analytics.

The Analytics Imperative—The Birth of Data Warehousing

The original vision was to create a "warehouse" that would store all the data and thus all the history about an enterprise, and make it available for analytics. In 1990 Walmart created its now-famous data warehouse that helped it to take over the retail world by managing its logistics, and kicked off the analytics gold rush. Every enterprise soon realized that it could get tremendous value from its data and, hopefully, use it to crush its competition. Equally importantly, enterprises realized that if they did not invest in analytics, their competitors might crush them. Suddenly, everyone was building a data warehouse. Unfortunately, as with many multi-year, multi-million-dollar projects driven by fear and hope rather than sound use cases and business needs, many of these projects were spectacular and well-publicized failures.

Fortunately, the industry learned from these failures and continued to innovate and improve. Various specialized techniques were developed to optimize these analytical platforms for specific use cases and solve the problem of efficiently storing and analyzing large quantities of data: breaking large data warehouses into data marts, inventing appliances that exploit hardware optimizations to process queries, and using columnar stores and in-memory databases. Over time, a large ecosystem of tools was developed to create and manage data warehouses, to manage data quality, and to keep track of data models and metadata. Some of the more prominent technologies include:

- Extract, transform, load (ETL) and extract, load, transform (ELT) tools
- Data quality (DQ) and profiling tools
- Data modeling tools
- Business glossaries
- Metadata repositories
- Data governance tools
- Master data management (MDM) systems
- Enterprise information integration (EII), data federation, and data virtualization tools

In addition, tools were developed to help create reports and analytics, including:

- Reporting tools
- Online analytical processing (OLAP) tools
- Business intelligence (BI) tools
- Data visualization tools
- Advanced analytic tools

We'll look at some of these in the following section.

The Data Warehouse Ecosystem

Figure 2-1 illustrates the flow of data through the data warehouse ecosystem. Subsequent sections will explore the function of and data flow in each component. These tools are not the subject of this book, but must be understood and put into context so that you know what data processes are in place today in most organizations, and what functions we are trying to reproduce or replace with a data lake.

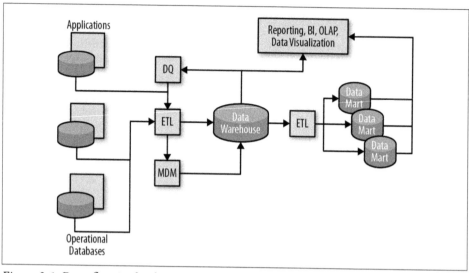

Figure 2-1. Data flow in the data warehousing ecosystem

In addition to a data flow, the data warehouse ecosystem has a rich metadata flow as well as a number of metadata-specific tools, as illustrated in Figure 2-2. Subsequent chapters will describe the metadata flow between various tools. The two end user-facing components in the ecosystem are the ones at the top of the diagram: the business glossary and various reporting tools. A wide swath of IT staff—ETL developers, data and system architects, data modelers, data stewards, report and BI developers, and database administrators—use the rest of the tools to make sure the end users get their reports and analytics. Note that I am not including general administration, backup, management, and other tools that are not specific to data warehouses and am simplifying some of the components—for example, I include data profiling in DQ, lineage in ETL, and so on.

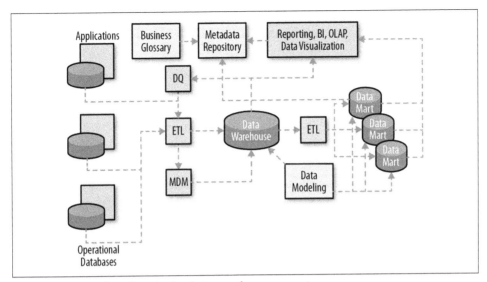

Figure 2-2. Metadata flow in the data warehouse ecosystem

Storing and Querying the Data

The database is at the heart of a data warehouse. Usually, it is a relational database optimized for analytics-type processing: large, long queries; aggregation; and multi-table joins. The database is usually heavily indexed and tuned to ensure optimal performance for the most common queries.

Dimensional modeling and star schemas

When relational databases are used to support operational systems and applications, data is usually stored in highly normalized data models. Normalized data models attempt to create tables with minimum redundancy and the smallest possible number of fields; this makes updates very fast.

For instance, a table representing sales might contain very little information except some generated keys for product, buyer, retail location, and the like. In order to find useful information, such as the city corresponding to a retail location, one has to join the table to another in an expensive computation.

On the other hand, most data warehouses favor *denormalized* data models, where each table contains as many related attributes as possible. In this way, all the information can be processed by a single pass through the data.

Next, because data warehouses typically contain data from many sources and applications, each with its own schema, data from these sources has to be normalized to convert it to a single schema. A popular data model used by data warehouses is the *star schema*, introduced by Ralph Kimball and Margy Ross in 1996 in the first edition of *The Data Warehouse Toolkit* (Wiley). This schema consists of a set of *dimension* and *fact* tables.

The dimension tables represent the entities being analyzed: in a sales context, there might be a customer dimension table containing all the attributes of a customer (name, address, etc.), a time dimension table with all the attributes of time (date, fiscal year, etc.), and a product dimension table with all the attributes of a product (make, model, price, etc.).

The fact table contains all the activities that involve the dimensions. For example, a transaction fact table would have a record for every line item in every order. The record would contain the customer key from the customer dimension table for the customer who placed the order, the time key from the time dimension table for when the order was placed, and the product key from the product dimension table for the product being ordered, as well as the attributes of the transaction itself (order and line item ID, quantity, price paid, etc.). The structure of the tables is symbolically represented by Figure 2-3. With data organized into a star schema, even general-purpose relational databases such as Oracle, IBM DB2, and Microsoft SQL Server can achieve reasonable performance, and many now include specialized query optimizations for handling star schema–like joins.

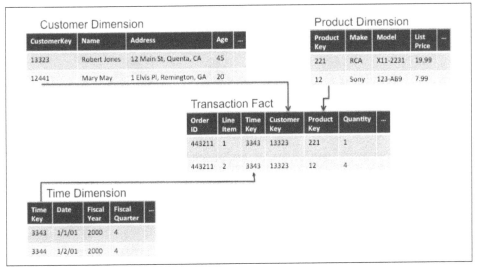

Figure 2-3. Tables in a simple star schema

Slowly changing dimensions

To allow accurate data analysis, it's necessary to keep track of a person's state over time. This ensures that each transaction corresponds to the person's state at the time of the transaction. Since the person's state does not change very often, a special construct has been developed to represent those changes: *slowly changing dimensions*. This concept was also introduced by Kimball and Ross in *The Data Warehouse Toolkit*.

The goal of a slowly changing dimension is to keep track of a dimension entity's (e.g., person's) state over time, so that the transactions (or facts) corresponding to the entity's state reflect that state over time, thus making analysis more accurate in the long term.

This section illustrates the basic concept by describing the most common type of slowly changing dimension, which tracks historical data by creating multiple records. This is called a type 2 dimension.

Let's say we have a store that has kept track of customer purchases along with customer demographics. For our example, a hypothetical Mary is a single person who has been shopping at the store for five years. After five years, Mary gets married and becomes a homeowner; two years later she becomes a parent. She continues shopping at the store.

In Figure 2-4, Mary's purchases for years 1–5 reflect those that might be made by a single person; for years 5–7 they reflect those of a homeowner; and for the subsequent years those of a new parent.

Figure 2-4. Shopping data with slowly changing dimensions

Without slowly changing dimensions, we would have one single record for Mary in our customer table that reflects her current state as a parent (see Figure 2-5). So, if we were to analyze how many people with children spend money on expensive travel or sports gear, we would mistakenly attribute her purchases from years 1–7 (as a person without children) to her current category.

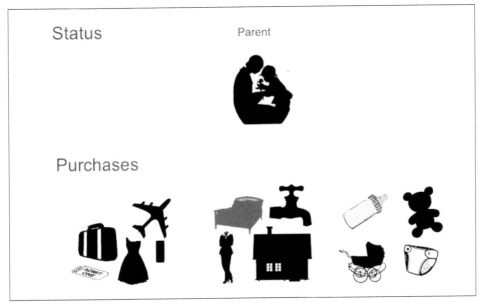

Status   Parent

Purchases

Figure 2-5. Shopping data without slowly changing dimensions

However, with the help of slowly changing dimensions, designed to capture the state of the person at the time of the transaction, the customer table will have a different record for Mary for each change in her state, as shown in Figure 2-6. So, when Mary's purchases are analyzed, they will be attributed to a person with the correct state.

Customer Key	Name	Address	Status	Start	End	...
12441	Mary May	1 Elvis Pl, Remington, GA	Single	1/7/2008	4/1/2013	
19223	Mary May Lee	1 Elvis Pl, Remington, GA	Married	4/2/2013	9/1/2015	
21221	Mary May Lee	1 Elvis Pl, Remington, GA	Parent	9/2/2015	current	

Figure 2-6. Every change in status creates a new record for Mary in the customer dimension table, with fields including the start and end date of the record's validity

Because slowly changing dimensions add so much complexity to both ETL jobs and analytic queries, only the history for the most critical attributes (such as family status in the previous example) are tracked. That means that if one of the untracked attributes becomes critical, the history of its evolution will not be available.

Massively parallel processing (MPP) systems

An alternative to using star schemas is to use a cluster of massively parallel computers that appear to the end user or BI tool as a single database. Teradata quickly became the database of choice for the largest data warehouses after developing such MPP technology. By using proprietary hardware, software, and networking protocols,

Teradata data warehouses were able to achieve a scalability unmatched in the industry prior to the advent of Hadoop. Since Teradata was able to operate computers in parallel, it did not require the users to model the data a certain way. Instead, it relied on its query optimizer to execute complex queries in the most efficient way possible.

Data warehouse (DW) appliances

DW appliances try to solve the problem of taking a high-performance database running on proprietary hardware and software and making it easier to deploy and manage than a standard off-the-shelf database. IBM Netezza is a good example of such a DW appliance. While not as scalable as MPP systems such as Teradata and IBM DB2, these appliances are much easier to deploy and tune and can address the needs of the majority of data warehouses and data marts.

Columnar stores

Relational databases model data as tables with rows (sometimes called records) and columns (sometimes called fields). For example, suppose you have a Customers table with 300 columns each containing a piece of data about a customer, such as Name, Address, Age, Date_Of_First_Purchase, and so on. Traditional relational databases store each row of data together, so all the information about the first customer is stored, then all the information about the second customer, and so on. In order to store 300 attributes with an average size of, say, 5 bytes/attribute, the database would need to use 1,500 bytes, or roughly 1.5 KB, for each user. If there were a million customers, the database would need at least 1.5 TB of storage to store all the customer data (in reality, it would need even more storage because the records won't fit neatly into disk blocks, and because there are underlying data structures and indexes that take up space as well). If the user wanted to find out how many customers were under the age of 30, the database would have to read each record in the table—in other words, it would have to read all 1.5 TB.

A *columnar* database would store all the data for each column together instead of storing all the data for each row together. For example, it would store the age for each customer together with a record identifier that indicates which customer record this value belongs to in the same storage blocks. If age takes 2 bytes and a record identifier is, say, 6 bytes, the database would need 8 bytes per field, or 8 GB for a million customers. Since it would have to read only 8 GB to answer the question of how many customers are under 30, it would be able to perform this query about 200 times faster. Of course, this improves performance only for queries requiring a few columns. If the query wanted to return all the information (all 300 columns) for a single user, a row-oriented database would just have to read a single block, while a columnar database would have to read 300 blocks. In other words, columnar databases are employed for very specific query patterns, unlike the relational model, which is more general-purpose. Some well-known vertical databases include Sybase IQ and Vertica.

In-memory databases

Although traditionally memory access was many orders of magnitude faster than disk, it was also more expensive. Hence, much of database development focused on optimizing disk access. As my Stanford database professor Gio Wiederhold was fond of repeating, "Any database engineer worth his salt always counts block reads." A lot of work went into minimizing those block reads by optimizing disk access, caching and pre-caching, creating indexes to reduce the number of block reads, and so on.

As the prices for memory fell and it became practical to store larger amounts of data in memory, the first database systems designed to keep and process data in memory came along. TimesTen was one of those pioneers; as the name suggests, it attempted to achieve 10 times the performance of traditional disk-based systems by focusing on storing and processing data in memory. Recently, there has been a renewed push for in-memory databases from vendors like SAP with its HANA system and the Apache Spark project, among many other efforts.

Loading the Data—Data Integration Tools

One important thing to keep in mind is that the data in a data warehouse is loaded from applications and operational systems. Therefore, the first order of business is loading the data warehouse with data.

There are various approaches, tools, and techniques for this.

ETL

ETL technology has been around for more than 20 years. Most modern ETL tools were developed in the mid- to late 1990s as part of the data warehousing movement. When relational databases were used to support operational systems and applications, data was usually stored in highly normalized data models. We won't go into too many details that are available in most relational database books, but normalized data models attempt to create tables with a minimum amount of redundancy and the smallest possible number of fields, so the updates are very fast. On the other hand, as we saw in "Dimensional modeling and star schemas" on page 31, most data warehouses favor denormalized data models where each table contains as many related attributes as possible, so all the information can be processed by a single pass through the data.

Data that comes from an operational system may contain customer information in several tables with different formats and representations. It would be the job of an ETL tool to convert the various representations into a common customer dimension, like the one we saw in Figure 2-3, and to make sure that the same customer record from different systems is used to create or update a single customer record in the customer dimension (Figure 2-7). Such a dimension is called a *conforming dimension*, because the customer dimension would make all incoming data conform to a single format and the same customer would be identified across the various records in different systems. In Figure 2-7, the operational system is using two tables to store customer data. Furthermore, these tables have different representations of the customer information. For example, first and last names are in different fields, there is a date of birth instead of an age, and multiple addresses are kept for each customer. The job of the ETL tool is to convert this representation into the representation expected by the data warehouse's customer dimension table by concatenating names into one field, calculating age from date of birth, and choosing the best address and concatenating it into a single string.

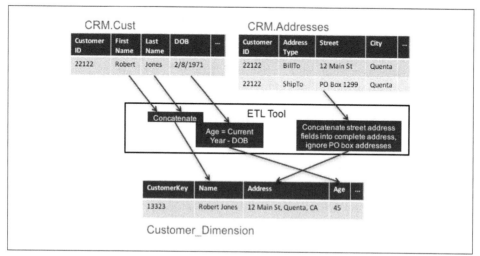

Figure 2-7. An ETL tool extracts data from multiple tables to create the customer dimension

Furthermore, because data warehouses typically contain data that comes from many different sources and applications, each with its own schema, data from each of these sources has to be normalized and converted to the single schema.

ETL versus ELT

For many years, Teradata and other high-end database vendors encouraged their customers to use their database engines to do the required transformations instead of leaving this to ETL tools. They argued that only highly scalable systems like theirs could handle the volume and complexity of loading their data warehouses. This processing is called ELT (extract, load, transform). In other words, the data gets loaded into the data warehouse as is and then converted into the right representation using the database engine (Figure 2-8).

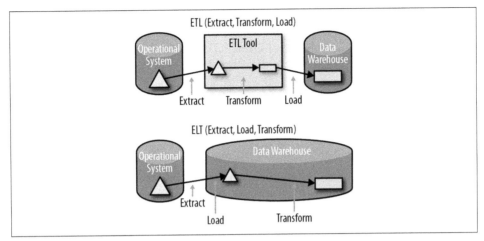

Figure 2-8. Comparison of ETL and ELT

Federation, EII, and data virtualization tools

When data comes from multiple systems, the data warehouse approach is to bring it all together in one place, integrate it into a single conforming schema, and then use it for analytics queries. An alternative approach is to create a logical or virtual schema across multiple systems and then issue queries against that virtual schema. This approach goes by many names, the most common being federation, enterprise information integration (EII), and data virtualization. The main scenarios where this approach is more appropriate than using a data warehouse are:

- When data must be kept fresh in the face of changes. Because these tools execute queries against original sources, the results are always up to date, while data warehouses usually have a lag depending on how often they are refreshed.
- When data access is infrequent. Building very expensive data warehouses for data that may only be used once a year or even less is not cost-effective.
- When compliance and data residency clauses may constrain data from being copied from one source location to a target destination.

On the other hand, this approach has several important drawbacks:

Labor-intensive manual process
    Virtual tables must be manually defined across disparate systems.

Schema and logic changes
    Although a schema change can cause ETL jobs loading a data warehouse to break, it will affect only the latest data, and the bulk of the data will still be available for analysis. With data virtualization tools, a schema change can break the queries and make all data unavailable until the queries are fixed.

Performance

Some queries that span multiple systems (called *federated queries*) have significant performance challenges. For example, complex multi-table joins and correlated subqueries across multiple databases can take a lot longer to execute than when all the tables are in the same database. Furthermore, while a data warehouse can be optimized for analytics with additional indexes and tuning, the operational source systems usually cannot be optimized for analytic queries without slowing down the operations that they were designed for.

Frequency

Each query is effectively executing a full integration job every time it runs. Therefore, if there are a lot of queries against the virtual schema, it becomes much more advantageous to extract the data once, store it in a data warehouse, and query it there. Doing so substantially reduces the load on the source systems and is far more computationally effective than reading and integrating the source tables again and again for each query. Some data virtualization tools mitigate the waste by caching data in some staging area, but in general, if the access frequency is very high and data freshness is not critical, a data warehouse may be a better choice.

As data volume and variety keep growing, data virtualization tools try to keep up by improving query optimization and adding in-memory processing and caching.

Figure 2-9 illustrates a data warehouse approach versus a data virtualization approach. In the top diagram, the two tables from different databases are combined during the ETL process and the result is persisted as a table in the data warehouse. All queries are then executed against this table. In the bottom diagram, a virtual view is created through data virtualization while the data physically remains in the original databases.

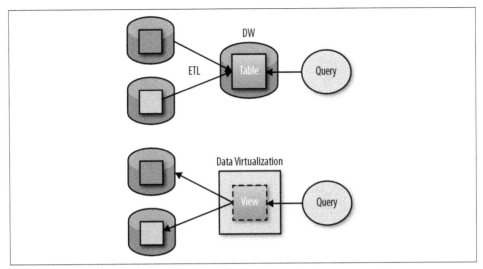

Figure 2-9. Comparison of data warehouse and virtualization approaches

Organizing and Managing the Data

The size and complexity of data warehouses has led to the development of a wide range of tools to organize them, check the quality of the data, and govern access. This final section explains the purpose and basic operation of these tools.

Data quality tools

Data quality is a mature discipline within data management. It involves defining quality rules, applying those rules to data to detect violations—often called exceptions—and fixing those exceptions. Data quality is a big topic, and entire books have been written about it, so this section provides just a quick summary designed to get the general approach across.

Data quality rules come in many shapes and sizes, but can generally be broken into several broad categories:

Scalar
> Applied to a specific value. For example, Name is a required field and should have a value; Salary should be a number; Age should be between 0 and 150.

Field level
> Applied to all the values in a field. The most common examples have to do with field uniqueness (for example, Customer_ID should be unique) and field density (for example, Name cannot be empty), but there may be other rules, such as that Income should fall in the range of X to Y. While some of these rules, like that of density, may seem redundant—for example, Name not being empty can be

expressed as a scalar test—the advantage of doing it at the field level is that we can provide tolerances; for instance, we can tolerate up to 10% of customer names being empty.

Record level

Applied to all the fields in a single record. For example, we can specify that if the US_CITIZEN field is True then the Social_Security_Number field should not be empty, or that a root element in the Orders record in a JSON file should have exactly three children.

Data set (table/file) level

Applied to the entire data set. These are not common and usually involve the number of records. For example, a data set containing sensor data should have at least one event per sensor per hour.

Cross–data set level

Applied across data sets. Referential integrity rules are very common in relational systems. They basically state that a primary key should be unique and that a foreign key field should not have any value that does not exist in the primary key field: select count(distinct order_id) from orders where fulfilled = 1 should be the same as select count(distinct order_id) from shipments, or the number of rows in file 1 should be smaller than or equal to the number of rows in file 2.

Some of the data quality rules can be fixed programmatically, while others require manual intervention. For example, a missing customer name may be looked up in a master customer list or a missing gender can be deduced from the salutation or first name. On the other hand, sometimes there is no way of programmatically fixing data quality problems. In such cases, data needs to either be fixed manually or be fixed differently depending on the project it is being used for. For example, if a transaction for an account number is missing a digit, the analyst curating the data may need to manually search through the accounts to see which one(s) it might match, and then look at the account history to see whether there is a transaction for that amount on that date. If customer income information is missing and the analyst has no way to get it, they may decide to take out the records with missing income values, to treat the income as 0, or to replace the missing income values with an average income, depending on the type of project they are working on.

In the absence of data quality rules, *data profiling* is a technique of automatically gathering statistics about data to then ascertain its quality. Profiling tools usually read all the data and, for each field, keep track of how many values are of which type (string versus number versus date), how many values are empty (NULLs), the minimum and maximum values, as well as the most frequent values for each field and some other statistics depending on the field. The advantages of using profiling are that it does not require the design of any quality rules, and that analysts can use the results to ascertain the quality of the data with regard to the specific project they are working on. For example, if the Age field is mostly empty but is not needed for a specific project, the data set may have acceptable quality levels. While pretty much all data quality tools include profiling, profiling is also used by a variety of other tools, for everything from data prep to data discovery.

Popular profiling and data quality tools include IBM Information Analyzer, Informatica DQ, SAS DataFlux, and many others.

MDM systems

A special class of data quality tools called master data management systems are used to create *master lists* of various entities: primarily customers, but also products (these are called product information management, or PIM, systems), suppliers, and many others. These are very sophisticated systems that take data from one or more systems, harmonize the data to a common schema and representation (units of measure, codes, etc.), and perform what's called *entity resolution*: finding multiple records that apply to the same entity. For example, some systems have multiple records for the same customer because of duplicate data entry, acquisitions (one customer firm bought another and they became a single customer), human error, or a variety of other reasons. Furthermore, different systems may use different identities for the customers—one may use tax IDs, while another relies on name and address and a third uses account numbers. Reconciling all of these is the job of an MDM system.

Once the records for the same entity have been identified, often it's found that they contain conflicting information—addresses are different, names are spelled a little differently, and so forth. So, another task of the MDM system is to fix these conflicts, either automatically or by triggering a manual intervention, to create the *golden record*: the one correct record for an entity that everyone should use.

MDM suppliers include traditional vendors such as IBM, Oracle, and Informatica, and some next-generation vendors such as Tamr that provide machine learning capabilities to automate the process.

Data modeling tools

Data modeling tools are used to create a relational schema. While theoretically data modelers can use tools such as Erwin and IBM InfoSphere Data Architect to create physical, logical, and semantic models, in practice, most of the time these tools are used to create an entity relationship model of the data with primary and foreign keys (also called referential integrity constraints).

Schema design is a very important activity for operational databases. Well-designed schemas improve database performance, while poorly designed ones slow it down— sometimes quite dramatically. A schema has to be designed with usage in mind: if it's operational, it must be well normalized and optimized for many small transactions; if it's for data warehousing, dimensional design should be used to optimize for analytical queries. The schema designer must also consider understandability and extensibility. Schemas change, and well-designed schemas are usually easy to change by adding new columns, while poorly designed ones frequently require expensive rearchitecting.

We discussed referential integrity and normalization earlier in this chapter. Because it is such a core concept, all relational databases provide facilities to enforce referential integrity. Unfortunately, to do that, every time a new order is added to the Orders table in our previous example, the database has to check the Customers table to make sure the Customer_ID in the Orders table exists in the Customers table and, if the value is not there, abort or reject the transaction. This adds significant performance overhead to Orders table updates. It also complicates all the applications that process orders, because they need a way to deal with such rejected transactions. In practice, I haven't seen any production databases that enforce referential integrity. Instead, the information about primary and foreign keys is kept in data modeling tools and data quality tools are used to check referential integrity.

Metadata repositories

Metadata repositories contain technical metadata (data about data) across the data assets. The metadata is collected manually or by integrating with various other tools, such as ETL tools, BI tools, and so forth. There are three main use cases for metadata repositories:

Finding data assets
> For example, a data architect may want to know which tables in which databases contain a Customer_ID.

Tracking lineage (provenance)
> Many regulations require enterprises to document the lineage of data assets—in other words, where the data for those assets came from and how it was generated or transformed.

Impact analysis
> If developers are making changes in a complex ecosystem, there is always a danger of breaking something. Impact analysis allows developers to see all the data assets that rely on a particular field or integration job before making a change.

Metadata repository vendors include IBM, Informatica, ASG Rochade, and many others. However, these are quickly being supplanted by a new class of products called *data catalogs*, covered in Chapter 8.

Data governance tools

Data governance tools record, document, and sometimes manage governance policies. The tools usually define who the *data steward* is for each data asset. Data stewards are responsible for making sure the data assets are correct, documenting their purpose and lineage, and defining access and lifecycle management policies for them.

In some companies, data steward can be a full-time, dedicated role. In other companies, the role may be assigned to someone with direct business responsibilities related to the data. The organizational structure also varies: some data stewards belong to a formal data governance organization, often managed by a chief data officer (CDO), whereas others belong to functional teams or business units or, more rarely, to the IT department. For example, a data steward for sales data may be a member of the sales ops team.

Data stewardship is often complex and cross-functional. For example, each sales group may have its own customer relationship management (CRM) system and its own data steward, while a data warehouse that combines all the sales and customer data from all systems may have its own data steward too. The most important function of the data governance tool is to identify who is responsible for what, so they can be consulted and can authorize access and other data policies.

Once ownership has been documented, the next step in rolling out a data governance program is to document data governance policies. Broadly speaking, these usually include the following aspects:

Access control and sensitive data regulatory compliance
> Who can see what. This is particularly important for sensitive data and for complying with regulations that address sensitive data. For example, the credit card industry has Payment Card Industry (PCI) regulations that define how sensitive credit card data should be handled, the medical industry in the US has government regulations called the Health Insurance Portability and Accountability Act (HIPAA), and any company that has any European customers must comply with a new regulation called the General Data Protection Regulation (GDPR).

Documentation or metadata management
> What has to be documented about each data set, usually including lineage and, again, regulatory compliance. For the financial industry, the Basel III compliance requirement is documented in rule BCBS 239, requiring detailed lineage to be maintained for all financial results reported by a company.

Data lifecycle management
> Retention policies, backup policies, and so on.

Data quality management
> The acceptable levels of quality and what data quality rules to use.

The business glossary

The various terms represented by the data. The glossary organizes and documents these terms: it usually contains the official names and descriptions for each term and their data representations (for example, the "profit" term may describe how profit is calculated, while the "customer status" term may describe a list of legal statuses and how these statuses are assigned).

Consuming the Data

Once data is loaded and made available, the analysts can use it to produce reports, run ad hoc analytics, and create dashboards. There are a plethora of such tools available, including many open source and free products.

Historically, these tools used to be separated into reporting tools such as Crystal Reports and Jasper Reports, which produced print-ready reports; BI tools such as Business Objects and Cognos, which created ad hoc reports and charts; and OLAP tools such as those that created in-memory cubes and allowed the users to "slice and dice" or analyze data along various dimensions. These cubes were built either in memory (e.g., ArborSoft/Hyperion) or on demand from a relational database (also called ROLAP; e.g., MicroStrategy). Eventually, most of these capabilities became consolidated into one tool, so these days a tool like MicroStrategy provides all of them.

The first generation of these tools were designed for developers to create reports, dashboards, or OLAP cubes and let analysts work with these artifacts. In the 2000s, a new generation of products such as Tableau and Qlik came to prominence by providing analysts with simple tools that allowed them to work directly with data tables and files without having to wait for IT to code up a report. This ushered in the era of self-service analytics that we will cover extensively in Chapter 6.

Advanced analytics

Advanced analytics have been around for years in many industries. From engineering to insurance to finance, statistical models and predictive models have been used to measure risk and simulate real-life scenarios. Many of the natural sciences, from anthropology to physics, employ statistics to measure, extrapolate, and predict. Wall Street quants have been building automated trading models for decades. Insurance actuaries have been modeling risk and probabilities for over a century. An entire segment of computer science called data mining has been around for over 20 years. A multi-billion-dollar industry has grown up around providing specialized tools for statistics and advanced analytics, including such vendors as SAS, MATLAB, SPSS (now part of IBM), and many others.

Traditionally the realm of statisticians and scientists, advanced analytics have slowly been making their way into the mainstream. Popular consumer packages such as

Excel now include basic statistical functions like regular regression. More importantly, many consumer-facing applications showcase predictive or statistical models. From real estate websites like Zillow.com that use statistical models to calculate the value of a home to credit scoring applications and money management packages that model savings and retirement incomes, people are increasingly encountering the results of predictive analytics in their daily lives and are beginning to wonder how they can incorporate them into their business lives.

There is increasing talk of "citizen data scientists"—basically business analysts who apply advanced analytics to address their problems without hiring statisticians and professional data scientists. Just as programming is now taught in many high schools and most analysts are comfortable using Excel macros, SQL queries, and even simple scripting languages, advanced analytics are slowly but surely making their way from "advanced" to commonplace.

Conclusion

This brief history of data and data management techniques has brought us to the early 2010s. In the next chapter, we will cover the big data phenomenon and the disruption that it caused in data management practices.

CHAPTER 3

Introduction to Big Data and Data Science

The popular use of big data can be traced to a single research paper published in 2004: "MapReduce: Simplified Data Processing on Large Clusters" (*https://ai.google/ research/pubs/pub62*), by Jeffrey Dean and Sanjay Ghemawat. In this 13-page paper (including source code), two engineers at Google explained how the company had found a way to bring its gigantic indexing needs down to reasonable processing requirements through a radically new type of algorithm running on massively parallel clusters. The basic idea of MapReduce is to break work into *mappers* that can run in parallel and *reducers* that take the output of mappers and process it. The first operation is called "mapping" because it takes each element of input data and "maps" a function onto it, leaving the output for the reducer to handle.

For example, to count words in all the documents on all the nodes in a cluster, assuming each document is stored on a single node, we can have thousands of mappers, running in parallel, produce a list of documents and the word count of each, and send that list to the reducer. The reducer will then create a master list of all documents with their word counts and calculate the total word count by adding all the counts for all the documents together (Figure 3-1). Assuming that the disk is much slower than the network and that the mapper reading documents is much slower than sending a total to the reducer, this program would scale very nicely to a large cluster without any perceptible performance degradation.

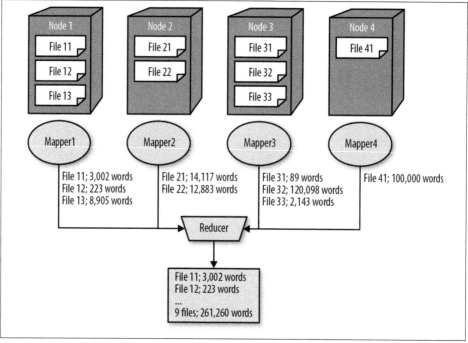

Figure 3-1. The basic architecture behind MapReduce

Hadoop Leads the Historic Shift to Big Data

Although Google did not release its internal MapReduce tools, developers inspired by the paper created a free, open source implementation called Hadoop that quickly became central to the processing of big data by organizations everywhere.

The Hadoop File System

A special filesystem is needed to provide data efficiently to MapReduce, and the most popular one is the Hadoop File System (HDFS). It is a massively parallel, highly available, self-healing filesystem. However, it makes no attempt to implement the relational model (although SQL-like interfaces were later built on top of it). Instead, like many of the other NoSQL databases that were growing up at the time, HDFS is a sophisticated kind of key/value store.

It makes multiple copies of each block (by default, three copies) and stores these copies on different nodes. This way, if one node dies, two other copies are still available and the block will be copied to a third node once the failure is detected without affecting availability. The multiple copies also facilitate load balancing, because we can choose to send the work to the least busy node that contains the data. For example, in Figure 3-2, file 11 is stored across different nodes. It has two blocks. Block 1 is stored on nodes 1, 2, and 3, while block 2 is stored on nodes 1, 3, and 4. When the file is being processed, work for block 1 can be performed on any of nodes where it is stored—whichever is less busy. Similarly, work on block 2 can be performed on any of the three nodes where it is stored. If one of the nodes—say, node 3—were to get corrupted or otherwise become unavailable, HDFS would still have access to the two other copies of each block stored on node 3 and would make sure to create replacement copies for the blocks originally stored on node 3 on other nodes that are still up and running.

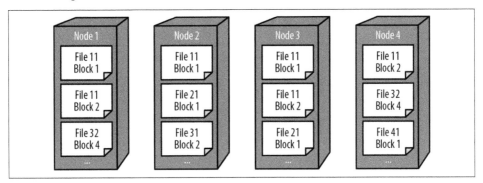

Figure 3-2. Example of distributed storage in HDFS

How Processing and Storage Interact in a MapReduce Job

In our previous example of counting words, a job will be created that contains a list of all the blocks in all the files and the job manager will send the work for each block to the least-loaded node that contains it, evening the load across the cluster. Of course, to create a file list, we now have to reassemble the files from the blocks. Assuming that's too much for a single node, we can have multiple reducers processing the work. In order to make sure that the same reducer gets all the blocks for a single file, we will leverage what's called the *shuffle* step of MapReduce, where the output of the mappers contains a key and a value and a shuffle function is applied to the key to send all work with the same key to the same reducer. For example, we can use a hash function that takes a filename and returns 0 or 1, perhaps by adding all the ASCII values for the letters in the filename and dividing by 2. All output for files whose names hash to 0 goes to reducer 1, whereas output for files whose names hash to 1 goes to reducer 2.

When there are multiple reducers, in order to create a single file we will need to channel all of the reducers to a single reducer that will assemble the final output into one file, adding complexity and processing time. Instead, to optimize for multiple reducers working in parallel, most MapReduce jobs generate multiple files, typically in the same directory. To enable this, most Hadoop components work on directories rather than files. For example, Pig scripts, Hive, and other projects expect a directory as input rather than a file, and treat all files in that directory as a single "logical" file. In

Figure 3-3, a folder called *WordCount* is created, and files with unique names contain the output of the two reducers. The names of the files are usually generated automatically, so they aren't meaningful and are never used directly except by the internal program code that needs to read them. All work is done on the *WordCount* folder, treating it as a single logical file. This is equivalent to concatenating all the files in the folder.

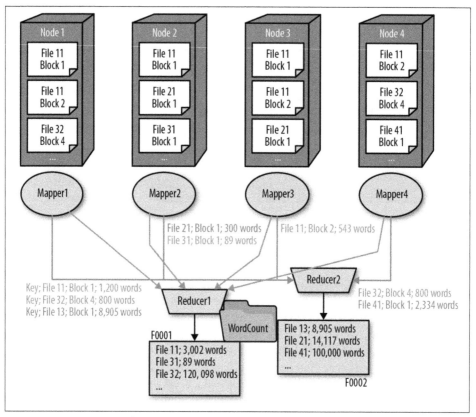

Figure 3-3. Mappers, reducers, and file storage in Hadoop

Because so much work is done on the block level, Hadoop usually has a large block size, defaulting to 64 or 128 MB. Since only one file can be stored in a block, this makes Hadoop not very efficient for storing small files—a 1 KB file would still take a whole block of 64 or 128 MB. To optimize storage, *sequence files* were introduced. A sequence file is a collection of key/value pairs and is often used to store lots of small files in one large file by using the smaller files' names as the keys and the contents as the values.

While very efficient and elegant, MapReduce requires developers to think about their logic carefully and divide the work correctly. If the work is not distributed properly, the job can suffer from significant performance degradation. For example, if we have 1,000 mappers running on a 1,000-node cluster and 999 of the mappers take 5 minutes to run but the last mapper takes 5 hours, the entire job will still require 5 hours to run.

Schema on Read

In relational databases, the schema (a list of columns, their names, and their types) of a table is defined when the table is created. When data is inserted into the table, it has to conform to this predefined structure. This requires a very formal and careful approach to schema management because if the data does not match the table schema it will not be inserted or stored in a data warehouse. In fact, there won't be any place it can be inserted, since inserting it will require the definition of a schema that matches the data.

Since HDFS is a filesystem (it basically looks like a Linux filesystem to the user), it can store all sorts of data. Of course, in order to do any processing, the data has to be given a schema or structure. To achieve this, Hadoop takes a "schema on read" approach—it applies the schema to the data when it reads it. For example, a user can define an external Hive table for a file in HDFS. When that table is queried, Hive will attempt to map the data in the file to the table definition, giving it a schema. If the data does not match the schema definition, the query will fail. However, unlike with a relational database, the data is still stored in HDFS and preserved. It just cannot be used until the correct schema is applied. Because of this approach, data can be added to HDFS with minimal effort, without any checks and without any schema being defined.

Hadoop Projects

Hadoop has spawned a rich ecosystem of projects to do everything from ingestion to administration to management. Tables 3-1 and 3-2 cover some of the most popular projects traditionally included with Hadoop distributions. Most are open source, although some components of Cloudera and MapR require a commercial subscription (indicated with a * in Table 3-1).

Table 3-1. Popular on-premises tools related to Hadoop and HDFS

	Apache Hadoop	Cloudera	Hortonworks (including IBM, Microsoft Azure, and Pivotal)	MapR
Ingestion	Sqoop, Flume		NiFi	
Relational interface/DB	Hive	Hive, Impala*	Hive	Hive, Drill
NoSQL	HBase	HBase, Kudu	HBase	MapRDB (variant of HBase)
Security	Ranger	Sentry*	Ranger	
Governance	Atlas	Navigator*	Atlas	Resells Waterline*
Filesystem	HDFS	HDFS	HDFS	MapR-FS

Table 3-2. Popular cloud-based tools related to Hadoop and HDFS

	AWS	Azure	Google Cloud Platform
Ingestion	Kinesis	Event Hub	Cloud Pub/Sub
Integration	Glue	ADF	Cloud Dataflow
Relational interface/DB	Hive, Presto, RedShift, Aurora	Hive	Cloud Spanner
NoSQL	DynamoDB	AzureNoSQL	Bigtable
Security		Security Center	
Governance	Glue	Azure Governance	
Filesystem	EBS, EFS	ADLS	ECFS
Object store	S3	Blob Storage	GCS

One of the most important developments in the Hadoop ecosystem was *Spark*, an extension of the concept that offers both more speed and more flexibility than Map-Reduce. Spark originated as network speeds improved and reduced the need to tightly couple compute and storage. Spark was started at UC Berkeley's AMPLab in 2009 and is now a top-level Apache project. It is commercially supported by Databricks and is included in every Hadoop distribution.

The core idea of Spark is to create a large in-memory data set across a cluster of computers. If HDFS strove to create a single persistent filesystem across a cluster, Spark effectively creates one large memory space across the cluster. At the core of Spark is the Resilient Distributed Dataset (RDD), which appears as a single data set to the programs using Spark.

Another improvement in Spark is the generalization of the old MapReduce model. Instead of a single pipeline consisting of mapper, shuffler, and reducer (with multiple instances potentially running in parallel), complex pipelines can pass data through multiple different instances of each stage. For instance, Spark can easily pass the output of one reducer to another reducer, which in Hadoop would require cumbersome manual coding and slow writes and reads to and from the disk.

Although Spark is written in Scala, it can be used through interfaces in Java, Python, R, and other languages as well as SparkSQL, a SQL interface to RDDs based on a layer of abstraction called a DataFrame.

Data Science

A lot of analytics are *descriptive*: they look back at what has happened and rely on human experts to examine the history and make decisions about the future. Sometimes humans do a good job of this, but sometimes they don't. Often they rely on their intuition and personal experience and have very little opportunity to validate their decisions. Imagine if, instead, you could *predict* what was going to happen before it happened and validate it against the historical data? Or if you could actually test things on a small subset of users before rolling them out on a large scale?

The idea of data science is to make recommendations about actions to take based on factual information represented as data. Even the name of the discipline is indicative of the underlying principle. When I asked DJ Patil, who coined the phrase, why he called it "data science," he told me how he'd started a new group at LinkedIn focused on using data and advanced analytics to answer all sorts of questions about LinkedIn's user experience and business. To decide what to call this group, they placed three different wanted ads describing the person they were looking for. All three ads were for the same position with the same job description and preferred experience, placed on the same job sites. The only difference was the name: "Data Scientist," "Data Analyst," and "Data Engineer." The ad that drew the most applicants was "Data Scientist," so they named the group "Data Science."

This is a good example of what's commonly referred to as *A/B* or *split testing*: you try A and B on different groups of people and rigorously measure which one is better, before making a decision. Most data-driven companies, like LinkedIn and Google, do not allow any code to be released without instrumentation that allows them to measure its effectiveness. They also traditionally test new features in several different markets before rolling these out to the broader user base.

At the core of data science is a combination of math (specifically statistics), computer science (especially data handling and machine learning), and domain or business knowledge. The domain knowledge is crucial for the data scientist to understand what problems need to be solved, what data is relevant, and how to interpret the results. Many books and articles have been written on the technical aspects of data science, but in this book we will focus on data science as it can be practiced by large enterprises. To introduce the central concepts, I'll reprint here the following essay by Veijko Krunic, who consults with large enterprises about how to start practicing data science.

What Should Your Analytics Organization Focus On?

 *Veljko Krunic is an independent consultant and trainer helping his clients to get the best business results from data science and big data. He has worked with organizations ranging from the Fortune 10 to early-stage startups, guiding them through the complete lifecycle of big data and analytical solutions, from early proof-of-concept efforts to the improvement of mission-critical systems. His previous employers include Hortonworks, the SpringSource division of VMware, and the JBoss division of Red Hat. He has a PhD in computer science and an MS in engineering management from the University of Colorado at Boulder, with a focus on strategic planning and applied statistics in quality sciences. He is also a Six Sigma Master Black Belt.*

Many companies are making investments in big data and data science, and are rightfully expecting significant business benefits. At the same time, the resulting big data systems and data science methods may be among the most complex technologies to enter the enterprise market in recent memory. The size of the effort makes it hard to match the tools and techniques you adopt to the organization's goals.

As an executive, you will be exposed to a huge variety of new technologies and concepts. You may have been bombarded with such terms as deep learning, HMMs, Bayesian networks, GLMs, SVMs, and more. On the big data infrastructure side, you may have heard terms like Spark, HDFS, MapReduce, HBase, Cassandra, Hadoop, Impala, Storm, Hive, Flink, and many others. The Hortonworks Hadoop distribution alone packages 26 Apache projects as of the end of 2018, and the Apache Software Foundation has over 300 active projects, many of which are data-related. There are also hundreds of commercial products fighting for a place in the ecosystem. It's easy to get lost in all the noise. Even your technically trained staff can be overwhelmed. It's rare to find a data scientist or architect who possesses excellent (or even strong practitioner-level) skills in *all* those areas. It is much more likely for knowledge about various parts of the system to be fragmented among different members of the team. It may even happen that this is the first time the team is working on a project similar to what you are doing now.

This essay is meant to keep you focused on the important questions you need to answer as an executive. How do you know that you are directing your project down the road to optimal business success, as opposed to simply following the direction determined by the preexisting knowledge your team happens to possess? When no single person has expertise in all the areas covered by a project, how do you know that you are investing in the areas that will give you the best payoff? How can you avoid playing the unfortunate "knowledge poker" game, in which various team members are assumed to hold cards that the project needs for success, but no one is actually sure what you collectively know as a team and whether the full scope of the project is covered?

The previously mentioned technologies are important to many projects, to be sure. However, if these terms are the only ones that you are hearing when you are talking with your data science and big data teams, you should ask yourself whether the right focus is being put on the system as a whole, or whether your team is overfocusing on certain components of the system at the expense of the system as a whole. In particular, *is the focus on things you need as the executive, or on things your team knows (or hopes to learn)*? Thinking about the relationship of engineering to your business, with a focus on final results, is the discipline of *whole system engineering.*

It is not your team's fault if it is not focused on the system as a whole. It is fair to say that as of now, industry in general suffers from the same absence of focus on systems. Most presentations, meetups, and marketing materials focus on only a few of the technologies that are in turn only a *part* of the successful analytical stack. Much less time is devoted to system engineering. For that matter, how much do we even talk in our community about the simple but fundamental notion that big data systems are engineering *systems* that have to be fit for *business* purposes?

As an example of the current tendency to focus on various parts of the system, with the goal of making the right choice between alternative methods, a lot of ink is spilled discussing the relative strengths and weaknesses of individual machine learning methods. These are important tactical decisions, but your job is to avoid getting trapped in technical decisions before you know your strategy.

Let's take as an example the MNIST data set, which presents a classification problem: handwritten digits that the computer should classify as digits from 0 to 9. It is probably the most widely used data set in computer vision today, used to test computer vision algorithms developed in settings that range from classroom projects to major internet corporations. The period between 1998 and 2016 saw improvement in the accuracy of classification from an error rate of 2.4% (achieved with a relatively simple *k*-nearest neighbors algorithm) to 0.21% (achieved with an ensemble of deep neural networks).[1] For 18 years, some of the brightest minds in machine learning worked hard to improve the error rate by 2.19%. That is a significant improvement, allowing, for instance, a computer scanner to read most of the addresses written on mail envelopes automatically, versus a human having to look at almost every envelope.

---

1 See *http://yann.lecun.com/exdb/mnist/* and *http://rodrigob.github.io/are_we_there_yet/build/classifica tion_datasets_results.html.*

However, when you are running a business project, you are not interested in the behavior of a single classification algorithm. The underlying question you need to ask is: "Does that difference of x% significantly contribute to the success of the project?" Sometimes it will, sometimes it won't. Sometimes you don't need the best classification method known to humankind; you may benefit more from simply collecting additional data sources that might produce better overall results.

The reality of system engineering is that it is much more important to avoid big pitfalls from which you cannot recover than it is to make the best possible choice between two close competitors, whether they are methods or products. Certainly, if you don't make the best decision about a particular part of the system, you might be giving a significant advantage to your competitors, and such an error might even kill you down the road. But before "down the road" can even become an issue, you must first have the ability to develop a viable product that could start moving down that road.

And while big data and data science do bring important new elements to the table, they don't significantly change the best practices of system engineering. As an executive, you are on a good course to developing a viable product if, after meeting with your data science team, you are able to clearly and concisely answer the following questions:

1. How are the data science concepts they are talking about related to your business?

2. Is your organization prepared to act on the results of the analysis? (Business results don't magically materialize just because you've completed an analysis —they materialize when you take *appropriate business actions* based on the results of the analysis. Both at the start and throughout the project, you need a clear understanding of the business actions available to your organization.)

3. What part of your machine learning system should you invest in to get best "bang for the buck"?

4. If the team needs to do more research to answer the previous questions, what exactly is that research, what is the range of possible answers they expect to get, and what are the things they need to complete that research (time to try methods, additional data, etc.)?

Key to your success is distinguishing whether you are running a system engineering effort that is able to produce predictable results (or a spectrum of possible results), or a *research project* whose results might be great, but are not exactly predictable or marketable. While there is a place for both in business and industry, you certainly should not mistake the two types of project. And you should also guide your team so that the members focus on executing the right type of project. An inability to clearly answer the previous questions is a major red flag, and until you can "ace" them, better methods will not help you much.

The process of whole system engineering is beyond the scope of this book, but there is one critical component that you will get right if you apply the techniques advised here. That critical component is an appreciation of the need to understand your data, and that getting to know your data is a non-trivial challenge.

Some teams make the error of assuming that by the simple virtue of having recorded their data in some database or data lake, they are automatically experts on the data. Starting with that as a premise, it may appear logical to devote all attention to "other, more important issues." The reality is that cataloging and interpreting modern enterprise data is a complex problem, and organizations must make substantial investments in data governance to carry out these tasks. Essentially, if you have the wrong data, improving classification by 2.19% will not necessarily help. If you're working with the wrong data or have misinterpreted your data, you must change course as soon as possible. Luckily, you may be able to reuse the investments you've made in tools.

Finding and implementing the right approach to your data is a key aspect of system engineering, and the approach should be evaluated near the beginning of your project to make sure you are on the right track.

Machine Learning

Machine learning refers to the process of training a computer program to build a statistical model based on data. It is a very broad and deep topic, and we are not going to do it justice here; this section aims simply to give you a flavor of what machine learning is about.

Machine learning can be supervised or unsupervised. *Supervised* machine learning involves feeding training data to create a model. For example, if we want to predict prices of homes in a specific area, we could feed historical sales data to the model and create a formula that should accurately predict values for other similar homes.

Various machine learning algorithms have been around for years and are well understood and trusted. While there are thousands of algorithms and they can always be improved, the most common algorithms, such as linear regression, are available even in common tools such as Microsoft Excel. The difficult part of machine learning is usually not the model, but the data.

Without the right data, the model is going to be *unstable*. A model is said to be unstable if it seems to work well on test data but does not accurately predict results on real data out in the field. A common technique is to break historical data into two random data sets, train the model on one (the training data set), and then apply the model to the other (the test data set) to see whether it accurately predicts the results. This may catch some of the problems, but if the entire data set is biased, the model will still be unstable when used against real-world data. Furthermore, the conditions that the model was trained on may change and the model may no longer apply. This is called "model drift." For instance, in the housing example a new road or a new business might dramatically affect the prices, and we would need to retrain the model to incorporate this new information.

In general, the key to creating good models is having the right features—the inputs to the model that determine the outcome. Imagine if, in our house pricing example, the quality of schools was not considered. Two identical houses on the same street but on opposite sides of the school district boundary might have significantly different prices if one school is dramatically better than the other. No matter how much data we get to train our model, if this variable is missing, we will not be able to accurately predict the prices. And even if we have the right features, we have to have representative data. For example, if all our data is from districts with similar-performing schools, the model will be trained to ignore school scores because they will not produce any variations in home prices. To accurately train the model, we would need data from a representative mix of high- and low-performing school districts. Feature engineering is one of the most critical tasks every data scientist has to perform.

Not only is it important to have the right data, but it should be of high quality. Unlike in regular analytics, where data problems often jump out as results that do not make sense, it can be very difficult to spot bad data in machine learning unless it makes the models unstable. For instance, in our case if the school district information was corrupted or wrong, we might be able to build a stable model as long as it was corrupted consistently for both the training and the testing data sets, but the model would likely be useless on real live data where this information is not corrupted.

Unsupervised learning refers to machine learning that is not trained. For example, customer segmentation is often done using unsupervised machine learning. The program is given a set of customers and huge amounts of different demographic information, and then breaks the data into buckets of "similar" customers. Just as with supervised learning, if segmentation is performed on bad data, it may produce unreliable results and it may be very difficult to figure out that, say, the 7 segments you produce of 100,000 customers each are somehow wrong. Because models tend to be so complex that they are impenetrable to human understanding, *explainability* has become a major topic in machine learning.

Explainability

I had an interesting discussion once with a data scientist who told me how he was hired to do customer segmentation. When he presented the results of his model to his client, the VP of marketing picked two customer records out of the same segment and asked why those two were grouped together. The data scientist couldn't explain the results beyond going over how he had trained the model, and the VP announced he wasn't going to invest hundreds of thousands of dollars into a campaign based on this segmentation if no one could explain it to him.

Explainability is not just a matter of curiosity or an aid to debugging. It is a fundamental question of trust. Users of analytics are often asked to prove that the models they use are not making inappropriate or illegal decisions. Discrimination is one of those tricky areas. Imagine a town where one ethnic population has on average about a quarter of the income of another ethnic population. Should the model be allowed to consider ethnicity as a variable? Most people (and anti-discrimination laws) would say no. But what if we make decisions based on income? People with more income might get higher credit limits at local banks or stores; this seems to be fair and common sense. However, what if we don't know people's true income levels when they apply for credit? Most store credit applications do not require a copy of an income tax return or paycheck. In addition, some people may be part of the gig economy and not earn formal income even if their household income is quite high, while other people might not have a credit history or score to use for verification purposes. What to do?

A clever data scientist might be tempted to infer ethnicity from the first and last names and cross-reference average income for that ethnicity in that town against the income reported by the applicant. If the inferred income and reported income are far apart, the application process would require additional credit checks. Is that legal? Are we now discriminating by ethnicity? How would a credit officer even know why "the computer" is requiring additional credit checks? What if the data scientist was not consciously checking ethnicity, but the algorithm uncovered correlations between names and income level blindly?

Such problems require explainability. Which variables caused the decision? What were the values of those variables? This is a difficult, but promising, area of machine learning. A lot of work is being done in academia as well as at machine learning companies such as FICO.

Change Management

Since the real world rarely stays the same, models that represented it at one point in time may well lose their predictive abilities. This is known as *model drift*. And since the outputs of the models are predictive, it is difficult to tell how good the predictions are and, therefore, whether the model is still relevant until the actual events happen. Thus, constant monitoring is critical to keep the model performing accurately. If drift is detected, the model needs to be retrained on new data. Even the data may drift. For example, IoT sensors in harsh conditions such as oil fields might go bad. Some of them may start spewing incorrect data, which must not be allowed to affect the outcome of the model. This data drift must be checked for outliers, so incorrect data does not corrupt the model.

Unfortunately, rerunning the existing model on the new data may not produce a stable model because the model won't reflect any new variables that may be introduced into the mix to affect the outcomes. For example, a model that once accurately predicted house sale prices in a neighborhood may not consider the fact that a new highway is being constructed through the neighborhood, and that proximity to this highway significantly affects the prices. Until this new variable (proximity to the new highway) is added to the model, the model may not be able to predict prices accurately. In short, one must regularly construct new models or retrain existing ones using the most appropriate current machine learning algorithms.

Conclusion

Advanced analytics, machine learning, predictive analytics, recommendation engines —the list is long and there are still many challenges to overcome, but this technology is very promising. It is already changing our lives, with applications ranging from self-driving cars, to much improved voice recognition and visual recognition technology, to looking for disease signals in genetic codes, reading IoT signals to provide predictive maintenance, or predicting what our houses are worth. All of this runs on data—and what better place to get that data than an enterprise data lake?

CHAPTER 4

Starting a Data Lake

As discussed in the previous chapter, the promise of the data lake is to store the enterprise's data in a way that maximizes its availability and accessibility for analytics and data science. But what's the best way to get started? This chapter discusses various paths enterprises take to build a data lake.

Apache Hadoop is an open source project that's frequently used for this purpose. While there are many other alternatives, especially in the cloud, Hadoop-based data lakes provide a good representation of the advantages they provide, so we are going to use Hadoop as an example. We'll begin by reviewing what it is and some of its key advantages for supporting a data lake.

The What and Why of Hadoop

Hadoop is a massively parallel storage and execution platform that automates many of the difficult aspects of building a highly scalable and available cluster. It has its own distributed filesystem, HDFS (although some Hadoop distributions, like MapR and IBM, provide their own filesystems to replace HDFS). HDFS automatically replicates data on the cluster to achieve high parallelism and availability. For example, if Hadoop uses the default replication factor of three, it stores each block on three different nodes. This way, when a job needs a block of data, the scheduler has a choice of three different nodes to use and can decide which one is the best based on what other jobs are running on it, what other data is located there, and so forth. Furthermore, if one of the three nodes fails, the system dynamically reconfigures itself to create another replica of each block that used to be on that node while running current jobs on the remaining two nodes.

As we saw in the previous chapter, MapReduce is a programming model that has been implemented to run on top of Hadoop and to take advantage of HDFS to create massively parallel applications. It allows developers to create two types of functions, known as mappers and reducers. Mappers work in parallel to process the data and stream the results to reducers that assemble the data for final output. For example, a program that counts words in a file can have a mapper function that reads a block in a file, counts the number of words, and outputs the filename and the number of words it counted in that block. The reducers will then get a stream of word counts from the mappers and add the blocks for each file before outputting the final counts. An intermediate service called *sort and shuffle* makes sure that the word counts for the same file are routed to the same reducer. The beautiful thing about Hadoop is that individual MapReduce jobs do not have to know or worry about the location of the data, about optimizing which functions run on which nodes, or about which nodes failed and are being recovered—Hadoop takes care of all that transparently.

Apache Spark, which ships with every Hadoop distribution, provides an execution engine that can process large amounts of data in memory across multiple nodes. Spark is more efficient and easier to program than MapReduce, much better suited for ad hoc or near-real-time processing, and, like Map-Reduce, takes advantage of data locality provided by HDFS to optimize processing. Spark comes with an array of useful modules, like SparkSQL, which provides a SQL interface to Spark programs, and supports universal processing of heterogeneous data sources through DataFrames.

However, the main attraction of Hadoop is that, as Figure 4-1 demonstrates, it is a whole platform and ecosystem of open source and proprietary tools that solve a wide variety of use cases. The most prominent projects include:

Hive
    A SQL-like interface to Hadoop files

Spark
    An in-memory execution system

Yarn
    A distributed resource manager

Oozie
    A workflow system

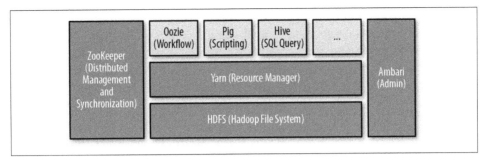

Figure 4-1. A sample Hadoop architecture

Several properties of Hadoop make it attractive as a long-term data storage and management platform. These include:

Extreme scalability

At most enterprises data only grows, and often exponentially. This growth means more and more compute power is required to process the data. Hadoop is designed to keep scaling by simply adding more nodes (this is often referred to as "scaling out"). It is used in some of the largest clusters in the world, at companies such as Yahoo! and Facebook.

Cost-effectiveness

Hadoop is designed to work with off-the-shelf, lower-cost hardware; run on top of Linux; and use many free, open source projects. This makes it very cost-effective.

Modularity

Traditional data management systems are monolithic. For example, in a traditional relational database data can only be accessed through relational queries, so if someone develops a better data processing tool or a faster query engine, it cannot leverage existing data files. RDBMSs also require tight schema control— before you can add any data, you have to predefine the structure of that data (called the schema), and you have to carefully change that structure if the data changes. This approach is referred to as "schema on write." Hadoop, on the other hand, is designed from the ground up to be modular, so the same file can be accessed by any application. For example, a file might be accessed by Hive to perform a relational query or by a custom MapReduce job to do some heavy-duty analytics. This modularity makes Hadoop extremely attractive as a long-term platform for managing data, since new data management technologies will be able to use data stored in Hadoop through open interfaces.

Loose schema coupling, or "schema on read"

Unlike a traditional relational database, Hadoop does not enforce any sort of schema when the data is written. This allows so-called *frictionless ingest*—data can be ingested without any checking or processing. Since we do not necessarily know how the data is going to be used, using frictionless ingest allows us to avoid the cost of processing and curating data that we may not need, and potentially processing it incorrectly for future applications. It is much better to leave the data in its original or raw state and do the work as needed when the requirements and use case are solidified.

If you're building a long-term storage and analytics system for your data, you'll want it to be cost-effective, highly scalable, and available. You'll also want adding data to require minimal work, and you'll want the system to be extensible to support future technologies, applications, and projects. As you can see from the brief preceding discussion, Hadoop fits the bill beautifully.

Preventing Proliferation of Data Puddles

With all the excitement around big data, there are many vendors and system integrators out there marketing immediate value to businesses. These folks often promise quick return on investment (ROI), with cloud-based solutions. For many business teams whose projects languish in IT work queues and who are tired of fighting for priority and attention or finding that their IT teams lack the necessary skills to do what they are asking, this may seem like a dream come true. In weeks or months, they get the projects they have been demanding from IT for years.

Many of these projects get started and produce quick wins, causing other teams to undertake similar projects. Pretty soon, many business groups have their own "shadow IT" and their own little Hadoop clusters (sometimes called data puddles) on premises and in the cloud. These single-purpose clusters are usually small and purpose-built using whatever technology the system integrators (SIs) or enterprise developers are familiar with, and are loaded with data that may or may not be rigorously sourced.

The unfortunate reality of open source technology is that it is still not stable enough, or standard enough, for this proliferation. Once the SIs move on and the first major technical challenge hits—jobs don't run, libraries need to be upgraded, technologies are no longer compatible—these data puddles end up being abandoned or get thrown back to IT. Furthermore, because data puddles create silos, it is difficult to reuse the data in those puddles and the results of the work done on that data.

To prevent this scenario, many enterprises prefer to get ahead of the train and build a centralized data lake. Then, when business teams decide that they need Hadoop, the compute resources and the data for their projects are already available in the data lake. By providing managed compute resources with preloaded data, yet giving users autonomy through self-service, an enterprise data lake gives businesses the best of both worlds: support for the components that are difficult for them to maintain (through the Hadoop platform and data provisioning), and freedom from waiting for IT before working on their projects.

While this is a sound defensive strategy, and sometimes a necessary one, to take full advantage of what big data has to offer it should be combined with one of the strategies described in the following section.

Taking Advantage of Big Data

In this section, we will cover some of the most popular scenarios for data lake adoption. For companies where business leaders are driving the widespread adoption of big data, a data lake is often built by IT to try to prevent the proliferation of data puddles (small, independent clusters built with different technologies, often by SIs who are no longer engaged in the projects).

For companies trying to introduce big data, there are a few popular approaches:

- Start by offloading some existing functions to Hadoop and then add more data and expand into a data lake.
- Start with a data science initiative, show great ROI, and then expand it to a full data lake.
- Build the data lake from scratch as a central point of governance.

Which one is right for you? That depends on the stage your company is at in its adoption of big data, your role, and a number of other considerations that we will examine in this section.

Leading with Data Science

Identifying a high-visibility data science initiative that affects the top line is a very attractive strategy. *Data science* is a general term for applying advanced analytics and machine learning to data. Often, data warehouses that start as a strategic imperative promising to make the business more effective end up supporting reporting and operational analytics. Therefore, while data warehouses remain essential to running the business, they are perceived mostly as a necessary overhead, rather than a strategic investment. As such, they do not get respect, appreciation, or funding priority. Many data warehousing and analytics teams see data science as a way to visibly impact the business and the top line and to become strategically important again.

The most practical way to bring data science into an organization is to find a highly visible problem that:

- Is well defined and well understood
- Can show quick, measurable benefits

- Can be solved through machine learning or advanced analytics
- Requires data that the team can easily procure
- Would be very difficult or time-consuming to solve without applying data science techniques

While it may seem daunting to find such a project, most organizations can usually identify a number of well-known, high-visibility problems that can quickly demonstrate benefits, taking care of the first two requirements.

For the third requirement, it is often possible to identify a good candidate in two ways: by searching industry sites and publications for other companies that have solved similar problems using machine learning, or by hiring experienced consultants who can recommend which of those problems lend themselves to machine learning or advanced analytics. Once one or more candidate projects have been selected and the data that you need to train the models or apply other machine learning techniques has been identified, the data sets can be reviewed in terms of ease of procurement. This often depends on who owns the data, access to people who understand the data, and the technical challenges of obtaining it.

Some examples of common data science–driven projects for different verticals are:

Financial services
> Governance, risk management, and compliance (GRC), including portfolio risk analysis and ensuring compliance with a myriad of regulations (Basel 3, Know Your Customer, Anti Money Laundering, and many others); fraud detection; branch location optimization; automated trading

Healthcare
> Governance and compliance, medical research, patient care analytics, IoT medical devices, wearable devices, remote healthcare

Pharmaceuticals
> Genome research, process manufacturing optimization

Manufacturing
> Collecting IoT device information, quality control, preventive maintenance, Industry 4.0

Education
> Admissions, student success

Retail
> Price optimization, purchase recommendations, propensity to buy

Adtech
> Automated bidding, exchanges

Once a problem is identified, most organizations invest in a small Hadoop cluster, either on premises or in the cloud (depending on data sensitivity). They bring in data science consultants, run through the process, and quickly produce results that show the value of a data lake.

Typically, two or three of these projects are performed, and then their success is used to justify a data lake. This is sometimes referred to as the "Xerox PARC" model. Xerox established PARC (the Palo Alto Research Center in California) to research "the office of the future" in 1970. In 1971, a PARC researcher built the first laser printer, which became the main staple of Xerox business for years to come. But even though many other industry-changing technologies were invented at PARC, none were successfully monetized by Xerox on the scale of laser printing. The point of comparing data science experiments with PARC is to highlight that the results of data science are inherently unpredictable. For example, a long, complex project may produce a stable predictive model with a high rate of successful predictions, or the model may produce only a marginal improvement (for example, if the model is right 60% of the time, that's only a 10% improvement over randomly choosing the outcome, which will be right 50% of the time). Basically, initial success on a few low-hanging-fruit projects does not guarantee large-scale success for a great number of other data science projects.

This approach of investing for the future sounds good. It can be very tempting to build a large data lake, load it up with data, and declare victory. Unfortunately, I have spoken to dozens of companies where exactly such a pattern played out: they had a few data science pilots that quickly produced amazing results. They used these pilots to secure multi-million-dollar data lake budgets, built large clusters, loaded petabytes of data, and are now struggling to get usage or show additional value.

If you choose to go the analytical route, consider the following recommendations that a number of IT and data science leaders have shared with me:

- Have a pipeline of very promising data science projects that you will be able to execute as you are building up the data lake to keep showing value. Ideally, make sure that you can demonstrate one valuable insight per quarter for the duration of the data lake construction.

- Broaden the data lake beyond the original data science use cases as soon as possible by moving other workloads into the lake, from operational jobs like ETL to governance to simple BI and reporting.

- Don't try to boil the ocean right away. Keep building up the cluster and adding data sources as you keep showing more value.

- Focus on getting additional departments, teams, and projects to use the data lake.

In summary, data science is a very attractive way to get to the data lake. It often affects the top line, creating ROI through the value of the business insight and raising awareness of the value of data and the services offered by the data team. The key to building a successful data lake is to make sure that the team can continue producing such valuable insights until the data lake diversifies to more use cases and creates sustainable value for a wide range of teams and projects.

Strategy 1: Offload Existing Functionality

One of the most compelling benefits of big data technology is its cost, which can be 10 or more times lower than the cost of a relational data warehouse of similar performance and capacity. Because the size of a data warehouse only increases, and IT budgets often include the cost of expansion, it is very attractive to offload some processing from a data warehouse instead of growing the data warehouse. The advantage of this approach is that it does not require a business sponsor because the cost usually comes entirely out of the IT budget and because the project's success is primarily dependent on IT: the offloading should be transparent to the business users.

The most common processing task to offload to a big data system is the *T* part of *ETL* (extract, transform, load).

Teradata is the leading provider of large massively parallel data warehouses. For years, Teradata has been advocating an *ELT* approach to loading the data warehouse: extract and load the data into Teradata's data warehouse and then transform it using Teradata's powerful multi-node engines. This strategy was widely adopted because general ETL tools did not scale well to handle the volume of data that needed to be transformed. Big data systems, on the other hand, can handle the volume with ease and very cost-effectively. Therefore, Teradata now advocates doing the transformations in a big data framework—specifically, Hadoop—and then loading data into Teradata's data warehouse to perform queries and analytics.

Another common practice is to move the processing of non-tabular data to Hadoop. Many modern data sources, from web logs to Twitter feeds, are not tabular. Instead of the fixed columns and rows of relational data, they have complex data structures and a variety of records. These types of data can be processed very efficiently in Hadoop in their native format, instead of requiring conversion to a relational format and uploading into a data warehouse to be made available for processing using relational queries.

A third class of processing that's commonly moved to big data platforms is real-time or streaming processing. New technologies like Spark, which allows multi-node massively parallel processing of data in memory, and Kafka, a message queuing system, are making it very attractive to perform large-scale in-memory processing of data for real-time analytics, complex event processing (CEP), and dashboards.

Finally, big data solutions can be used to scale up existing projects at a fraction of the cost of legacy technologies. One company that I spoke with had moved some complex fraud detection processing to Hadoop. Hadoop was able to process 10 times more data, 10 times faster for the same compute resource cost as a relational database, creating orders of magnitude more accurate models and detection.

An example of the benefits of the move to a data lake involves a large device manufacturer whose devices send their logs to the factory on daily basis (these are called "call home logs"). The manufacturer used to process the logs and store just 2% of the data in a relational database to use for predictive modeling. The models predicted when a device would fail, when it would need maintenance, and so forth. Every time the log format or content changed or the analysts needed another piece of data for their predictive models, developers would have to change the processing logic and analysts would have to wait months to gather enough data before they could run new analytics. With Hadoop, this company is able to store all of the log files at a fraction of the previous cost of storing just 2%. Since the analysts can now access all the data as far back as they like, they can quickly deploy new analytics for internal data quality initiatives as well as customer-facing ones.

Once IT teams move such automated processing to big data frameworks and accumulate large data sets, they come under pressure to make this data available to data scientists and analysts. To go from automated processing to a data lake, they usually have to go through the following steps:

- Add data that's not being processed by automated jobs to create a comprehensive data lake.

- Provide data access for non-programmers, enabling them to create data visualizations, reports, dashboards, and SQL queries.

- To facilitate adoption by analysts, provide a comprehensive, searchable catalog.

- Automate the policies that govern data access, sensitive data handling, data quality, and data lifecycle management.

- Ensure that service-level agreements (SLAs) for automated jobs are not affected by the work that analysts are doing by setting up prioritized execution and resource governance schemes.

Strategy 2: Data Lakes for New Projects

Instead of offloading existing functionality to a big data platform, some companies use it to support a new operational project, such as data science, advanced analytics, processing of machine data and logs from IoT devices, or social media customer analytics. These projects are usually driven by data science teams or line-of-business teams and frequently start as data puddles—small, single-purpose big data environments. Then, as more and more use cases are added, they eventually evolve to full-fledged data lakes.

In many ways, the path of starting with a new operational project is similar to the off-loading process for an existing project. The advantage of a new project is that it creates new visible value for the company. The drawback is that it requires additional budget. Moreover, a project failure, even if it has nothing to do with the data lake, can taint an enterprise's view of big data technology and negatively affect its adoption.

Strategy 3: Establish a Central Point of Governance

With more and more government and industry regulations and ever-stricter enforcement, governance is becoming a major focus for many enterprises. Governance aims at providing users with secure, managed access to data that complies with governmental and corporate regulations. It generally includes management of sensitive and personal data, data quality, the data lifecycle, metadata, and data lineage. (Chapter 6 will go into a lot more detail on this topic.) Since governance ensures compliance with governmental and corporate regulations and these regulations apply to all systems in the enterprise, governance requires enterprises to implement and maintain consistent policies. Unfortunately, implementing and maintaining consistent governance policies across heterogeneous systems that use different technologies and are managed by different teams with different priorities presents a formidable problem for most enterprises.

Data governance professionals sometimes regard big data and Hadoop as a far-removed, future problem. They feel that they first have to implement data governance policies for legacy systems before tackling new technologies. This approach, while not without merit, misses the opportunity of using Hadoop as a cost-effective platform to provide centralized governance and compliance for the enterprise.

Traditionally, governance has required convincing the teams responsible for legacy systems to commit their limited personnel resources to retrofitting their systems to comply with the governance policies, and to dedicate expensive compute resources to executing the rules, checks, and audits associated with those policies. It is often much more straightforward and cost-effective to tell the teams responsible for legacy systems to ingest their data into Hadoop so a standard set of tools can implement consistent governance policies. This approach has the following benefits:

- Data can be profiled and processed by a standard set of data quality technologies with uniform data quality rules.

- Sensitive data can be detected and treated by a standard set of data security tools.

- Retention and eDiscovery functionality can be implemented in a uniform way across the systems.

- Compliance reports can be developed against a single unified system.

Furthermore, file-based big data systems such as Hadoop lend themselves well to the idea of *bimodal IT*, an approach that recommends creating different zones with different degrees of governance. By creating and keeping separate zones for raw and clean data, a data lake supports various degrees of governance in one cluster.

Which Way Is Right for You?

Any one of these approaches can lead to a successful data lake. Which way should you go? It usually depends on your role, your budget, and the allies you can recruit. Generally, it is easiest to start a data lake by using the budget that you control. However, regardless of where you start, for a data lake to take off and become sustainable, you will need a plan to convince analysts throughout the enterprise to start using it for their projects.

If you are an IT executive or big data champion, the decision tree in Figure 4-2 should help you formulate a data lake strategy.

At a high level, the steps to take are as follows:

1. Determine whether there are any data puddles (i.e., are business teams using Hadoop clusters on their own?).

    a. If there are, are there any projects that would agree to move to a centralized cluster?

        i. If so, use the cost of the project to justify a centralized cluster.

        ii. If not, justify building a data lake to avoid proliferation of data puddles. Use previous proliferations (e.g., data marts, reporting databases) as examples. If you cannot get approval, wait for puddles to run into trouble—it won't take long.

    b. If there are no data puddles, are there groups that are asking for big data and/or data science? If not, can you sell them on sponsoring it?

2. Look for the low-hanging fruit. Try to identify low-risk, high-visibility projects.

3. Try to line up more than one project per team and more than one team to maximize the chances of success.

4. Go down the data science/analytics route:

    a. If there are no groups ready to sponsor a big data project, is there a data governance initiative? If yes, try to propose and get approval for the single point of governance route.

b. Otherwise, review the top projects and identify any that require massively parallel computing and large data sets and would be more cost-effective using Hadoop.

5. Finally, find existing workloads to offload.

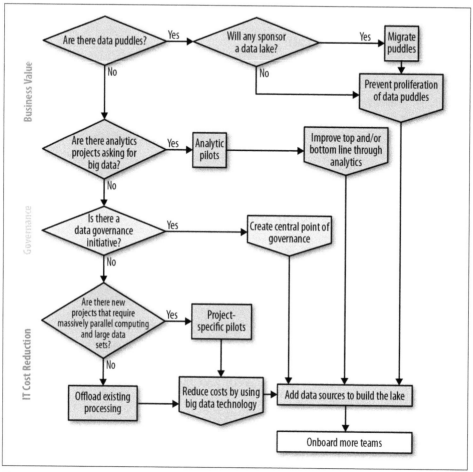

Figure 4-2. Data lake strategy decision tree

Conclusion

There are many ways to get to a data lake. Although each situation is different, successful deployments tend to share several traits: a clear and deliberate plan, recruiting enthusiastic early adapters, and demonstrating immediate value.

CHAPTER 5

From Data Ponds/Big Data Warehouses to Data Lakes

Although when they were introduced over three decades ago, data warehouses were envisioned as a means of providing historical storage for enterprise data that would make it available for all types of new analytics, most data warehouses ended up being repositories of production-quality data used for only the most critical analytics. The majority could not process the vast amount and wide variety of data they contained. Some particularly high-end systems like Teradata could provide admirable scalability, but at very high costs. A lot of time and effort was spent tuning the performance of the data warehousing systems. As a result, any change—whether a new query or a schema change—had to go through elaborate architectural review and a lengthy approval and testing process. The ETL jobs that loaded the data warehouse were just as carefully constructed and tuned, and any new data required changes to those jobs and a similarly elaborate review and testing procedure. This prevented ad hoc querying and discouraged schema changes, and meant that data warehouses lacked agility.

Data lakes attempt to fulfill the original promise of an enterprise data repository by introducing extreme scalability, agility, future-proofing, and end user self-service. In this chapter we will take a closer look at data ponds—data warehouses implemented using big data technology—and explain how these ponds (or the data lakes that encompass them) can provide the functions for which organizations currently use a traditional data warehouse.

Data lakes are ideal repositories for enterprise data because they house different types of data in appropriate ways, to be used for different purposes by different processing systems within one massively parallel interoperable system. We will discuss adding data that it was difficult or impossible to add to a data warehouse, integrating a data lake with data sources, and consuming the data in a data lake with other systems.

Essential Functions of a Data Warehouse

Since many data lakes aim to complement or even replace data warehouses, and since data warehouses are frequently the easiest, biggest, and best sources of data in the enterprise, it is important to understand why they do things a certain way, how data lakes are constrained from doing these things, and what techniques can be used in big data technology to address these challenges.

The original vision for data warehouses was to host (or warehouse) all historical data for future use. As the concept became formalized, data warehouses became highly managed systems with carefully controlled schemas and time-consuming change processes. Modern data warehouses generally focus on supporting analytics on high volumes of historical data read in from multiple sources. In order to achieve this, data architects need to make sure that:

- Data is organized to facilitate high-performance analytics. This is usually accomplished by means of dimensional modeling that creates star schemas. In addition, because of cost and performance implications, data warehouses usually cannot keep a complete history and have to aggregate or archive older data.

- Data from multiple systems can be analyzed in a consistent way. This is accomplished by integrating data from different systems into a consistent representation using techniques that include conforming dimensions, harmonization, and normalization.

- Managing changes in a way that preserves the accuracy of historical analysis. This is usually accomplished using a technique called slowly changing dimensions, described in Chapter 2.

- Making sure that data is clean and consistent. This is accomplished using data quality tools and techniques, also discussed in Chapter 2.

As described in previous chapters, an ETL (extract, transform, load) process is used to convert data from source systems into a form that can be loaded into a data warehouse. This conversion can be done either externally to the data warehouse or internally. External solutions make use of a range of ETL tools, many of which have been on the market for decades. Internal solutions load raw source data into the warehouse and apply transformations using SQL scripts executed by the data warehouse, a technique known as ELT (extract, load [into the target data warehouse], transform). In both cases, data quality tools are frequently integrated with the ETL tools and executed as part of the process.

Since a data pond or lake based on big data technology is massively scalable and cost-effective, it can easily overcome the performance and data volume limitations of a data warehouse. Therefore, good performance does not require either dimensional modeling or aggregation (summarizing) of older data, as it does in most data warehouses. However, with regard to historical analysis, many of the challenges of data warehousing still apply. These include:

- Modeling data for analytics
- Integrating data from disparate systems to a common representation
- Managing changes without losing data's history

A data pond or data lake is the ideal place to store data for future use and perform large-scale analytics—but its use of big data technologies like Hadoop also makes it a great place to transform vast amounts of data. Data ponds often begin life as a result of performing the transformations required to create a data warehouse schema (known as ETL offloading). They evolve into data ponds by making both the raw and the transformed data warehouse data available for analytics, then eventually expand to include data from external or internal sources that was not in the original data warehouse and grow into full-fledged data lakes.

Before we examine how data ponds deal with the aforementioned challenges, let's take another look at the issues in the context of traditional data warehouses.

Dimensional Modeling for Analytics

As we saw in Chapter 2, when relational databases are used to support operational systems and applications such as enterprise resource management (ERM) and customer relationship management (CRM), data is usually stored in highly normalized data models. Operational systems tend to do many small reads and writes. This activity is part of the reason for normalized data models, which attempt to create tables with minimum redundancy and the smallest possible number of fields. In addition to making updates and reads very fast, normalization eliminates the risk of inconsistent data.

In contrast, most data warehouses favor denormalized data models, with each table containing as many related attributes as possible. This makes it possible to process all the information needed by an analytical application with a single pass through the data. Furthermore, data warehouses typically receive data from many sources and applications, each with its own schema, and data from these different sources has to be converted to a single common schema.

This topic was covered in detail in Chapter 2, but as a brief refresher, a popular data model used by data warehouses is the star schema, consisting of dimension tables representing the entities being analyzed (e.g., customer, time, product) and one or more fact tables representing the activities that involve the dimensions (e.g., orders placed).

The difficulty is that the sources of data often represent the same information in different ways: for example, one may break each address into multiple fields such as street, city, and state, whereas another stores the address in a single field. Similarly, some may keep a date of birth, while others store an age for each customer. In such cases, data needs to be converted to the format used by the data warehouse. For example, all the address fields might need to be concatenated, or a person's current age might need to be calculated based on their date of birth. If data from all the source systems is kept in the same dimension tables in the same destination format, these tables are said to be *conforming*.

Integrating Data from Disparate Sources

Most modern ETL tools were developed around two decades ago, as part of the data warehousing movement, with the aim of converting data from different operational systems with different schemas and representations to a single common schema. Thus, the first challenge solved by ETL tools is converting records from the normalized schemas favored by operational systems to the denormalized schemas favored by data warehouses, as described in the previous section.

The second challenge is converting data from many different operational applications to a single common schema and representation—the "conforming" data mentioned in that section. We saw an example in Chapter 2 of how an ETL job might be used to convert an operational system's representation of customer data into the representation expected by the data warehouse's customer dimension table (see Figure 2-7).

Data warehouses often contain data from many different sources and applications, each with its own schema, and data from all of these sources has to be normalized and converted to the data warehouse's preferred schema differently, using a different ETL process for each source system. This leads to a rapid growth in the number of ETL scripts that have to be maintained and versioned.

Preserving History Using Slowly Changing Dimensions

Most dimensional data in a data warehouse is fairly static (customer data, data about retail or geographic locations, etc.). However, changes can occur in this data over time, and for accurate data analysis it's necessary to keep track of them. A special construct has been developed to represent dimensional changes when considering historical data, called *slowly changing dimensions*. This ensures that, in the event of changes in certain aspects of the data (marital or job status, address, etc.), the correct state is taken into account for the analysis. The use of slowly changing dimensions in data warehouses is described in detail in Chapter 2.

Limitations of the Data Warehouse as a Historical Repository

With legacy systems and data warehouses, because of the high cost of storage and processing, enterprises are forced to keep historical data at a coarser granularity than their more recent data. For example, a data warehouse may hold individual transactions for the last three years, daily totals for the last seven years, and monthly totals for data that's more than seven years old. This causes a number of problems:

- Data aggregation loses a lot of useful detail, limiting the types of analysis that can be performed.
- Most historical analysis has to be done at coarse granularity (at a level all the data can support, which will be either daily or monthly in our example, depending on whether the analysis extends back beyond seven years).
- Writing reports and queries that account for different levels of granularity is complex and error-prone.
- Managing this system and moving data into various levels of granularity increases processing and administration overhead.

Most advanced analytic applications can benefit from having more historical data. Even simple analytics and historical trends give a more complete picture when given more history, both in terms of duration and number of attributes.

A scalable and cost-effective storage and execution system like Hadoop allows enterprises to store and analyze their historical data at the finest granularity, thus increasing the richness and accuracy of analytical results.

For example, fraud detection algorithms rely on analyzing large numbers of transactions to identify patterns of fraud. One well-publicized case study (*https://on.wsj.com/ 2RMdspZ*) describes how Visa started using Hadoop for fraud detection and went from analyzing 2% of customer transactions across 40 attributes using a single model to analyzing 100% of the transactions across 500 attributes using 18 models, thereby allowing the company to identify billions of dollars' worth of fraudulent transactions.

Moving to a Data Pond

Now that we have discussed the challenges of working in a traditional data warehouse, we can explore how to solve these problems with a data pond, or some combination of data warehouse and data pond. In this section we'll cover alternative ways to organize data for efficient intake and processing, and how to preserve history (traditionally implemented using dimension tables).

Keeping History in a Data Pond

Let's first examine how history is kept in the data pond using partitions, and the limitations of this approach for keeping track of slowly changing dimensions. A new approach, using snapshots, is then discussed as a solution.

In a data pond, as data is ingested, it is typically stored in multiple files or partitions. Each ingestion batch is typically loaded into a separate folder. All the files from all the folders are treated as a single "logical" file or table. Hive, the most popular SQL interface to Hadoop data, has a special construct called *partitioned tables* for working on these files. Partitioned tables allow Hive to intelligently optimize queries based on the partitioning structure.

Figure 5-1 illustrates a typical partitioning schema used for daily loads of transaction data. A *transactions* directory contains all the transactions. The files are organized by year (for instance, */transactions/Year=2016*), inside a year by month (e.g., with */transactions/Year=2016/Month=3* containing all transactions for March 2016), and inside a month by day (with */transactions/Year=2016/Month=3/Day=2* containing all the transactions for March 2, 2016). Because Hadoop does a lot of parallel processing, to avoid contention for a single file, it generates multiple files in a */transactions/Year=2016/Month=3/Day=2* directory. These files are all concatenated to form a single file of transactions for that day.

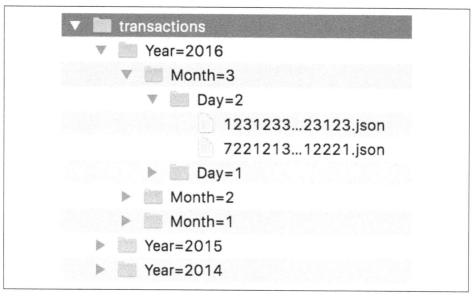

Figure 5-1. Directory structure for partitioned tables in Hive

In Hive, the user would create a single table (say, `all_transactions`), associate it with the *transactions* folder, and specify partition keys (`Year`, `Month`, `Day`). This `all_transactions` table would include all the data from all the files in the *transactions* folder. For example, the SQL statement `select * from all_transactions` would return all rows in the table by returning every single record in every single file in every subfolder under *transactions*, from the oldest file in the directory tree— say, */transactions/Year=2014/Month=1/Day=1/99312312311333.json* to the latest— say, */transactions/Year=2016/Month=3/Day=2/722121344412221.json*.

In addition, the naming convention of Field=Value (e.g., Year=2016) allows Hive to intelligently direct each query to the files that may contain the data needed by the query. For example, a SQL query of select * from all_transactions where Year = 2016 and Month = 3 and Day=2 would read data only in the files in the */transactions/Year=2016/Month=3/Day=2* folder, instead of reading all the files in all the folders and then filtering out the transactions for March 2, 2016.

Implementing Slowly Changing Dimensions in a Data Pond

Now we have to handle the dimensional or reference data, such as a customer's marital status or other life changes. If we are loading dimension tables from a data warehouse that has used slowly changing dimensions, we can load the changed records—new customers and customers who have undergone a state change—into a separate file or append them to a single file containing all the customer data, because all the work of figuring out and handling changes to customer state has already been done.

However, if we are loading data directly from operational systems, we need some way to identify changes. The technique used for data warehouses, creating slowly changing dimensions, complicates ingestion and analytics in the data pond. Each read can potentially add a record not only to the main data table, but to the dimensional data. Even worse, during later analytics, reads must join the temporal data in one table to the correct records in the other table.

Denormalizing attributes to preserve state

Another option is to denormalize the data and add all the important attributes to the file containing the transaction data. For example, when we load transactions from operational systems, we add information about customer demographics, marital status, and the like at the time of the transaction. This avoids the need for expensive and complicated joins. To save space and processing, we can optimize by adding attributes only where state information is important—in other words, we can add only the fields for which we would provide slowly changing dimensions in a data warehouse.

The big drawback of this approach is that including these attributes in a data set with transaction data makes them available for use with the data in that particular data set, but not with other data. For example, we may have a separate data set for returns, a separate one for warranties, and so forth. To apply this technique, we would have to add all the customer attributes to each of these data sets, increasing storage and processing costs and adding complexity to our ingestion process. We would also have to remember to update all these data sets whenever we introduced a new customer attribute or made changes to the use of an existing attribute.

Preserving state using snapshots

Yet another alternative is to ingest the latest version of the data every day. To support this, we would have a directory tree of dimensional data, but instead of a folder for each day being part of the data set (a partition), each day's folder would be a complete version or snapshot of the data set. In other words, we could create a structure to keep changed data for customers using the same process as described earlier for transactions. Thus, the */customers/Year=2016/Month=3/Day=2* folder in Figure 5-2 would contain files that, when concatenated, would have the version of the customers data set for March 2, 2016.

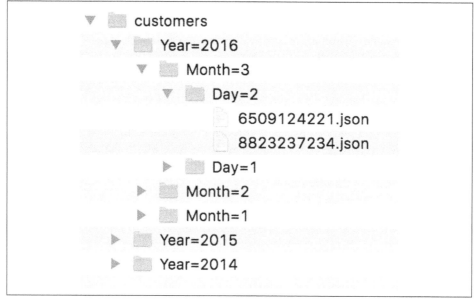

Figure 5-2. Partitioned folders for dimension table

To get the appropriate representation of a customer record, we have to join each *transactions* record with a *customers* record from the same date. For example, if we'd created Hive tables for our *transactions* and *customers* data sets, we would join them using a SQL query on both customer ID and transaction date (e.g., `all_transac tions.customer_id = customers.customer_id and transactions.Year = custom ers.Year and transactions.Month = customers.Month and transactions.Day = customers.Day`) to get the customer state at the time of the transaction.

The easiest way to see all the data is to create a Hive table that includes all the files in the folder. However, if for whatever reason using Hive or a similar tool is not an option, we will have to write custom code to correlate each partition of the *transactions* data set with the corresponding snapshot of the *customers* data set to make sure that we are considering the correct state of customer data at the time of a transaction.

Although this is an expensive way to track changes because we have to store complete customer data for every day, it has several advantages over creating slowly changing dimensions. First, ingestion is straightforward and can use simple tools like Sqoop. Second, the snapshots preserve history for all attributes of the customer (whereas slowly changing dimensions track only some attributes). Additionally, this approach does not require us to assign a new customer key every time an important attribute changes, making it easier to do certain customer-related analytics, such as figuring out how many real customers we have over time. The final advantage of the snapshot approach is that if at some point storage becomes too expensive, this snapshot tree can be converted to a data set that captures only the slowly changing dimensions.

Growing Data Ponds into a Data Lake—Loading Data That's Not in the Data Warehouse

Most data in the enterprise today is thrown away because there is no known business use case for it yet. Without clear business value, there is no budget to cover the cost of keeping data, and without a use case in mind, it is not clear what schema to create to store it or how to transform or cleanse it. The data lake paradigm makes it possible to keep this data inexpensively and process it efficiently using the scalable computing model of Hadoop MapReduce or Spark.

Raw Data

As we discussed previously, a data warehouse keeps only clean, normalized data. Unfortunately, a lot of important information is lost as part of the normalization process. Issues include:

Data breadth
Typically, operational systems have many more attributes than a data warehouse. Only the most critical and common attributes end up in the data warehouse. The main reason for this is to reduce the cost of storing and processing all the attributes, as well as the management, ETL development, and other costs associated with loading anything into a data warehouse.

With the scalability and cost efficiency of a data lake, it becomes possible to store and process much more information. And with frictionless ingestion (where the new data is loaded without any processing), the cost of ETL development is eliminated until there is a need to use this data.

Original or raw data
In a data warehouse, all data is treated the same and converted to a single format. For example, some systems may indicate that salary is not known with a NULL value or an illegal value such as -1, but since many databases cannot perform aggregation on NULL fields and since -1 is not a legal salary, these values may be

replaced with a default value of, say, 0, either during the ETL process or as a separate data cleansing step. Data scientists would prefer to be able to tell the difference between someone who is really not earning any money and someone whose income is unknown—say, so they can replace the unknown income with an average income for that demographic to create a more accurate model. (This type of change is known as *data interpolation*, a routine analytic activity.)

A data lake typically keeps both original or raw data and processed data, giving the analysts a choice.

Non-tabular formats
A lot of big data (for example, social media data like Twitter feeds) is not in a tabular format but instead is represented as documents (e.g., JSON or XML), in columnar formats (e.g., Parquet), as log files (e.g., Apache log format), or as one of many other specialized representations. Thus, it cannot be easily translated to a relational data warehouse schema.

Because a data lake is typically built using big data technology like Hadoop, it can easily accommodate non-tabular formats. In fact, these formats are popular and are handled well by Hive, Spark, and many other big data projects.

External Data

External data has been a multi-billion-dollar industry for decades. From Nielsen ratings to Equifax, TransUnion, and Experian credit reports, and from Morningstar ratings to Dun and Bradstreet business information to Bloomberg and Dow Jones financial transactions, enterprises have been buying and utilizing external data for years. Recently, the range of sources and data providers has expanded to include social media companies such as Twitter and Facebook, plus free government data available through Data.gov and other portals.

Enterprises face big challenges with external data, including:

Data quality
Quality issues range from incorrect and missing data to conflicting data from different suppliers. Data quality remains a major hurdle to incorporating external data into decision-making processes.

Licensing costs
Data is expensive. To make matters worse, in many enterprises the same data is purchased multiple times by different groups because there is no easy way to share data sets or know whether the company has already purchased a specific data set.

Intellectual property

Data providers sell subscriptions to data feeds, and many require their customers to remove all their data from their systems when they stop subscribing. Usually this includes not only the original purchased data sets, but any sets generated using that data. To accomplish that, the enterprises need to know where the data is and how it has been used.

As Figure 5-3 illustrates, two different teams can purchase the same external data set, paying the vendor twice. Each team addresses quality problems differently and the resulting data is used in a variety of data sets and reports, which introduces conflicting information into the ecosystem. Even worse, lineage information is usually lost, so the enterprise cannot find all the instances where the data is used or trace the data back to the original data sets.

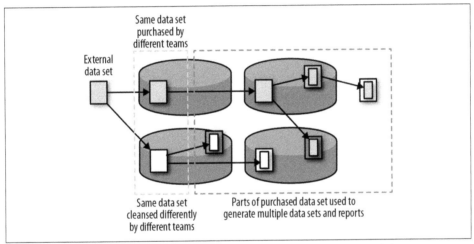

Figure 5-3. Two different teams purchasing and using the same external data set

A Hadoop data lake can become a central place to load external data, address quality issues, manage access to original and clean versions, and track how the data is used. A simple approach is to create a folder hierarchy for keeping external data, such as */Data/External/<vendor_name>/<data_set_name>*. So, for instance, if the company purchases credit rating data from CreditSafe, it can place this data in */Data/External/CreditSafe/CreditRatings*. Additional folders can be used to capture more detail. For example, 2016 data for the United Kingdom could go into */Data/External/CreditSafe/CreditRatings/UK/2016*. If anyone in the organization needs 2016 UK credit ratings, they'll know where to look before buying the data set again, as illustrated in Figure 5-4.

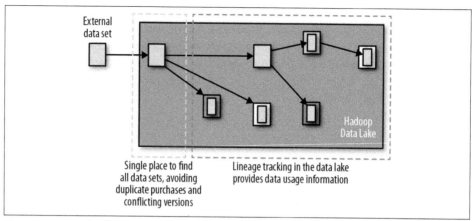

Figure 5-4. Single place to keep external data in order to avoid duplicate purchases

One drawback of this approach is that similar information might be provided by different vendors—so, analysts looking for UK credit ratings for a particular year would have to check the folder for each vendor to see if the data they need is already available. However, if we instead organize data by subject (e.g., */Data/External/CreditRatings/UK/2016/CreditSafe*), we run into other challenges. Vendor data sets do not always align well with predefined subjects, and may contain additional attributes. For example, the *CreditRatings* data set might also contain demographic data. If another analyst wanted to buy demographic data from CreditSafe, the company could well end up paying for this data twice. Even if someone noticed that the company had the data already, it would then have to be stored in two partitions.

Additionally, the data owner (the department that purchased the data for the organization) may require other information, like vendor ID or name, to uniquely identify a data set, and this information is difficult to capture in a single fixed folder hierarchy.

A more elegant and productive approach is to create a *catalog* of the external data sets that can capture multiple aspects of the data through properties, tags, and descriptions. For example, all data sets in the catalog can have common properties such as *vendor* and *owning department*, as well as properties specific to each data set such as *country* and *year*. This way, the data sets can physically live wherever the organization wants to keep them, but still be findable through their properties. In addition, because the catalog usually captures all the attributes or fields of a data set, analysts will be able to find the relevant data sets easily regardless of the purpose for which they want to use them.

Internet of Things (IoT) and Other Streaming Data

Data lakes are especially appealing for the human interaction data within social media and web logs. This data usually far exceeds typical business transaction data in volume and complexity. Data lakes are even more appealing for the data that comes automatically from digital IoT devices. Because machines can produce data so much faster than humans, machine-generated data is bound to dwarf human-generated data and is expected to be the main source of data going forward. Most complex machines, from computer equipment to airplanes, medical devices, and elevators, generate log files that are sent back to the factory when problems arise. Increasingly, this data is being streamed back for real-time automated monitoring. This data is used to monitor and address problems as well as to make machines smarter. From self-driving cars to automated temperature controls, smart machines are increasingly using data and analytics to self-manage their operations.

While monitoring is performed in real time, it is difficult to interpret real-time behavior without comparing it to historical data. For example, to identify unexpected or anomalous behavior, we first have to establish a baseline of normal behavior, which requires analyzing historical data and comparing it to what we are seeing in real time. If a malfunction occurs, it will need to be handled right away. In addition, the behavior leading up to it—sometimes over many days, months, or even years—should be analyzed for clues, with the aim of understanding, detecting, and preventing such malfunctions in the future. Since a data lake is an ideal place to keep this history, a number of approaches and architectures have been developed to combine real-time data processing and historical analytics.

In the following essay, big data visionary Michael Hausenblas discusses some best practices for such real-time data lakes.

Real-Time Data Lakes

Michael Hausenblas is a long-term big data visionary and practitioner who first got involved with Hadoop and other big data technologies in 2008. Currently, Michael handles DevOps relations at Mesosphere. He is an Apache Contributor for Mesos and Drill, and former Chief Data Engineer for MapR in EMEA.

Traditionally, data lakes have been associated with data at rest. Whether the data itself was machine-generated (for example, log files) or is a collection of manually generated data such as spreadsheets, the basic idea was to introduce a self-service approach to data exploration, making business-relevant data sets available across the organization.

Increasingly, there is a need to take streaming data sources into account, be it in the context of mobile devices, constrained devices such as sensors, or simply human online interactions (think, for example, embedded customer support chats): in all these cases, the data should usually be processed as it arrives. This is in contrast to the rather static idea of data sets manifesting themselves in dumps and being processed in a batch fashion. The question is, how can one build such real-time data lakes (for lack of a better term)? What guiding architectural considerations exist for building them so as to derive insights that you can act on instantly?

In the past couple of years, several principal architectures have been proposed that allow the processing of data at rest and in motion together, at scale. Notably, Nathan Marz came up with the term *Lambda Architecture* for a generic, scalable, and fault-tolerant data processing architecture based on his experience working on distributed data processing systems at BackType and Twitter. The Lambda Architecture aims to satisfy the need for a robust system that is tolerant of hardware failures and human mistakes and able to serve a wide range of workloads and use cases for which low-latency reads and updates are required. It combines a *batch layer* that spans all the (historical) facts and a *speed layer* for the real-time data. You can learn more about it at *http://lambda-architecture.net*.

Another related and relevant architecture is the *Kappa Architecture*, introduced by Jay Kreps (*https://oreil.ly/2LSEdqz*) in 2014. In essence, it has a distributed log at its core and is simpler than the Lambda Architecture. Further variations of architectures relevant for realizing real-time data lakes can be found in Martin Kleppmann's excellent book *Designing Data-Intensive Applications* (*http://datain tensive.net/*) (O'Reilly).

No matter what architecture you choose, at the end of the day you'll need to select concrete technologies for the implementation part. Here I've grouped them into three buckets, and you'll likely end up with at least one technology from each:

- Data stores: HDFS, HBase, Cassandra, Kafka
- Processing engines: Spark, Flink, Beam
- Interaction: Zeppelin/Spark notebook, Tableau/Datameer

Last but not least, in a data lake scenario, provenance is of paramount importance. Being able to tell where a data set (or data stream) comes from and what it contains, and having access to other related metadata, is crucial to enable data scientists to select and interpret the data correctly and provide confidence measurements along with the results.

Real-time data lakes have been successfully implemented in a variety of domains, including the financial industry (from fraud detection to bonus programs), telecommunications, and retail. Most organizations start out with a small and focused application, learn from the outcomes, and proceed to grow these application-specific data sets into data lakes that span different departments and applications, providing organizations with a data infrastructure that's scalable both in terms of technology and human users. The technological aspect of scalability is satisfied by the properties of the data infrastructure, including the ability to scale out on commodity hardware and the inherently distributed nature of the processing and storage systems. The human aspect, however, can turn out to be more challenging. Firstly, without metadata, one risks turning a data lake into a data swamp. Further, the smooth interplay of data scientists, data engineers, and developers deserves special attention. Akin to the DevOps philosophy (*http://itrevolution.com/book/the-phoenix-project/*), a culture of sharing and joint responsibility should be in place.

The Lambda Architecture

Let's take a closer look at the Lambda Architecture that Michael Hausenblas describes. It combines real-time and batch processing of the same data, as illustrated in Figure 5-5.

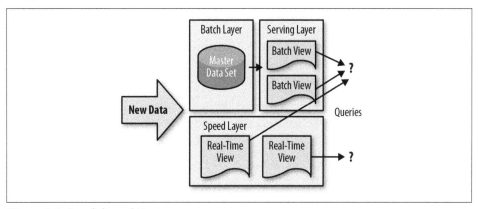

Figure 5-5. Lambda architecture

An incoming real-time data stream is stored in master data batch layers as well as being kept in a memory cache in a speed layer. Data from the master data set is then indexed and made available through batch views, while real-time data in the speed layer is exposed through real-time views.

Both batch and real-time views can be queried either independently or together to answer any historical or real-time questions. This architecture is well suited to Hadoop data lakes, where HDFS can be used to store the master data set, Spark or Storm can form the speed layer, HBase can be the service layer, and Hive creates views that can be queried.

To learn more about the Lambda Architecture, see *Big Data: Principles and Best Practices of Scalable Realtime Data Systems* by Nathan Marz and James Warren (Manning).

Data Transformations

When using operational data for analytics, it can be useful to transform it for several reasons:

Harmonization

> Data from different sources is converted to a common format or schema. This requires data architects to understand and carefully map every single attribute from every source system to that common schema. Because of the amount of work required to harmonize data, as a practical matter, most analytic schemas contain only a small subset of attributes; most of the attributes are thrown away.

Entity resolution and reconciliation

> Different instances of the same entity (e.g., customer) coming from different sources need to be recognized as referring to the same instance. For example, the names and addresses of the same customer may be slightly different in different systems and have to be recognized and matched. Once an entity is resolved and all instances are grouped together, any conflicts have to be resolved (e.g., different sources may have different addresses for the same customer, and conflict resolution involves deciding which address to keep).

Performance optimization

> In certain systems, such as relational databases, some schemas facilitate faster analytic queries. A star schema, as mentioned earlier in this chapter, is one such common optimization.

Fortunately, in a data lake, because schemas are imposed only as data is read (and not enforced when data is written, as described in Chapter 3), operational data can be ingested from various sources as is and harmonized as necessary for analytics. Instead of throwing away attributes that we cannot afford to harmonize now, we keep them in the data lake until there is a need for them and we can justify doing the work.

The same approach can be taken for entity resolution. Instead of going through the effort and expense of reconciling all the entities from different systems and resolving conflicts for all the attributes, we reconcile only the entities that we need for our project and consider only the conflicts for the attributes we care about. We can then resolve them in the way that's most appropriate for the project. For example, general entity resolution might focus on finding the current address for a customer. However, if we are identifying target customers for a promotion around the San Francisco 49ers football team, having all the past addresses for customers is a huge benefit. Our conflict resolution will focus on determining whether a person ever lived in San Francisco, rather than trying to figure out their current address.

Finally, because Hadoop is such a powerful transformation engine and can efficiently execute massive queries that require significant transformations during analysis, we will less often need to transform data to an analytics-friendly schema for performance reasons.

However, interestingly enough, Hadoop is frequently used to perform transformations to feed other systems, such as data warehouses. As described earlier, this process of transforming operational data into the analytic schema required by a data warehouse is a form of ETL offloading. The operational data is ingested into Hadoop as is and then transformed and loaded into the data warehouse. A practical approach is to ingest all or most of the operational data into the data lake, not just the data needed by the data warehouse. Then some of the data can be used to load the data warehouse, while all of the data is available for analysis and data science in the lake. In addition, if this data needs to be added to the data warehouse later, it is already present in the data lake.

Figures 5-6 through 5-9 illustrate the expansion of pure ETL offloading to a more generalized data lake. We start with the traditional data warehouse (DW) design illustrated in Figure 5-6, where an ETL tool is used to extract data from operational systems, transform it into the data warehouse schema, and load it into the data warehouse.

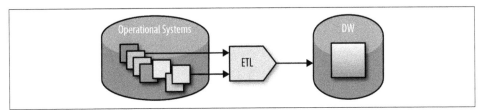

Figure 5-6. Traditional ETL process

For many years, high-end database vendors encouraged their customers to use their database engines to do the transformations (the ELT model discussed in Chapter 2 and shown in Figure 5-7) instead of leaving it to external ETL tools. These vendors argued that only highly scalable systems like theirs could handle the volume and complexity of loading their data warehouses.

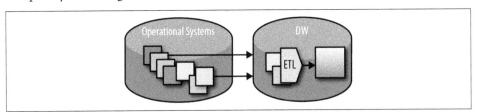

Figure 5-7. ELT process

With ETL offloading, Hadoop-based ETL jobs built using MapReduce or Spark or one of the existing projects like Hive, Pig, or Sqoop replace the ETL tool or the work done by the data warehouse in ELT, as illustrated in Figure 5-8. Operational data is ingested into Hadoop as is, then transformed into the required schema and loaded into the data warehouse.

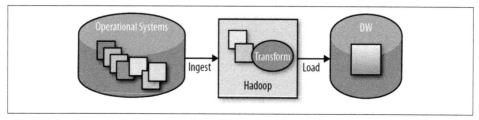

Figure 5-8. Using Hadoop for ETL offloading

At this point, Hadoop contains the original source data used to load the data warehouse in the original format. If we add the remaining operational data as well, we have the beginnings of a data lake that will contain the original (raw) data in the landing zone, plus the cleansed and transformed data in the curated or gold zone, as illustrated in Figure 5-9.

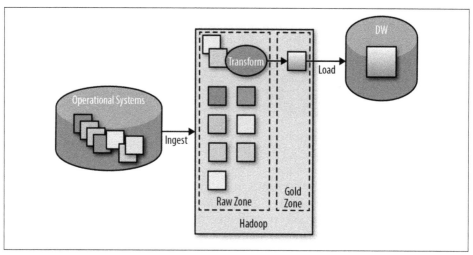

Figure 5-9. A Hadoop ETL offloading project containing raw, cleansed, and transformed data

Target Systems

Data from the data lake can be consumed by a variety of target systems. These systems are commonly data warehouses and specialized analytical databases and data marts, but consumers of the information can also be operational applications such as ERP or CRM and real-time applications, or even data scientists who want raw data for their models.

We will examine the consumption paradigms for the following target systems:

- Data warehouses
- Operational data stores (ODSs)
- Real-time applications and data products

Data Warehouses

We covered ETL offloading in the previous section. The data generated by the offloaded ETL jobs running in the lake typically gets loaded into the data warehouse by creating files that can be bulk-loaded using native database utilities or by creating simplistic ETL jobs that just load the data without any transformations.

Operational Data Stores

An operational data store is used to consolidate, cleanse, and normalize data. It addresses a disadvantage of the ELT approach, wherein the ELT jobs interfere with and affect the performance of analytics jobs. By moving all the processing to a separate ODS, enterprises can protect analytics queries from being slowed down by ELT jobs. While a data lake can be used to feed processed data to an ODS, it is actually a very attractive replacement for the ODS, and offers the side benefit that the resulting data can be kept in the data lake as well, to be used by analytics there. In many ways, using Hadoop or another big data platform as an ODS is a natural extension of ETL offloading. In this configuration, more functionality, such as data quality and master data management, is offloaded to Hadoop and the results are distributed to the other data systems that used to get their data from an ODS.

Real-Time Applications and Data Products

Real-time applications process incoming data streams. Various industry-specific use cases exist for processing real-time information, from automated inventory replenishment to health monitoring. Data products are production deployments of statistical models created by data scientists. Data products can process data in real time or in batches.

We can roughly generalize the output of real-time applications and data products into several categories, as illustrated in Figure 5-10:

Dashboards
    These display the current state of a system. Stock tickers, real-time election results, and airport arrival and departure displays are examples of real-time dashboards. As real-time events are processed, the state is continuously updated.

Automated actions

As events are being processed, based on specific conditions, these systems automatically respond. This is also called *complex event processing* (CEP) and can control anything from factory operations to inventory management, automated replenishment, transportation logistics, and climate control. This kind of data product is often used to perform automated stock trading or advertising auction bidding, where millions of bids are placed in seconds.

Alerts and notifications

These are an alternative to both human-intensive processes—making staff constantly monitor dashboards—and writing complex automated programs to handle any possible condition. Many real-time systems augment human intelligence with automation, specifying notification conditions and sending notifications to human users when those conditions are triggered. Conditions can vary from simple ones (e.g., when a temperature gets to a certain point, pop up a warning on the control panel) to very complex ones that incorporate historical and real-time data (e.g., when the website traffic exceeds 20% of normal traffic for this time of the day and day of the year, send an email message to the administrator).

Data sets

Data products frequently perform bulk operations that produce data sets, such as generating a list of customers for an email campaign by doing customer segmentation, or producing reports to estimate house prices.

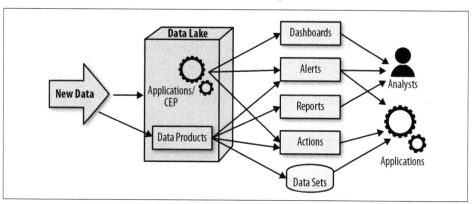

Figure 5-10. Results of processing in the data lake

Conclusion

As laid out in this chapter, data lakes can be attractive replacements for data warehouses and can subsume some existing legacy systems and processes, like ETL and ODSs. However, their true power and incredible value are realized when data lakes are used to address different needs that arise in the enterprise, like advanced analytics, ad hoc analysis, and business user self-service, that will be covered in subsequent chapters. The journey is not simple, but the processing power of the data lake, the benefits of centralizing and sharing data and processing, and the economics of big data are compelling and make it eminently worthwhile.

CHAPTER 6

Optimizing for Self-Service

The power of data can be realized only if decision makers can base their actions on the data. In the past, business users had to wait for specialists to prepare data and run analyses. This effectively prevented many worthwhile queries from being run, and routinely led to delays, mistakes, and misinterpretations.

I once spoke to a doctor from a leading medical research hospital who had used a week's vacation to take a SQL class. He explained that he was concerned about the efficacy of a specific medical treatment protocol, but he couldn't change the protocol without proving that the changes were safe. He'd spent a year trying to explain what he wanted to IT—waiting weeks to receive the data sets, realizing that they weren't what he was looking for, requesting more data, waiting for it, then investing more time only to discover that it wasn't what he needed either. He eventually became so frustrated that he took the SQL class so he could explore the data himself. Within two weeks of applying his newly acquired knowledge, he was able to find the data he needed to improve the treatment protocol. This is just one of many stories that showcase the value of self-service and the amazing breakthroughs that analysts can make if they are able to explore the data directly.

This chapter delves into how an organization has to reconsider its ways of collecting, labeling, and sharing data in order to achieve the self-service model required to empower business users. We'll explore issues such as helping users find useful data in the data lake, establishing trust that the data is correct and valuable, and helping users do their own analyses. Without establishing this trust in the data, business analysts will be reluctant to use the available data to make decisions, or may end up making the wrong decisions.

The Beginnings of Self-Service

In the past, the rule of thumb was that the first set of requirements for the data warehouse were always wrong—this was a well-known Data Warehouse 1.0 problem. To start the journey to a functioning data warehouse, IT had to build the first-generation schema, along with the accompanying reports. This gave users something tangible to figure out what they really needed so IT could produce "real" requirements. Except for a few power users, most analysts did not have the skills or the tools to work with the data directly.

The lengthy response times from IT that so many users experienced, like the doctor in my previous story, arose from the growing interest in and number of requests for the data. We've witnessed an explosion in the amount of data generated by applications and acquired from external providers, and a concomitant increase in business users' expectations to be able to leverage that data at near-real-time speeds. This simultaneous increase in data volume and user expectations made it impossible for IT to keep up.

However, the new generation of analysts, subject matter experts (SMEs), and decision makers are more technical and computer savvy than any previous generation, as they've grown up in the digital age and most have had some exposure to programming as part of their high school or college curriculums. This generation of users would rather have "self-service" access to the data; they want to find, understand, and use the data themselves. In addition, the cloud makes it possible for the business users to sidestep their IT departments and provision the infrastructure needed to run their analyses themselves.

In this chapter we will contrast the old approach, where IT departments provided analytic services for business analysts who performed analyses for business users, with the new self-service approach, where business users expect to be able to do their own analyses. To avoid unnecessary complexity, I'll refer to whoever is performing the analyses as analysts—this may include anyone from people with formal analyst titles, to business users doing their own analyses, to data scientists doing advanced analytics.

While the previous ETL versions of data modeling and business intelligence (BI) tools were created for programmers and architects, the new generation of tools are designed for power users to access directly. In the past, specialists did most of the work:

- Data modelers designed the schema for the data warehouse.
- ETL developers created ETL jobs to extract data from source applications, transform it, and load it into the data warehouse.
- Data quality analysts created validation jobs to check the correctness of the data.

- BI developers created reports and online analytical processing (OLAP) cubes that the users could slice and dice.
- Metadata architects created business glossaries to try to capture the meaning of various data elements and metadata repositories to try to keep track of the data in the enterprise.

The only analysis that an analyst could perform was through semantic layers such as Business Objects Universes that allowed end users to combine data by using higher-level prebuilt constructs (the business objects, such as *customer* and *order*), while the complexity of the actual data manipulations was hidden. For example, a user could add business objects for both a customer and an order to a report and would be able to see the orders for each customer. While very convenient, this approach was restricted to whatever business objects the IT staff created. Any changes required multi-person reviews and approvals that sometimes took months.

The data self-service revolution has upended this brittle situation. Self-service data exploration and visualization tools such as Tableau, Power BI, and Qlik, which allow analysts to visually explore data and work with it directly to create charts, are rapidly replacing traditional BI offerings. Analysts are now using self-service data prep tools like Excel, Trifacta, and Paxata to transform data into whatever shape they need.

Furthermore, self-service catalog tools such as Waterline Data and IBM Watson Catalog are now allowing the analysts to annotate, find, and understand data sets themselves without having to request them from IT.

Figure 6-1 illustrates how analysts' reliance on IT, and the consequent load on IT, is significantly reduced in the self-service analytics world. The self-service tools available today were almost all developed with the analyst in mind as the target user, and they often do not require any IT involvement to deploy and use (one exception is the catalog tools that straddle IT and business, which are usually administered by IT but used by analysts). The underlying data infrastructure remains squarely in the hands of IT, however, which keeps the data stable.

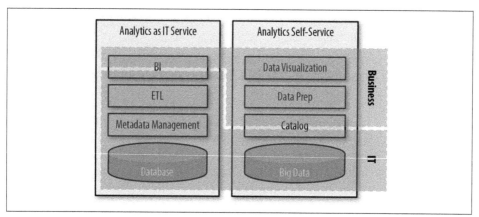

Figure 6-1. Enabling analysts and reducing the load on IT with self-service analytics

Business Analysts

Unfortunately, most enterprises today don't really support the self-service model, because the data warehouses are not designed to handle a large volume of ad hoc queries and analytics. As we discussed earlier, they are carefully tuned to support mission-critical production reports and analytics. Allowing hundreds or even thousands of users to issue random and sometimes ill-formed queries would interfere with those functions. Furthermore, analytics often require combining data in the data warehouse with other data sets, but adding anything to a data warehouse is an expensive and lengthy process that requires a lot of design work, architectural and security approvals, and ETL development.

Therefore, one of the main purposes of a data lake in many enterprises is to create an environment where such self-service is possible. To understand self-service, we need to examine the workflow of a typical business analyst (Figure 6-2).

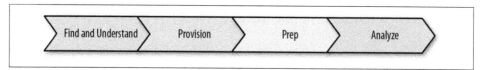

Figure 6-2. The business analyst's workflow

As we saw in Chapter 1, first the analyst has to *find and understand* the required data. The next step is to *provision* the data—that is, obtain it in a usable form and format. Next, the data needs to be *prepared* for analysis. This may involve combining, filtering, aggregating, fixing data quality problems, and so on. Once the data is in the correct shape, the analyst can *analyze* it using data discovery and visualization tools.

We'll look at the first three steps in this workflow in more detail here, along with the important issue of establishing trust in the data that's identified.

Finding and Understanding Data—Documenting the Enterprise

Analysts want to search for data using business terms that they are familiar with (for example, "I need customer demographics including annual spend, age, and location"), whereas data sets and fields are often exposed through cryptic technical names. This makes it very challenging for analysts to find and understand data. To bridge that gap, many enterprises are investing in data catalogs that associate business terms or tags with data sets and their fields, allowing analysts to quickly find data sets using such tags and to understand these data sets by looking at the tags associated with each field. Usually, multiple data sets contain the data that analysts need, so the next step becomes selecting which one to use. Analysts usually include judgments about how complete, accurate, and trustworthy the data is when making their choices (we'll consider the issue of establishing trust in the next section).

While catalogs are critical to enabling self-service for business analysts, they are challenging to build and maintain. This is because in most enterprises the knowledge about where data is, which data sets to use for what, and what data means is locked in people's heads—this is commonly referred to as "tribal knowledge."

Without a catalog, in order to find a data set to use for a specific problem, analysts have to ask around until they find someone—if they're lucky, a subject matter expert —who can point them to the right data. SMEs can be difficult to find, though, so the analyst may instead run into someone who tells them about a data set that they used for a similar problem, and will then use that data set without really understanding what was done to it or where it came from.

This is sort of like playing Russian Roulette with your project—it's akin to asking around if anyone knows a doctor who might know anything about the pain in your right side, running into someone who says that they had a pain in their right side and took a particular medicine, and then taking some of their medicine. Not only may their medicine not be right for you, but you have no idea what it is, where it came from, or how old it is. Even if you find a doctor who claims to know something about your pain, you have no idea if this doctor is qualified to diagnose it. Needless to say, this is an incredibly painful (pun intended), time-consuming, and error-prone process, whether applied to physical or data doctoring.

One thing we have going for us in this age of Google, Yelp, and Wikipedia is that we are used to capturing knowledge through crowdsourcing. The same approach has been applied by enterprises to crowdsourcing tribal knowledge about data from analysts, so the information in their heads can be captured in glossaries and metadata repositories. These efforts are time-consuming, however, and run into two obstacles. First, only the most important data gets documented—typically called *critical data elements* (CDEs). These usually include descriptive fields found in master data lists, such as customer and product attributes, and core transaction fields, such as order

IDs, dates, and amounts. Second, even for CDEs, the repositories quickly become out of date as data sets, business processes, and rules change and technology evolves.

The best practices for overcoming these challenges are:

- Crowdsourcing all tribal knowledge and making it available to everyone
- Automating annotation of data sets

Ten years ago, analysis was typically performed by dedicated staff who spent all their time working with data, so knowledge about the data was concentrated in analytics and data architecture teams. In the enterprise today, analysis is done by everyone who needs to make decisions. Combined with proliferation of data, this makes it more difficult to find subject matter experts who are knowledgeable about the data. SME is usually not a full-time job or an official role. Some enterprises have developed a formal data stewardship framework where people are assigned full-time or, more often, part-time responsibility for stewarding data—that is, making sure it is used appropriately, complies with governmental and internal regulations, and is kept at high levels of quality. However, most SMEs and even most official data stewards do not get compensated for helping other teams, yet are still expected to complete their primary work. The SMEs frequently resent this role and don't really enjoy explaining the same material over and over to different groups. Analysts have been known to bribe SMEs with lunches or other incentives in exchange for their time and knowledge. But at the end of such a lunch, the analyst may have only part of the knowledge they need, and, if they're lucky, have been given pointers to other SMEs they can consult for the remaining knowledge. Which leads to more expensive lunches!

Since enterprises are beginning to recognize the value of SMEs and their knowledge, they are experimenting with various ways of incentivizing crowdsourcing. Some of the best practices include:

- Making it as easy and efficient as possible for SMEs to document their knowledge. Commonly, this is achieved by creating glossaries or taxonomies of terms and letting SMEs tag data sets with those terms instead to having to write elaborate descriptions for each field.
- Enhancing tags further through a practice called "folksonomy," which allows SMEs to use the terms that they are familiar with as tags instead of forcing them to learn an imposed taxonomy (whether homegrown or industry-standard, like FIBO for financial services). For example, an American analyst may look for a "first name" and "last name," while a European one looks for "given name" and "family name." While these are simple synonyms, sometimes the terms have additional connotations and semantics. For example, one business may consider "due date" and "default date" the same, while another business may have a "grace period," such that "default date" is "due date plus grace period." The variety and

complexity introduced by different geographies, businesses, functions, and acquisitions are quite astounding.

- Encouraging SMEs to share their knowledge by giving public recognition for their work—from gamification and badges to simple recognition by projects that they've helped.

- Making it easy to find out whom to ask about which data sets. This not only helps analysts find the right people to ask, but encourages SMEs to document their data sets, so they do not have to explain them to every new user. For example, when Google implemented a searchable catalog where users could find SMEs for each data set, they found that the frequently used data sets got documented quickly as SMEs got tired of responding to questions.

- Making it easy for the analysts who talk to SMEs to document what they've learned as tags and annotations, so they can retain it for the future and avoid bothering SMEs again. This is probably the most effective technique—in this way, knowledge quickly spreads and becomes institutionalized.

While crowdsourcing SMEs' knowledge is an important step toward self-service, the sheer volume of data in the enterprise makes it prohibitive to manually document everything. As a consequence, often only a few well-known and frequently used data sets become well documented, while the majority of data remains dark. This also causes problems with new data sets, which may not get documented right away and thus may not be found by analysts.

The answer to this problem is automation. New tools effectively combine crowdsourcing and automation to do "automated data discovery"—the automated tagging and annotation of data sets based on the tags provided by SMEs and analysts. These tools leverage artificial intelligence (AI) and machine learning to identify and autotag elements in dark data sets, so analysts can find and use them. Waterline Data's Smart Data Catalog and IBM's Watson Data Catalog are good examples of this approach. Catalogs are explored in more detail in Chapter 8.

Establishing Trust

Once an analyst finds the pertinent data set, the next question becomes whether the data can be trusted. While analysts sometimes have the luxury of access to clean, trusted, curated data sets, more often than not they have to independently ascertain whether they can trust the data. Trust is usually based on three pillars:

- Data quality—how complete and clean the data set is
- Lineage (aka provenance)—where the data came from
- Stewardship—who created the data set, and why

Data quality

Data quality is a wide and complex topic. In practice, quality can be defined as compliance of data to policies, which can range from simple (e.g., the customer name field should never be empty) to complex (e.g., sales tax must be correctly calculated based on purchase location). The most common data quality rules are:

Completeness
> The field is not empty.

Data type
> The field is of the correct type (for example, age is a number).

Range
> The field is in a specified range (for example, age is between 0 and 125).

Format
> The field has a specific format (for example, a US postal code is composed of either five digits, nine digits, or five digits followed by a dash and four digits).

Cardinality
> The field has a specific number of unique values. (For example, if a US states field has more than 50 unique values, we know there is a problem. We may still not know whether every value is a legal state name, but if we already have every legal state name represented, checking the cardinality is enough of a sanity check to catch any illegal names because they will push the number of values above 50.)

Selectivity
> The values for the field are unique (for example, customer IDs should be unique in a customer list).

Referential integrity
> The values for the field are in the reference value set. (For example, all the customer status codes are legal, and each customer ID in the order list refers to one of the customers in the customer list. While for some values, like states, we may get away with a cardinality check, customer status codes may have significant implications for how we treat the customer, what we charge, and so on, so when making sure each customer has a legitimate status code it's important to check every value.)

The most common way to check data quality is called *data profiling*. This approach involves reading the data in every field and calculating metrics such as the number of empty fields (completeness), number of unique values (cardinality), and percentage of unique values (selectivity), as well as checking the data type, range, and format and performing referential integrity checks.

In addition to basic data profiling, custom rules can be defined to validate specific aspects of the data. The advantage of profiling is that it can be done automatically and universally for all fields, then reviewed by analysts who are considering whether to use a data set to ascertain quality levels. Custom rules, on the other hand, have to be manually designed, implemented, and applied to the data set in question.

Lineage (provenance)

While data quality checks tell the analysts how good the data is, lineage tells them where the data came from. For example, customer data from a CRM system is more trustworthy than a customer list from a specialized data mart because the former is a system of record for customer data, where the latter could be a subset of customers from a certain geography or demographic and might contain modified or out-of-date customer data.

In some industries, such as financial services, lineage is required as part of regulatory compliance. For example, the Basel Committee on Banking Supervision's rule 239 requires that financial services companies demonstrate to auditors the lineage of the data used for financial reporting. So, if data in the gold zone is used for financial reporting, it is imperative to document its lineage and keep it up to date.

There are many challenges with representing data lineage, especially around system identity and transformation logic. Because data passes through many systems and tools, it is often difficult to identify whether different tools are referring to the same system or to different systems. Furthermore, because different tools express their transformations differently—some visually, some using a programming language, some using a query language or script—it can be difficult to represent all the transformations that have been performed in a unified way.

Let's look at identity first. Imagine that one Hadoop file is created with an open source Hadoop utility called Sqoop that uses Java Database Connectivity (JDBC) to execute relational database queries and load the results into a file. However, another Hadoop file is created by reading data from the same table in the same database with an ETL tool that uses an Open Database Connectivity (ODBC) interface. There may be no programmatic way of recognizing that both files were extracted from the same database. Furthermore, because Sqoop may execute a free-form query, it may not be possible to recognize that Sqoop is ultimately reading the same table as the ETL tool.

One of the selling points of an ETL tool is that if all the transformations are performed by a single tool, the identity problem is resolved by that tool and technical lineage is easy to represent using whatever representation that ETL tool uses natively. However, if your enterprise, like most, is using multiple ETL tools, you have to resolve the identity problem as well as the representation problem. There are many ways to represent lineage, depending on the target audience. Business analysts, for example, prefer business-level lineage that describes how the data was generated using business terms and simple explanations. Most technical users prefer technical lineage that shows the specific code that was used to generate the target data set, or a rigorous equivalent graphical representation of that code.

Technical lineage is challenging because the data set may be generated through multiple steps using a variety of programs and programming languages, scripts, and tools. Two aspects of technical lineage need to be considered: granularity and transformation representation.

There are two levels of granularity that you may encounter:

Data set–level granularity
> The lineage relationship between various data sets is usually captured and represented as a *directed graph*. In other words, each step in obtaining or transforming the data is shown as a node or box, with arrows showing the one-way flow of data through these nodes. Frequently, the programs used to generate data sets are represented as well, but as nodes on a graph rather than detailed pieces of code.

Field-level granularity
> The lineage of each field is captured and represented as a directed graph, often with different nodes representing different transformations. Sometimes, this level of lineage is combined with the data set level on a single graph, so the users can drill down from data set level to field level in the interface for a specific target data set.

There are also two transformation representations that you might see:

Normalized representation
> All transformations are translated to a common representation. This is difficult because the data set may have been generated using a variety of procedural and declarative languages, so the translation may be complicated (or even impossible).

Original representation
> All transformations are presented in the original language or script. This is also challenging because a data set may be generated using complex software, making it extremely difficult to programmatically extract just the logic that was used to generate that data set.

Let's look at an example. Imagine we have two Hadoop files: one downloaded from the data warehouse that contains our complete customer list with customer addresses and one from a public website called Data.gov that provides average income for each zip code.

Once we've downloaded the files, we create two Hive tables based on the directories where the files reside—Cust and IncomebyZip—to provide a relational (SQL) interface. We then execute a SQL query to select Californian customers from the Cust table and join it with the IncomebyZip table to generate a final table, CalCustRelIncome, that rates each customer based on how their household income compares to the average in their zip code.

The business lineage for this process will look something like Figure 6-3. It will skip all the intermediate steps and details and provide English (or whatever language is used) descriptions as callouts documenting what each major step accomplishes. Of course, the issue with verbal business-level descriptions is that someone has to write them up and, even more challenging, maintain them as the code changes. On the other hand, these descriptions are probably the only practical way to inform a business analyst how a data set was generated.

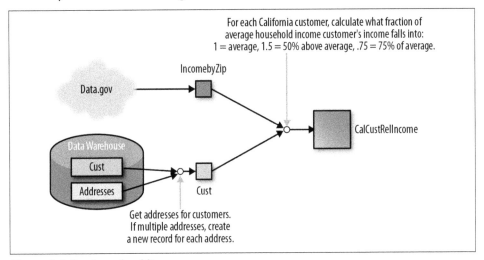

Figure 6-3. Business-level lineage

A more technical data set representation is illustrated in Figure 6-4. It gives a reasonably high-level view of what the major steps are and where the data comes from. It does not, however, give the details of the operations. For example, if we did not call the target table CalCustRelIncome, there would be no way from the data set–level lineage to infer that only Californian customers are being selected from the Cust table.

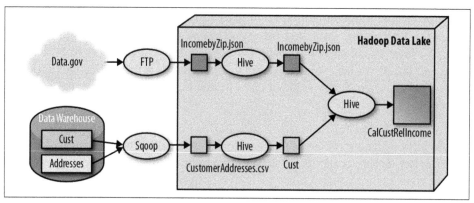

Figure 6-4. Data set–level technical lineage

Sometimes it is possible to add more details to this lineage—for example, a callout to the Sqoop node that shows the Sqoop query or a Hive node to show the Hive query, as illustrated in Figure 6-5.

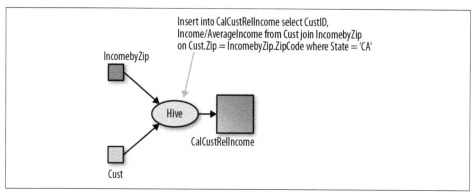

Figure 6-5. Adding detail to data set–level transformation nodes

Let's now take a look at how this single Hive query would be represented graphically as field-level lineage using a   normalized graphical representation, as illustrated in Figure 6-6.

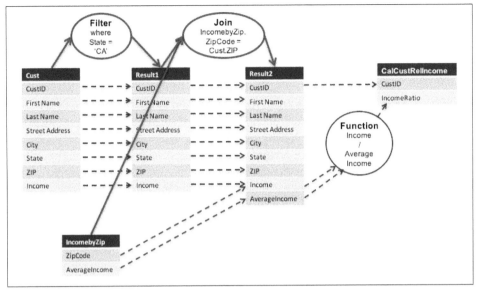

Figure 6-6. Field-level technical lineage

In Figure 6-6, the field-level operations are depicted using dashed blue lines and the data set operations using solid dark red lines. If a field is simply copied from source to target, it is represented with a dashed blue line from the source field to the target field. If there is an operation involved, it is represented by a blue oval, and the inputs and outputs of the operation are depicted using dashed blue lines. The inputs and outputs of set operations (in the red ovals) are indicated by solid red lines between the operations and specific data sets. A single Hive SQL query is represented as three steps or nodes:

Filter node

Applies a filter to the Cust Hive table to select only Californian customers.

Join node

Combines the results of the first operation and the IncomebyZip Hive table to add the AverageIncome for each customer based on their zip code.

Function node

Extracts the fields that will go into the CalCustRelIncome Hive table and calculates each customer's IncomeRatio by dividing the customer's income by the average income. Because the calculation is done in place as part of the query, the function does not have a name and is represented by the code that performs the desired calculation.

To generate this diagram, the lineage system has to be able to parse and understand Hive SQL and break it into separate operations. This is a nontrivial amount of work, especially since, instead of using a declarative language like SQL, the user may have chosen to write a Java MapReduce program or a Pig script, or used any of a number of other options that may be difficult or impossible to represent in a normalized way.

Stewardship

There is a strong social aspect to trust. Analysts rely on word of mouth to find trusted SMEs. Just as some bloggers, YouTubers, and industry experts stand out by developing credibility and a large following, some users' annotations and curation in a modern data lake may be more credible than others. These trusted users may have organizational responsibility for the data, they may be official data stewards, or they may be widely recognized and respected experts. Even in organizations with a mature governance structure and officially designated data stewards, some data stewards may be more knowledgeable than others, and sometimes analysts can have better insight and knowledge—especially about data sets they've created or use all the time—than the official data stewards. To address the distributed and unofficial nature of expertise, some enterprises are turning to paradigms used by consumer websites such as TripAdvisor and Yelp to identify credible reviewers by allowing users to rate whether they found the information helpful and accurate.

Provisioning

Once the right data set is identified, the analyst needs to make it available for use, or "provision" it. Provisioning has two aspects: getting permission to use the data and getting physical access to the data.

One of the big challenges with a data lake is deciding which analysts to give access to what data. In some industries, giving everyone access to all the data is perfectly acceptable and solves the first problem. Most industries, however, handle a lot of sensitive data. Data sets may contain personally identifiable information (PII), financial information such as credit card and account numbers, and business-sensitive information such as order sizes and discounts.

Traditional access control approaches create an account for each user and potentially add users to one or more groups, and specify access permissions for specific users and groups to each data set or field. For example, all US marketing analysts may get access to US sales data, but not EU sales data. When a new marketing analyst is hired in the US, they're added to the US marketing analysts group and get access to the US sales data. If they transfer to a different team or join a different project, their permissions and group memberships will have to be reviewed. When a new data set is received, the security team and data stewards have to figure out who should get access to it. There are many problems with this approach:

- It is very time-consuming. Large companies may be hiring people or moving them between projects all the time. Someone—usually a high-cost and highly responsible person—has to figure out who should have access to what.

- There is a lot of historical baggage, because someone who transfers to another project may still have responsibilities in the old team for a period of time. Analysts sometimes end up with access privileges for data that is no longer relevant to their work and to which they shouldn't have access.

- There is a lot of data, and it is sometimes difficult to figure out correctly who should have access to what data.

Ideally, the analysts should be able to request access to the data they need. However, if they cannot find the data without having access to it, we have a catch-22.

The solution is a more agile approach to access control that some enterprises are beginning to adopt. They create metadata catalogs that allow the analysts to find any data set without having access to it. Once the right data sets have been identified, the analysts request access to them and the data steward or data owner decides whether to grant access, for how long, and for which portions of the data. Once the access period expires, the access can be automatically revoked or an extension requested.

There are many advantages to this approach:

- No work has to be done detecting and protecting sensitive data inside a data set until someone requests this data set.

- The analysts can find any data in the data lake, including the newly ingested data sets, without having access to it.

- The data stewards and owners do not have to invest time in figuring out who should have access to what data unless there is an actual project requiring it.

- Access requests can require justification, creating an audit trail of who is requesting what data sets and why.

- Access may be granted to a portion of a data set and for a specific period of time.

- It is always clear which data sets are in use, so data quality and governance efforts can be focused on those data sets. For example, ETL jobs can update only the data sets that are currently in use, and sensitive data deidentification and data quality rules may be applied just to those data sets.

We'll talk more about catalogs in Chapter 8 and look at access control and provisioning in much more detail in Chapter 9.

Preparing Data for Analysis

While some data is usable as is, more often than not it requires some preparation. Preparation may be as simple as selecting the proper subset of data, or it may involve a complex cleansing and transformation process to get the data into the right form. The most common data preparation tool is Microsoft Excel. Unfortunately, Excel has significant limitations that make it impractical to use for working with large data lake files. Fortunately, new tools that scale better have been brought to market by newer companies like Alteryx, Datameer, Paxata, and Trifacta, as well as more established data integration vendors such as Informatica and Talend. Even some of the data visualization vendors, like Tableau and Qlik, are incorporating common data prep capabilities into their tools. Excel is evolving too—Microsoft is working on a Hadoop interface for Excel running in Azure.

Because traditional data warehouses were designed to do fairly narrow and predefined types of analysis, they relied on well-tested and optimized ETL jobs developed by IT to transform data to a single common schema and load it. Any data quality issues were resolved in the same way for everyone, and all data was transformed to a common set of measurements and representations. All the analysts had to make do with this one-size-fits-all approach.

Modern self-service analytics, and especially data science, are more agile and exploratory. Analysts can leverage more of the data that's available in the data warehouse and often seek out the original or raw data to work with, so they can prepare it in the way that fits their specific needs and use cases.

This need to create "fit for purpose" data is impossible for IT to accommodate. Fortunately, a set of tools called *data preparation* or *data wrangling* tools have become popular that make it easy for analysts to convert raw data into a format suitable for analytics without needing deep technical skills. These data preparation tools present a visual spreadsheet-like interface for the analysts to work with. The following essay by Bertrand Cariou describes different use cases for data wrangling and describes how one of the modern data preparation tools, Trifacta, provides sophisticated machine learning interfaces that try to guess and automatically suggest operations based on the user's data selections.

Data Wrangling in the Data Lake

 ***Bertrand Cariou*** *is Senior Director of Partner Marketing at Trifacta. Bertrand has focused on making data accessible and usable at Informatica and a number of other US and European companies.*

The term "data wrangling" is often used to describe the preliminary preparation that business professionals, such as business analysts, data analysts, and data scientists, do in order to get data ready for analytics. Data wrangling can thus be part of the "self-service" described elsewhere in this book. However, we also see an increasing amount of data wrangling done by data engineers to facilitate their work and improve collaboration with business users. Whoever carries out the task, data wrangling is the process of converting diverse data from its raw formats into a structured and consumable format for business intelligence, statistical modeling tools, and machine learning, or to supply data to business applications. New tools informed by machine learning, such as those offered by my company, Trifacta (*https://www.trifacta.com/*), take much of the effort out of data preparation by making suggestions and interacting with users to accelerate and automate data wrangling for their particular data-driven needs.

Situating Data Preparation in Hadoop

Data preparation sits between the data storage and processing layer—tools such as Hadoop, Spark, and other data computation engines—and the visualization or statistical applications used downstream in the process.

As pictured in Figure 6-7, data wrangling happens in various places within an analytical workflow:

Exploratory prep
> Data wrangling in the data lake typically occurs within a zone or during a move between zones. Users may access raw and refined data to combine and structure it for their exploratory work or to define new transformation rules they want to automate and run on a regular basis.

> Data preparation can also be used for lightweight ingestion, which brings in external data sources (e.g., spreadsheets and relational data) to augment data already in the data lake for the purpose of exploration and cleansing.

Consumption

Wrangling often occurs in the production zone to deliver data to the business insight layer. This can be done by SQL-based BI tools, or by exporting the data in a file format (e.g., CSV, JSON, or the Tableau Data Extract format) for further use with analytics tools including Tableau, SAS, or R.

Operationalization

In addition to the actual work of transforming data, data preparation tools are used within the operationalization layer, where teams can regularly schedule data preparation jobs and control their execution.

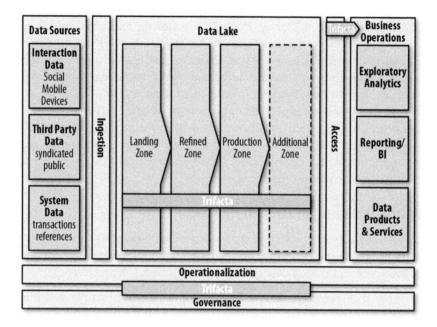

Figure 6-7. Trifacta ecosystem

All data access, transformation, and interaction within the solution is logged and made available to data governance tools so administrators can understand the lineage of data.

Common Use Cases for Data Preparation

The use of data preparation tools can be classified into three major scenarios (with variations) that may benefit from automation organized by a business team or an IT team. Here is a summary of three common use cases for data wrangling and corresponding Trifacta customer examples.

Use case: Self-service automation for analytics or business applications

For these types of initiatives, the business teams manage the analytical process, from initial data ingestion to the eventual data consumption, including data preparation. Often, their end goal is to create a "master report" for compliance purposes or to aggregate disparate data. In these initiatives, the IT organization is responsible for setting up the data lake and data ingestion so that, from there, the business team can handle its own data requirements and schedule data preparation tasks without IT involvement.

Customer example

PepsiCo needed to optimize its retail sales forecasts, which combine retailer point-of-sales (POS) data with internal transaction information. For PepsiCo, the major challenge sprang from the different formats provided by each retailer through automatically generated reports or email attachments. With Trifacta, the business analyst team assumes ownership of the ingestion of the retailer data into PepsiCo's data lake, can explore and define how the data should be transformed, and can execute jobs on demand or through routine scheduling to deliver a consumable outcome to the downstream applications or processes. Trifacta learns from the user's interactions, providing immediate feedback to better guide them through structuring, enriching, and validating the data at scale.

Use case: Preparation for IT operationalization

In this scenario, the data specialists—usually data analysts or data engineers—design the preparation work themselves, then test, validate, and run the rules at scale to produce the desired outcome. After end users create operational workflows, the IT team usually integrates them into enterprise workloads.

Customer example

A large European bank needed to extract chat logs from its website to improve customer service, as well as to analyze product and service needs. The bank used Trifacta to transform these complex formats into discrete attributes for a broader Customer 360 initiative that incorporated additional data channels. In this case, the teams provided their IT organization with the data wrangling rules they'd created so that IT could combine the various data flows consistently.

Use case: Exploratory analytics and machine learning

As their name suggests, exploratory analytics use data to explore various aspects of the business and involve using a data preparation tool on an ad hoc basis to explore the data, investigate use cases, find relevant third-party data, validate hypotheses, discover patterns in the data, or generate data sets for data scientist modeling.

Analyzing and Visualizing

There are a plethora of great self-service data visualization and analytics tools. Tableau and Qlik have been around for years, and a number of smaller vendors, like Arcadia Data and AtScale, deliver high-quality, easy-to-use functionality specifically for big data environments. The following essay by Donald Farmer discusses the self-service trends in business intelligence.

The New World of Self-Service Business Intelligence

Donald Farmer is VP of Innovation and Design at Qlik. He has been pushing the boundaries of data strategy for almost 30 years, developing, writing, and speaking internationally on advanced analytics and innovation strategy.

In the past few years, business users have dramatically transformed their relationship with IT. The change began, as so many have recently, with the iPhone and the iPad and the phenomenon known as Bring Your Own Device. BYOD, as it is often abbreviated, is a strategic response or a tactical adjustment to the realization that users now have easy access to better technology and faster upgrades than IT can provision. This new reality is also reflected in the world of data analysis. In a clear parallel with Bring Your Own provisioning of devices, business analysts have embraced self-service business intelligence. With self-service, users build their own solutions and may even choose their own tools, "with or without IT's permission," as the analyst firm Gartner has noted.

In the past, IT departments necessarily provisioned the reporting infrastructure, dashboards, and analytics for enterprises. Only the IT team could deploy the expensive storage and computing power needed. Only IT understood the technical issues involved in extracting and consolidating data or building the analytic models. And very significantly, only IT could secure the data and the resulting analysis to ensure the right people had the right insights. The workflow of BI followed the classic lifecycle model: IT gathered requirements, built solutions, deployed them into production, and started another round of requirements gathering.

In truth, there was always a secondary "dark side" to this IT-led model. As developers struggled to run this lifecycle quickly enough for increasingly agile businesses, analysts in finance and marketing departments simply used Excel as a good-enough tool. Often they exported data from reports for further analysis. Sometimes they had access to source data. Excel was effective, but not powerful. Its lack of security, compounded by the habits of business users, caused poor analyses or even confidential data to proliferate in the shadows of an organization.

Self-service BI tools brought this dark side not only into the light, but into the mainstream of enterprise analytics. From the mid-2000s, as 64-bit computing became established as the norm, applications such as QlikView, Tableau, and Microsoft's PowerPivot brought powerful analysis capabilities to any business user. These tools rolled the lifecycle of ETL and building data models into a single, simple environment. They used elegant visualizations to enable users to find patterns and communicate insights easily and effectively. Using in-memory storage and compression, the same tools could bring data capacity and computing power to the desktop that was once available only in the carefully managed server room. With this power (as the cliche says) comes great responsibility, but well-designed self-service applications can help with that too.

This transformation in the power of business users has brought about many changes, especially in the analytic workflow and, dramatically, the role of IT.

The New Analytic Workflow

As I have already noted, the workflow for analytic applications and reporting used to be a variation on the classic application lifecycle: requirements, design, deployment, and new requirements. However, with self-service, the business analysts know their own requirements and develop their own solutions, so the process may seem a little haphazard. Requirements can change at any time. A tweak to the frontend design (adding a new element to a chart, for example) can alter the data extraction process. An analyst may deploy and share a half-finished solution just to get moving.

Rather than thinking of this agile, ad hoc process as a lifecycle, I find it more useful to picture it as a supply chain, with data as the raw material flowing through a number of processes and value being added at each step. The great advantage of a supply chain is that sometimes steps may be consolidated for efficiency. When delivering food from farm to table, for instance, a wholesaler may not only resell, but also wash and partially prepare some vegetables. Similarly, each step of the supply chain may be simply operational (transport from farm to market) or may add value as it takes place, such as sorting by size or quality grade.

In a business analytics supply chain, with data as the raw material, business users may take data from wherever it is available. Self-service tools typically offer a simple wizard, script, or visual environment to view, join, consolidate, or clean data. Often this phase is known as data blending—or, more poetically, data wrangling. However, unlike traditional ETL processes, which loaded a data warehouse model from the sources in advance of any analytic work, blending and wrangling may happen before, during, or (with an analytic app used as a source) even after an analytic process.

For business analysts using self-service tools, blending data *is* an analytic process. As they see initial results in their visualizations, they form a better understanding of the data as they work. They then modify their scripts or data wizards in order to see the data differently, or to enable a better visualization. Note an important difference here. In the traditional data warehouse lifecycle, ETL populates a model, which then drives the analysis. The model may be a star schema or a sophisticated OLAP model requiring specialized design and engineering skills. In the self-service supply chain, the model is still there, but the user may not even be aware of it. The business analyst, typically, is not a conscious modeler.

The flexibility of this new approach is of particular value when business analysts work with a data lake. In a traditional model, with complex relational sources and expensive storage, data was often transformed through remarkably complex processes to get it into a shape that was efficient for both storage and querying. ETL and OLAP, for example, required substantial skills.

The data lake, on the other hand, can store vast quantities of data easily. With the flexibility of schema-on-read there is no need to try to model all scenarios in a single data warehouse. So long as the data can be presented to business analysts with effective semantics (they should never be required to write MapReduce!) and reasonable performance, they can work with a data lake and self-service tools.

Gatekeepers to Shopkeepers

At this point, we should consider the role of IT. It is important to say that IT will likely still deliver mission-critical intelligence. The enterprise data warehouse will still be with us for year-on-year consolidated financial reporting, tax analysis, and HR. IT will still need their OLAP and ETL skills for some years to come. They will need MapReduce skills too!

Naturally, IT has an important role to play in the analytic supply chain. At the very least, IT must "keep the lights on" with robust networking, storage, and data sources to make the process possible. However, its role is much broader than that.

In the past, as we have seen, IT teams provided the entire lifecycle of analytics, because they were the only ones who could. In addition, they secured systems, offering "data access" as needed and as permitted. IT departments took this role of "gatekeeper" very seriously, as well they might, to the extent that business analysts were often frustrated by their limited access to essential data.

This frustration with the IT gatekeepers led to professional tensions and frequently to exactly the "dark side" of unmanaged data sharing that the controls were meant to avoid. Spreadsheets got out of control, because they were the only tool left to the analysts that IT could not lock down.

With self-service, we need a new approach. IT teams must move from being "gatekeepers" to "shopkeepers."

A gatekeeper is concerned with keeping the wrong people out. A shopkeeper invites the right people in, preparing, presenting, and provisioning the shop's goods to encourage their appropriate use. In IT terms, a data provisioning team can build feeds and models designed for business users to serve themselves. Rather than opening the gate to give users access to source systems, an effective team can instead provision data out for the users, cleaned, consolidated, and even anonymized as needed for effective analysis and good governance. What IT doesn't need to do is prepare every source for a specific use case: the business analysts use their tools on the data supply chain to serve themselves those solutions.

Governing Self-Service

In this supply chain model, where IT teams act as shopkeepers, they still play a major role in securing and governing data. One of the most important moves they can make is to provision well-designed self-service tools for their users.

A well-designed, enterprise-ready application for self-service doesn't only provide powerful, simple tools for the business user—it must also feature a powerful server architecture, in the cloud or on premises, which gives IT the necessary insight and oversight to govern the use of the system.

IT's oversight includes managing the deployment, user permissions, server performance, and scaling. The insights a well-designed application offers include understanding what data sources analysts are using, who they are sharing their apps and visualizations with, and how the data is prepared and refreshed.

Remember that IT still provides the mission-critical analytics, such as financial reporting. They are still the gatekeepers of the inner sanctum. But much of the work of business analytics can be handled with a lighter touch—still secure and governed—with a new provisioning approach that is not only more agile, but simply friendlier to the rest of the business too.

Conclusion

If leveraging data to make better decisions is key to the success of the modern enterprise, the old practices of IT-built rigid analytics and data warehouses are not going to keep up. The only practical way to leverage data to make better decisions is to enable the analysts to do their own analytics without having to involve IT in every project (and thereby making IT a bottleneck and slowing things down). As you saw in this chapter, a new generation of analytics and data infrastructure tools—from data visualization tools to data prep tools and data catalogs—has arisen to make it possible for the analysts to work with data without involving IT. Methods of providing search, provenance, and trust can be built into the data lake for all its users.

CHAPTER 7

Architecting the Data Lake

There are many ways to organize data in a data lake. In this chapter, we will start with how to organize a data lake into zones. Then we'll compare and contrast on-premises and cloud data lakes. Finally, we'll discuss virtual data lakes, which minimize resource usage and the overhead of maintaining a data lake while providing equivalent functionality to physical data lakes.

Organizing the Data Lake

Once a data lake is established, the analysts need a way to find and understand the data it contains. This is a formidable task when you consider the wide variety of data in most enterprises (one large retailer I spoke with had over 30,000 data sources feeding its data lake, and said that each source might provide hundreds or even thousands of tables). Even if analysts find the right data set, they need to know whether they can trust the data. Finally, to enable users to freely roam the lake, sensitive data must be identified and protected so that it is not exposed inadvertently. All these tasks fall under the umbrella of data governance.

In the old days of data warehousing, data governance was implemented by a large team of data stewards, data architects, and data engineers. Changes had to be carefully reviewed and approved. Data quality, data access, management of sensitive data, and other aspects of data governance were carefully considered and managed. But in the era of self-service, this approach does not scale. In fact, the exploratory and agile nature of data science conflicts with the top-down, careful style of traditional data governance.

In response to this speedup of data use, enterprises have started applying the concept of *bimodal data governance*, defined by Gartner (*https://www.gartner.com/it-glossary/bimodal/*) as follows: "Bimodal is the practice of managing two separate but coherent styles of work: one focused on predictability; the other on exploration." To support this bimodal approach, the data lake is usually divided into multiple zones with different degrees of governance. In this section we will cover best practices for organizing a data lake into zones, helping users understand the governance levels of data, and protecting sensitive data.

Figure 7-1 reflects a pretty common data lake cluster architecture. Data from external sources is loaded first into a raw or landing zone, where it is filed in folders that reflect its provenance (for instance, time and source) without further processing. Then, as appropriate, this data is copied into the gold zone, where it is cleansed, curated, and aggregated; the work zone, where users run their projects; or the sensitive zone, where data that should be protected is kept in encrypted volumes.

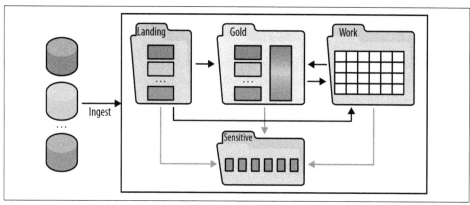

Figure 7-1. Sample breakdown of data lake into workspaces or zones

Different data lake users usually use dedicated zones, as illustrated in Figure 7-2.

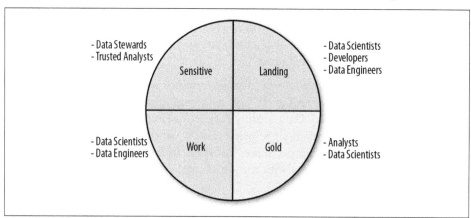

Figure 7-2. Different users use different zones

Landing or Raw Zone

The landing zone, sometimes also called the *raw* or *staging* zone, is used to house raw ingested data. The IT team usually creates naming conventions to identify where data comes from. For instance, all ingested raw data is usually kept in a single folder (e.g., */Landing*). Within that folder there is usually a subfolder per source (e.g., */Landing/EDW* or */Landing/Twitter*), and within those subfolders another folder per table or some other grouping (e.g., */Landing/EDW/Customer_dimension* or */Landing/Twitter/Mybrand1*).

If the table is reflected periodically, a partition may be created for each time new data is loaded (e.g., */Landing/EDW/Customer_dimension/20190101.csv* or */Landing/Twitter/Mybrand1/20190101.json* for data loaded on January 1, 2019). To avoid very large folders, a more elaborate folder tree may be created with a folder for each year and month, for example, and just that month's partitions as files (e.g., */Landing/EDW/Customer_dimension/2019/01/20190101.csv* or */Landing/Twitter/Mybrand1/2019/01/20190101.json*). Figure 7-3 shows a typical hierarchy of folders.

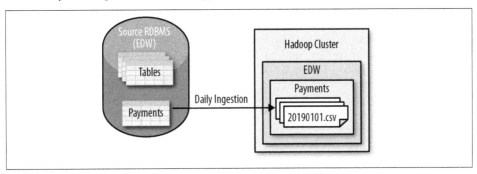

Figure 7-3. Ingesting raw or landing data into folders and files

Usually, only highly technical developers, data engineers, and data scientists get access to the landing zone. In general, users of the landing zone must have a compelling reason to perform their own data treatment and processing.

Analysts usually need cleaner data and use data from the gold zone, described next.

Gold Zone

The gold zone frequently mirrors the landing area, but contains cleansed, enriched, and otherwise processed versions of the raw data. This zone is sometimes also called *prod* to indicate that the data it contains is production ready, or *cleansed* to indicate that the data has been run though data quality tools and/or a curation process to clean up (or cleanse) data quality problems, as described in Chapter 2. Preparing the data for production use is often similar to the ETL jobs that create a data warehouse —data is harmonized and normalized into conforming dimensions or master lists, such as master customer or product lists. The operations might involve converting first, middle, and last names to a single field for the full name; converting kilograms to pounds; changing local codes to common ones; joining and aggregating data sets; or doing more sophisticated cleansing like address verification, filling in missing information from other sources, resolving conflicting information loaded from different data sources, detecting and replacing illegal values, and so forth. This is typically done using custom scripts or specialized data prep, data quality, or ETL tools. Transaction data is also often cleansed and summarized; for example, individual transactions may be aggregated into daily totals. However, unlike in a data warehouse, there may be many versions of the same data, used by different analytical models, that require different treatment. Like the landing zone, the gold zone often has a folder-per-source system (e.g., */Gold/EDW* or */Gold /Twitter*), with those top-level folders containing a folder per table or some other grouping (e.g., */Gold/EDW/Customer_dimension* or */Gold /Twitter/Mybrand1*).

If there are summarized or derived files, these go in subfolders here as well (e.g., */Gold /EDW/Daily_Sales_By_Customer* or */Gold /Twitter/BrandTwitterSummary*).

The folders may then be further subdivided by date, similar to in the landing zone. Figure 7-4 shows some processing that creates gold area repositories.

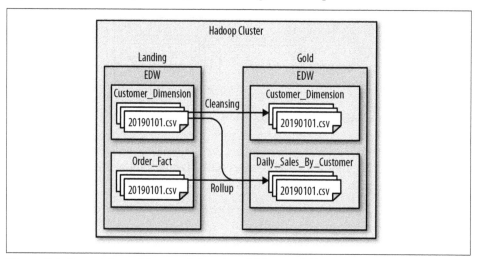

Figure 7-4. Organizing gold or prod data into folders and files

This is usually the most popular zone. Most non-developers are confined to this zone. Developers and data scientists also prefer to use cleansed data to avoid extra work, unless there is a compelling reason to do their own cleansing.

To make the gold zone more accessible, the IT staff commonly creates a SQL view of each file in the gold zone using Hive, Impala, Drill, or one of a dozen other systems.

SQL-like access makes the gold zone a natural starting point for most reporting and BI analysis, because even analysts who are not comfortable with SQL can usually use standard BI tools with Hive or other SQL interfaces on Hadoop files.

The gold zone is often managed by IT rather than users themselves and is documented the best, either through directory structures and naming conventions or through HCatalog (a data dictionary developed around the Hive Metastore that is being used by more and more other projects).

Data is typically read directly from the gold zone, but if changes need to be made, it is copied over to the work zone so it can be modified. If the resulting data sets need to be shared with a broader audience or productized for ongoing operations, they are then copied back to the gold zone and production-strength processes are developed to keep them up to date.

Work Zone

Most of the analysis happens in the work zone, also known as the *dev* or *projects* zone. This zone is usually structured to reflect the organizational structure of the enterprise. It is typically the domain of developers, data scientists, and data engineers, although analysts often make use of it to perform self-service data prep for their projects.

The work zone is typically organized into project and user folders, as follows:

- The top-level folder usually has a folder per project (e.g., */Projects/ Customer_Churn*), which in turn contains subfolders to reflect the details of the project.
- User folders are frequently located in some common directory with a folder per user (e.g., */Users/fjones112*) and provide a private space for each user.

These individual user and project folders contain both intermediate and final results of the work. This is usually the least-documented part of the data lake. Unfortunately, it is also frequently the largest part, since data science projects are explorative in nature and frequently require massive experiments. A typical data science project may create hundreds of experimental files before coming up with a good model or abandoning the approach altogether.

Sensitive Zone

A sensitive zone is sometimes created to keep files containing data that is particularly important to protect from unauthorized viewers, whether because of regulatory requirements or business needs. Usually, only data stewards and other authorized people can get access to data in the sensitive zone. For example, HR personnel may have access to employee data, finance employees to financial data, and so forth. This is usually accomplished through a combination of tag-based policies and Active Directory groups (we'll discuss access management more in the next two chapters).

The sensitive zone can contain explicitly encrypted data or utilize transparent encryption, which is described in more detail in Chapter 9. There are several best-practice approaches to structuring the sensitive zone:

- Have an encrypted copy of each sensitive file in the sensitive zone and a clear copy with redacted (removed or encrypted) sensitive fields in the gold zone. While redacting data may affect the ability to join different data sets—for example, if `Tax_ID` is the join key between employees and dependents, simply removing it would make it impossible to join the two data sets—there are different encryption techniques that will allow the data to be protected and yet remain joinable. Please refer to Chapter 9 for more information.

- Access to encrypted files is provided only explicitly and temporarily on an as-needed basis.

- If sensitive data is required for analytics, a process called deidentification, discussed next, may be applied to anonymize the data.

Deidentification

Deidentification is the process of replacing actual sensitive data with similar made-up data in a way that retains the properties of the original data. For example, female Hispanic first names may be replaced with different female Hispanic first names to protect the individuals' identity but still allow data scientists to infer missing gender and ethnicity information from the names if necessary.

Similarly, if geographical analysis needs to be done, an address may be replaced with a random valid address within a certain distance of the real address. This sometimes gets complicated because some regions are densely populated, so anonymization can be achieved by using any address within, say, 10 miles of the real one, whereas others are sparsely populated and may only have a handful of people living within a 10-mile radius. To address this, a concept of *cohorts* is used, where a population of a statistically meaningful size is identified either by geographic proximity or geographic type (depending on the type of analysis being done—e.g., farmland vs. suburbs vs. national parks) and the addresses are randomly assigned within the entire area covered by the cohort.

One difficult part of deidentification is maintaining consistency. The same value usually has to be replaced with the same identical value in all files, so it can be joined as part of the processing (e.g., so the same customer can be identified in multiple files). This adds complexity because the system has to maintain the mappings of real values to randomly generated values. Deidentification is also fragile, because a single-letter misspelling that might be easily handled by identity resolution systems can cause a deidentification system to generate two completely different values. Finally, it is vulnerable because if intruders get access to the deidentification software they can run a list of common names through it and get a table of value mappings for all the files.

Another consideration is that for certain types of files, it can be very difficult to identify sensitive data. For example, an electronic health record (EHR) is an XML file that may contain up to 60,000 elements. It is very difficult to review all the elements to find potentially sensitive ones and to regenerate the file to mask or deidentify them. In such cases, companies usually find it easier to just keep encrypted values in the sensitive zone.

Multiple Data Lakes

As we've seen, enterprises build data lakes for a variety of reasons. Some start as single-project data puddles created by a line of business or project team and grow into data lakes gradually. Some start as ETL offloading projects by IT and pick up additional users and analytic use cases along the way. Others are designed from the get-go as centralized data lakes by IT and analytic teams working together. Yet others are created in the cloud as shadow IT for business teams that don't want to wait for the official IT team.

Regardless of their origins, most enterprises end up with multiple data lakes. The question then becomes, should these be merged into one or kept separate? As with most things, there are pros and cons to both approaches.

Advantages of Keeping Data Lakes Separate

The reasons for separate data lakes are historical and organizational, not technical. Typical reasons include:

Regulatory constraints
In regulated industries and for personal data, regulatory constraints often forbid the merging or commingling of data from different sources or geographies. For example, the European Union has very strict data privacy guidelines that are implemented differently by every country. Medical institutions usually have very strict data sharing guidelines as well.

Organizational barriers
Sometimes there are organizational barriers to sharing the data, mostly around budgeting and control. Financing a common data lake and deciding on common technologies and standards between warring business units with greatly differing goals and needs may prove to be an insurmountable challenge.

Predictability

Keeping a data lake with a high-value production load separate from one used for ad hoc exploratory usage such as data science experiments can help ensure predictable performance and response times for the former.

Advantages of Merging the Data Lakes

If you are not constrained by the kinds of regulatory or business requirements mentioned in the previous section, you should try to restrict your organization to a single large data lake. There are several reasons for this:

Optimized resource usage

If, instead of two data lakes with 100 nodes each, you create one data lake with 200 nodes, you may be able to get better response times. For example, if the original data lakes each ran a job that required 10 minutes on 100 nodes, in theory you might be able to run those jobs for 5 minutes each on 200 nodes. In reality, clusters are usually executing multiple jobs using a subset of nodes, so for highly utilized clusters, the average performance will likely stay more or less the same because now there will be twice as many jobs competing for twice as many nodes. However, you will gain the ability to bring all 200 nodes to bear on critical and time-sensitive jobs. And if the different lakes have different, non-overlapping usage patterns (e.g., if one is used most heavily during business hours in the US, while the other is used during business hours in India), or if usage is sporadic, you may get quite a lot of performance benefit by combining the two.

Administrative and operational costs

When a lake grows twice as large, it doesn't usually take a team that's twice as large to manage it. Of course, the same team can manage multiple lakes, but if the lakes are there because of organizational and control issues, each organization tends to staff its own team so it can control its own destiny. This duplication raises costs.

Data redundancy reduction

Since both lakes belong to the same enterprise, chances are that both lakes contain quite a bit of redundant data. By merging the lakes, you can eliminate this and reduce the quantity of data stored. Data redundancy also implies ingestion redundancy, where the same data is extracted and ingested multiple times from the same source, so by consolidating, you can lessen the loads on the sources and the network.

Reuse

Combining the lakes will make it easier for the enterprise to reuse the work done by one project for other projects. This includes scripts, code, models, data sets, analytic results, and anything else that can be produced in a data lake.

Enterprise projects

Some groups work on an enterprise scale and may require data from different organizations. These projects will greatly benefit from having a single centralized data lake instead of having to merge data from multiple lakes.

Cloud Data Lakes

Over the last decade, there has been an unstoppable march to the cloud. Many new applications are now delivered using a hosted Software as a Service (Saas) model. Top cloud vendors such as Amazon, Microsoft, and Google are growing at incredible rates (Amazon now earns more from its cloud offering than from its retail sales), and other vendors are aggressively trying to get into the game. With all this excitement around the cloud, it is natural to ask whether it is also a good choice for a data lake. Actually, it's a great choice.

A cloud-based data lake offers a lot of advantages. One of these is that someone else takes care of setting up and maintaining the infrastructure, so you don't have to hire specialized experts for your enterprise. The compute infrastructure is managed and kept up to date for you. While levels of support and costs vary, you can review the options and make a choice based on the amount of assistance you and your IT staff will need—and if you find that the plan you choose isn't quite right, you can change it without doing any hiring or firing.

One of the most important advantages of the cloud is that new resources, both compute and storage, are provisioned on demand—you can create and use as much compute power as you need when you need it. This is called *elastic computing*. In addition, cloud providers offer different types of storage with different price points and different performance characteristics and seamlessly move data between different classes of storage as needed. To help you understand the advantages of these technologies to a data lake, let's compare an on-premises data lake to a cloud-based one.

In the on-premises data lake, both storage and compute power are fixed and dictated by the number of nodes, as illustrated in Figure 7-5.

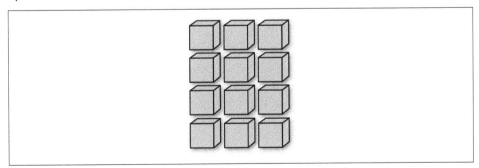

Figure 7-5. On-premises, fixed-size Hadoop cluster

Although there are flexible ways of decoupling storage and compute resources, there are hard boundaries on how much compute power can be brought to bear, and there are costs to storing the data that may not be used anytime soon, especially if it is duplicated or even triplicated for fault tolerance.

Let's compare that to a data lake built using the most popular cloud platform today, Amazon Web Services (AWS). Among its many offerings, Amazon provides scalable object storage with its Simple Storage Service (S3), scalable compute resources with Elastic Compute Cloud (EC2), and Elastic MapReduce (EMR), which can execute jobs on the allocated resources (Figure 7-6).

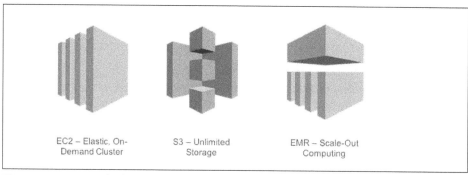

EC2 – Elastic, On-Demand Cluster   S3 – Unlimited Storage   EMR – Scale-Out Computing

Figure 7-6. Amazon's elastic cloud data lake offerings

Unlike the on-premises data lake, the cloud-based one provides virtually unlimited and very inexpensive storage with S3. Considering that you are saving data that may not be used for a while, or may never get used, storage costs are quite important. Furthermore, the compute resources are not limited by the number of nodes in the cluster.

With EC2, you can spin up a cluster of any size to run your job and pay only for the time you use it. For example, say you build a 100-node on-premises cluster to run a certain job for about 2 hours. If this job runs every day and the rest of the load on the cluster is small, those nodes will be sitting idle for up to 22 hours a day. With EC2, you can spin up a 100-node cluster dynamically, run it for 2 hours, and spin it down, so you pay only for the time it is running.

However—and this is even more exciting—for the same price, you can also spin up a 1,000-node cluster and run this job in only 12 minutes (assuming it scales linearly). This is the beauty of elastic computing, and it's available from all major cloud providers. You create and pay for the compute resources you need when you need them, so you can dynamically create huge clusters to execute your most challenging jobs without having to pay for them permanently.

For all their advantages, though, there are instances where cloud-based data lakes may not be the right solution:

- Not all data may be allowed in the cloud, for regulatory reasons.

- Data upload to a cloud-based lake may be a challenge. Companies often send disks or tapes to their public cloud vendors to load their initial data locally, and use the network subsequently for incremental uploads.

- Cloud data lakes are susceptible to network outages and internet provider failures. Therefore, in cases requiring 100% availability, such as medical devices in hospitals or industrial controls at a factory, a cloud data lake may be too risky. Granted, most historical data used for analytics probably doesn't require such high SLAs, but some data lakes support real-time data streams and may be used for real-time as well as historical analysis.

- The costs for projects that require constant compute resources with large amounts of data can be prohibitive. Cloud costs are much more favorable for ephemeral use cases requiring a certain number of compute nodes that can be scaled down when not needed. While most data lake use cases require just that type of elastic support, if your compute needs are more constant the cloud may not be the best option.

Virtual Data Lakes

One approach that has been gaining ground is creating a *virtual* data lake. In other words, instead of living with multiple data lakes or merging them into one centralized data lake, why not present them to the user as a single data lake, while managing the architectural details separately? There are two main ways to accomplish this: using data federation and using enterprise catalogs.

Data Federation

Data federation has been around for at least 20 years. IBM's DataJoiner product, introduced in the early 1990s, created a "virtual" database whose tables were really views on physical tables in multiple databases. The users of DataJoiner would issue SQL queries against these virtual tables, and DataJoiner would translate them into queries that it would apply against the different databases; it would then combine the results and present them back to the user, as illustrated in Figure 7-7.[1]

---

1 More details can be found in the paper "DataJoiner: A Practical Approach to Multi-database Access" (*https://ieeexplore.ieee.org/document/331706*) by Piyush Gupta and E. T. Lin.

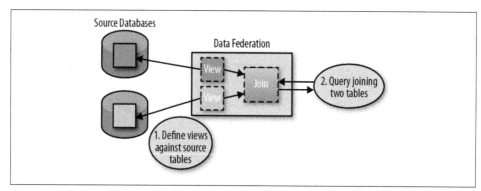

Figure 7-7. Example of a virtual database

DataJoiner eventually evolved into IBM InfoSphere Federation Server and was matched by products from Denodo, Tibco Composite, Informatica, and others. More modern versions of these products support RESTful APIs and can interact with applications and filesystems as well as databases. Nevertheless, at their core, these products are all designed to create a virtual database that, under the covers, can pull data from different systems and make it look like a single table.

There are several significant challenges to applying this technology to data lakes. The biggest challenge is that you have to manually configure each virtual table and map it to the physical data sets, be they files or tables. In a data lake with millions of files loaded through frictionless ingestion, that's simply not practical. Then there's the traditional distributed join problem: combining or joining large data sets from different physical systems requires very sophisticated query optimization and lots of memory and compute power. Finally, you have the schema maintenance problem: when the schema changes, the virtual tables have to be updated as well. Since a schema is applied only when data is read (so-called "schema on read"), the users may not know that the schema has changed until their queries fail. And even then, it may not be clear whether the problem was caused by a schema change, a data problem, human error, or any combination of these.

Big Data Virtualization

Just as data lakes arose as a way to cope with the massive growth in volume and variety of data, big data virtualization applies the big data principles of schema on read, modularization, and future-proofing to create a new approach to data virtualization that can cope with the massive volume and variety of data in the enterprise. At the heart of the new approach is a virtual filesystem that represents physical data sources as virtual folders and physical data sets as virtual data sets. This approach mirrors how staging zones are organized in data lakes, as described earlier in this chapter. This virtualization allows the data to stay in its original data source, while being exposed to other business users.

Because such a virtual filesystem can be massive and potentially contain millions of data sets, a search mechanism is needed to find and navigate them. This role is usually played by a data catalog that presents all the data in the enterprise, including the data lakes. With this approach, only the metadata (information describing the data) is in the catalog, so the users can find the data sets they need quickly. Once a data set is found, it can be provisioned to give the user access either by copying it to the user's project area or by giving the user permissions to access it in place. Figure 7-8 illustrates the process.

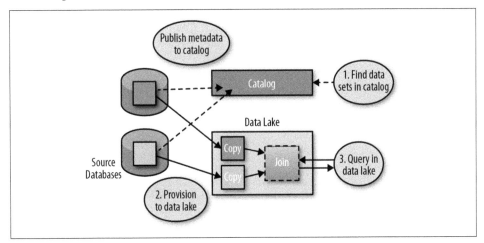

Figure 7-8. A virtual data lake

Because both tables in Figure 7-8 have been copied to the same physical system, the joins are local, much easier to implement, and faster to execute. Provisioning can involve an approval process where the user requests access for a period of time and specifies a business justification. The request is reviewed and approved by the data owners, and the data is then copied over. Finally, the copy of the data is kept up to date by ETL tools, customer scripts, or open source tools like Sqoop that connect to a relational database, execute a user-specified SQL query, and create an HDFS file with the results of the query.

Because the catalog is the main interface for finding and provisioning data in the data lake, it enables a very elegant solution to building a virtual data lake. When users look for a data set, it really does not matter to them where it is physically located—it looks the same and can be found exactly the same way. An intelligent provisioning system can be provided so if the user wants to use a data set in a tool, it may be provisioned in place (i.e., opened directly in the tool), while if it needs to be joined with other data sets or modified, it can be transparently copied over to the physical data lake and made accessible there.

Eliminating Redundancy

Two of the challenges of a physical data lake are completeness and redundancy. As Figure 7-9 illustrates, completeness is guaranteed only if all the data in the enterprise is loaded into the data lake. However, that causes a lot of redundancy because all the data is now stored in at least two places. While one might argue that traditionally data warehouses contained the same data as operational systems, that situation had different requirements because data was usually transformed before being loaded into the data warehouse. It was changed to conform to a common schema, denormalized, and merged with data from other systems. So, while it was more or less the same data, it was structured very differently, for a different purpose. In a data lake, on the other hand, if we implement frictionless ingestion, data in the landing zone is typically an exact copy of the source data and is completely redundant. We end up keeping multiple exact copies of the same data, regardless of whether anyone is using it, and keep paying the price of keeping these copies up to date.

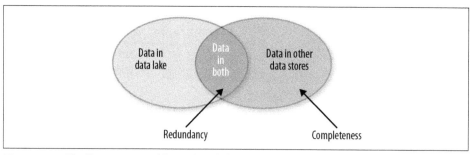

Figure 7-9. Challenges created by a data lake

Virtual data lakes help to alleviate this problem, because the data is brought into the data lake only when needed for specific projects. In other words, there is only one copy of the data (in the original source), unless someone needs to work on it in the data lake. Once the project is over and there is no more use for this data, it can be safely removed to save storage—or at the very least, we can stop updating the copy until someone needs it and then bring it up to date (Figure 7-10). With this model, most regularly used data will be in the lake and actively maintained, and only the rarely used or never before used data will not be in the lake. There may be a lag for loading very large files for the first time or updating them after a long period of not using them, but the trade-off is not having to pay for compute and storage resources to handle all the data that's not being used.

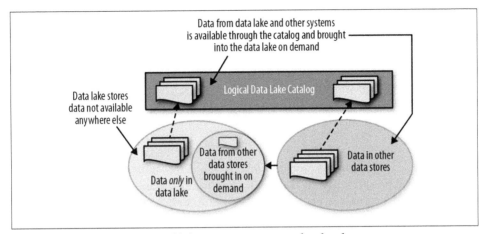

Figure 7-10. Effects of a virtual lake on consistency and redundancy

Unfortunately, redundancy does not stop with the data lake. The past 15 years have seen a proliferation of data marts and other project-specific databases. A typical data-related project starts with provisioning a database server, loading it with data from other systems, adding or changing a little bit of the data, and keeping it up to date by loading the latest data from other systems. Some enterprises have thousands or even millions of such databases. For example, I once worked with a small bank with 5,000 employees and 13,000 databases. All these databases cost money to run, including hardware and software costs, administration costs, backup costs, and so forth. Even worse, over time parts of these databases that start out the same inevitably diverge, whether because of human error, ETL logic differences, job or system failures, or other factors. Consequently, many a company spends time arguing about why finance, sales, and marketing all have different numbers for the same key measurements and whose numbers should be used or trusted (spoiler alert—finance usually wins).

Many enterprises have embarked on rationalization journeys, trying to consolidate almost identical databases, eliminate unnecessary ones, and converge diverging ones; an enterprise catalog is the first step on that journey. By capturing what data is where, where it came from, and who is using it, a catalog can help identify redundant and unused data.

Some common patterns that can be identified using a catalog are:

- Two almost identical data marts with a few additional measurements and properties. These can be combined into a single data mart by adding the unique measurements and properties from both to the combined data mart, reducing storage and administration costs. Furthermore, users of each data mart will now have access to all the fields that were previously in the other.

- A database that was once used for reports, but currently serves only as a staging database for another database. It can be eliminated completely, and the database that it populates can be populated directly from the upstream systems.

- A completely unused database that is generating reports and dashboards that no one is using. This can simply be retired.

Conclusion

While there are many options for data lake architecture, many enterprises are beginning to realize the attraction of the elasticity of the cloud and the efficiency of a virtual data lake. Next, we'll explore how data catalogs help enterprises create data lakes and expand them into virtual data lakes.

CHAPTER 8

Cataloging the Data Lake

Data lakes tend to suffer from a number of traits that make them difficult, if not impossible, to navigate. They contain a massive number of data sets. Field names are often cryptic, and some types of data sets—such as delimited files and unstructured data collected from online comments—may lack header lines altogether. Even well-labeled data sets may have inconsistent names and different naming conventions. It is virtually impossible to guess what particular attributes may be called in different files, and thus impossible to find all instances of those attributes.

As a result, data needs either to be documented as new data sets are ingested or created in the lake or to go through extensive manual examination, neither alternative being scalable or manageable for the typical size and variety found in big data systems.

Data catalogs solve the problem by tagging fields and data sets with consistent business terms and providing a shopping-type interface that allows the users to find data sets by describing what they are looking for using the business terms that they are used to, and to understand the data in those data sets through tags and descriptions that use business terms. In this chapter we'll explore some of the many uses of data catalogs, and take a quick look at some of the data cataloging products on the market today.

Organizing the Data

While the directory structure and naming conventions described in Chapter 7 can help analysts navigate a big data cluster, they are not sufficient. Here's what they lack:

- There is no search capability. Analysts have to browse to the right directory, which works when they know what they want but is not practical when they're just exploring the potentially thousands of sources/folders.

- Useful Hadoop utilities like Hue allow users to peek at an initial small segment of a file, but this may not be enough to understand what's inside large files. To decide whether a file is appropriate for their project, the analyst may need a better idea of what it contains. For example, is there any New York data? How many tweets are there? What are the order amounts? If the analyst is looking for customer demographics such as age, just previewing a few lines of a file and seeing some age data doesn't tell them whether this data is available for a substantial enough number of customers.

- The analyst also needs to be able to tell where a file came from. Not all data can be trusted. Some of it may come from failed data science experiments and some from systems that are notoriously inconsistent, whereas other data is from well-curated and trusted sources. Is the file in the landing zone, gold zone, or work zone? Depending on the analyst's needs, either raw or cleansed data may suffice. If the data is in someone's work folder, the analyst may have to carefully study the file description or talk to the file or project owner. And it's just as critical to understand what has been done to the data. Some attributes may already have been curated and treated in the way the analyst needs, whereas other attributes may need different treatment and need to be obtained from the raw files.

To address these shortcomings, just as every library is organized and cataloged, enterprises need to organize and catalog their data sets.

Finding the appropriate input data for analytics has been an unsolved problem for as long as I have been working in this space (more than 30 years). In the remainder of this section we'll look at different ways that data can be annotated and described with metadata to enhance findability, and we'll see how glossaries, taxonomies, and ontologies can be used to describe, organize, and search data sets.

Then, in the next section, we'll consider how automation can help. Given the sheer number of files in a data lake, and the fact that often there will be many years of history of people ignoring or circumventing processes and procedures designed to document and track data, the cataloging process has to be automated as much as possible, and whatever tool is used has to make it extremely easy for analysts to take notes and tag fields and data sets with meaningful business terms.

Technical Metadata

To help describe data sets, we turn to *metadata*, or data about data. For example, in a relational database, a table definition specifies the metadata, including the table name, column names, descriptions, data types, lengths, and so forth. The actual values in the table rows, then, are considered data. Unfortunately, the line between data and metadata is blurry. Consider the following example (Table 8-1), a table called Sales that contains quarterly and monthly sales data (in millions) for different years, for products identified by ID.

Table 8-1. The Sales table

ProdID	Year	Q1	Q2	Q3	Q4	Jan	Feb	Mar	...
X11899	2010	5	4.5	6	9	1.1	1.9	2.2	...
F22122	2010	1.2	3.5	11	1.3	.2	.3	.6	...
X11899	2011	6	6	6.5	7	4.5	2	.5	...
...	...	...	...	...	...	...	...	...	...

In this example, the field names ProdID, Year, Q1, Q2, Q3, Q4, Jan, Feb, and so on are all metadata, while the actual product IDs (X11899, F22122), years (2010, 2011), and sales amounts are data. If an analyst is looking for quarterly sales for products, by looking at the metadata, they can tell that they should be able to find it in this table. Similarly, if they are looking for monthly sales, they know they will be able to find that information in the table as well.

However, we could instead design the same table as shown next (Table 8-2).

Table 8-2. Sales table with more obscure metadata

ProductID	Year	Period	SalesAmount
X11899	2010	Q1	5
X11899	2010	Q2	4.5
F22122	2010	Q3	11
X11899	2011	Q1	6
X11899	2010	Jan	1.1
X11899	2010	Feb	1.9
X11899	2010	Mar	2.2
...	...	...	...

Instead of having a separate column for each period, we now have a row for each period. The Period column specifies what period we are looking at—either a quarter (Q1..Q4) or a month (Jan..Dec). Even though the two tables contain exactly the same information and can be used interchangeably, in this example quarter number and month are data, not metadata.

Of course, real life is much messier than this simplified example. Just as field names can be cryptic or misleading, so can data. For example, in real life, the second table is more likely to use codes and might look something like Table 8-3.

Table 8-3. Sales table with more obscure data

ProductID	Year	Period_Type	Period	SalesAmount
X11899	2010	Q	1	5
X11899	2010	Q	2	4.5
F22122	2010	Q	3	11

ProductID	Year	Period_Type	Period	SalesAmount
X11899	2011	Q	1	6
X11899	2010	M	1	1.1
X11899	2010	M	2	1.9
X11899	2010	M	3	2.2
...	...	...	...	...

Here, a `Period_Type` of `M` means "month" and an associated `Period` value of 2 means February, but a `Period_Type` of `Q` designates "quarter" and an associated `Period` value of 2 means the second quarter of the year. Profiling this table would not yield month names, although a clever analyst might be able to infer from the metadata (seeing that `Period_Type` is either `M` or `Q` and that there are three times more `M`s than `Q`s) that they are looking at monthly and quarterly sales data.

As this example illustrates, there is no hard boundary between data and metadata, and depending on the schema design, the same information can be captured as either. Relying solely on metadata provides no way to tell what kinds of periods the latter table contains, and analysts looking for monthly sales data won't know whether this table will help them until they look at the data and see that periods include months.

Data profiling

Since studying each table to understand what it contains significantly slows down the process of finding the right table to use, *profiling* is often used to bridge the gap between data and metadata. For example, if the analyst knew without having to look at the data that the `Period` field contained the values `Q1..Q4` and `Jan..Dec`, they would immediately recognize that they would be able to find quarterly and monthly sales data in that table. Profiling analyzes the data in each column to help round out our understanding of the data as well as its quality, as we covered in Chapter 6. Among other things (such as most frequent values and their counts), it calculates:

Cardinality
How many unique values are in each field. For example, if two tables are equivalent, the cardinality of the `ProductID` and `Year` columns should be the same in both.

Selectivity
How unique the values in each field are. This is calculated by dividing the cardinality of a field by the number of rows. Selectivity of 1 or 100% means that each value in the column is unique.

Density
How many NULLs (or missing values) are in each column. Density of 1 or 100% means that there are no NULLs, whereas density of 0% means that the field only contains NULLs (i.e., is empty).

Range, mean, and standard deviation
For numeric fields, the smallest and largest values are calculated as well as the mean and sigma or standard deviation.

Format frequencies
Some data has very distinctive formats—for example, US zip codes are either five digits, nine digits, or five digits followed by a dash and four more digits. Formats can be very helpful in identifying the type of data contained in a field.

The statistical information captured by profiling, together with other metadata such as the names of fields, tables, and files, is called *technical metadata*. While this helps us to understand the nature of the data, it does not address the problem of findability. In fact, to make matters worse, technical metadata is often abbreviated or obscure—for example, just as the columns in Table 8-1 were called Q1 and Q2 instead of First_Quarter and Second_Quarter, the Year column might just have been called Y; analysts would then have a hard time searching for it because Y might stand for Yield, Yes, Year, or any number of other things.

Profiling hierarchical data

Profiling information is very intuitive for tabular data—the stats are for each column, aggregated across all the rows—but it gets trickier for hierarchical data such as JSON or XML files.

While the format may be different, conceptually JSON files represent the same data as tabular files. For example, an order can be represented as a set of tables in a relational database or a set of tabular files related to each other by what are called *primary key–foreign key relationships*. In Figure 8-1, four tables are used to store information about orders, customers, and products. Primary key–foreign key relationships are captured with lines between primary key fields and foreign key fields with one-to-many relationships illustrated with 1:*N*, meaning that, for example, for each CustomerID in the Customers table, there may be many orders with the same CustomerID in the Orders table.

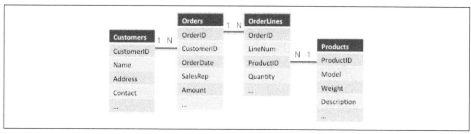

Figure 8-1. Entity relationship diagram

The same information may be presented in JSON format, with the hierarchy representing the relationships expressed by primary and foreign keys in relational systems. Instead of four different tables, a single JSON file will capture all the attributes and relationships. The following snippet captures all the information for an order. Note that there are no `CustomerIDs` and `ProductIDs` required to relate orders, customers, and products. Customer information is embedded in the `Order` records, product information is embedded in `OrderLine`, and so forth:

```
{"Order"
  {
    "OrderID" : "123R1",
    "Customer" {
      "Name" : "Acme Foods", "Address" : "20 Main St, Booville, MD",
      "Contact" : "Zeke Gan", ...
    }
    "OrderLine" {
      "LineNumber" : "1",
      "Product" {
        "Model" : "XR1900E", "Weight": "20",
        "Description" : "The XR1900E is the latest ...", ...
      }
      "Quantity" : 1,
      ...
    }
  }
}
```

Since the information in both cases is really the same, a simple process called *shredding* is often used to extract fields from hierarchical files. For example, a customer name may be extracted using its full hierarchical name, `Order.Customer.Name`. This name is an XPATH expression (XPATH is a query language to access specific parts of an XML document); shredding basically creates a unique field for each unique XPATH expression in a hierarchical file.

One problem with shredding is that it is what's called "lossy"—it loses information when transforming the data into tabular format. For example, if there happen to be two customers for one order and three line items, there is no simple way of shredding this data to preserve such information. Do we attribute all three line items to the first customer, or to each customer? Do we assign some to one customer and some to the other? There are no simple or universally correct answers.

Most profiling tools, such as the ones from Informatica and IBM, require hierarchical files to be explicitly shredded or converted to a tabular format before they can be profiled, while more modern tools like Trifacta, Paxata, or Waterline Data that were developed for non-relational big data environments either profile hierarchical data natively in a non-lossy way or at least shred hierarchical data automatically.

Business Metadata

To help analysts find data, we turn to *business metadata*, or business-level descriptions of the data. These can come in many forms.

Glossaries, taxonomies, and ontologies

Business metadata is often captured in glossaries, taxonomies, and ontologies. A business glossary is a highly formalized (usually hierarchical) list of business terms and their definitions. Some business glossaries are taxonomies, some are ontologies, and some are just grouping constructs without much semantic rigor. There are many spirited debates about what differentiates a taxonomy and an ontology. My goal here is to give you a flavor of the two, not to argue one side or another. With that in mind, you can think of a taxonomy as a hierarchy of objects where a child is a subclass of the parent. This is also known as an *is-a* (pronounced "izah") relationship. Figure 8-2 illustrates the biological taxonomy that most of us studied in biology class.

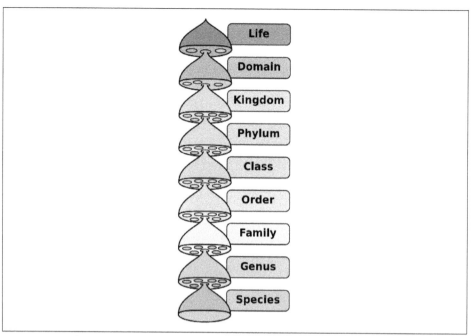

Figure 8-2. A biological taxonomy

An ontology is generally more elaborate than a taxonomy and supports arbitrary relationships between objects. For example, in addition to is-a relationships, it includes *has-a* relationships between objects and attributes (as in, an automobile has an engine). As another example of a relationship, a driver *drives* an automobile. Figure 8-3 illustrates a snippet of a possible automobile-related ontology, where an automobile has wheels and an engine and is a subclass of a vehicle.

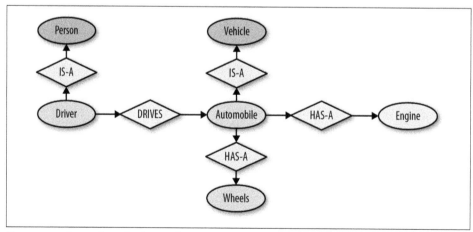

Figure 8-3. Part of a vehicle ontology

Industry ontologies

A number of standard ontologies have been developed for different industries. ACORD (*https://www.acord.org/*) is an insurance industry organization with over 8,000 organizations as members that helps insurance companies exchange data in a standard way. To describe the data being exchanged, ACORD developed a business glossary that describes each element in its forms, which cover many aspects of the insurance business. Another example is the Financial Industry Business Ontology (FIBO) (*http://bit.ly/2UJ9nF5*), developed by two well-respected industry organizations, the Object Management Group (OMG) and Enterprise Data Council (EDM).

Companies can also develop their own standards. When I was working at IBM, we developed a number of industry models that encapsulated both an industry-specific ontology and the corresponding analytical data model.

Folksonomies

The challenge with industry- or even company-standard ontologies is that, while they are great for contextual search, they are often very complex, with tens of thousands of terms, and keeping track of all the elements is difficult. Furthermore, adopting a standard ontology requires heavy training for the business teams on using a standard terminology.

Folksonomies are much less rigorous constructs that attempt to represent how employees think of their data. Instead of training analysts to use strict definitions, folksonomies collect current terms, organize them into coherent hierarchies, and use them as business metadata.

Another challenge is that different groups may legitimately have different names for the same thing. For example, marketing might refer to a field as a *prospect name*, sales as an *opportunity name*, and support as a *customer name*. Some systems may represent these as three different data sets dedicated to prospects, opportunities, and customers, respectively, while others may combine them in a single data set with a flag indicating the kind of contact this is.

To avoid confusion, different groups may use different folksonomies to search for the same data using the terms they are accustomed to. At Waterline Data, we chose to support this by creating different domains of tags or terms, dedicating some domains to certain groups and sharing other domains among multiple groups.

Tagging

Once we have a glossary, taxonomy, folksonomy, or ontology, in order to use it to find data sets, we have to assign the appropriate terms and concepts to those data sets. This process, known as *tagging*, consists of associating business terms with the fields or data sets that contain the data represented by those terms. For example, the `Period` field from our earlier example on technical metadata might be tagged with business terms `Number_of_Quarter` and `Month` that reflect its contents. Analysts could then find it by searching for "month," "quarter," or "quarter number." This tagging process is critical to building a catalog.

To be able to tag a data set, however, the analyst or data steward must understand it. Since there isn't a single person or even a team in any large enterprise that knows and understands every data set, this job must be crowdsourced among the enterprise's many data stewards, data analysts, and other subject matter experts.

Many companies, such as Google, Facebook, and LinkedIn, have catalogs where data stewards and analysts can manually tag data sets. There are also products from companies such as Alation, Informatica, and Waterline Data that support this kind of tagging and also allow the users of data to rate data sets, add comments, and more.

We explored the idea of crowdsourcing tribal knowledge in Chapter 6, and we'll look at some of the products that are available to help with cataloging later in this chapter.

Automated Cataloging

Although manual tagging and crowdsourcing are necessary, usually these processes are not sufficient and are much too time-consuming. Enterprises might have millions of data sets with hundreds of millions of fields, and even if each field could be tagged in a matter of minutes (in reality, sometimes this takes hours of investigation and discussion), we are still talking several hundred million minutes, or thousands of person years, of work! Clearly, this is not practical. From my discussions with teams at Google, LinkedIn, and other organizations, I have learned that when manual processes are relied upon only the most popular data sets end up being tagged, leaving a huge number "dark."

As mentioned in Chapter 6, the answer to this problem is automation. New tools leverage AI and machine learning to enable identification and automatic tagging and annotation of elements in dark data sets (based on tags provided elsewhere by SMEs and analysts), so that analysts can find and use these data sets. Waterline Data's Smart Data Catalog and Alation are probably the best examples of this approach. Alation tries to infer the meaning of fields from field names and to automatically interpret various field name abbreviations, while Waterline Data automatically tags fields based on field names (if available), field content, and field context, so it attempts to tag even the files that lack headers (field names).

We will use Waterline Data as an example that illustrates automated cataloging. The tool crawls through Hadoop clusters and relational databases and fingerprints every field (a fingerprint is a collection of the field's properties, including its name, content, and profile). It then lets analysts tag the fields while they are working with different files and tables. You can think of this like creating "wanted" posters.

Waterline Data's AI-driven classification engine, called Aristotle, then uses these fingerprints as well as field context to automatically assign tags to the untagged fields. Context is determined by the other tags in the same data set. For example, a numeric field with three-digit numbers ranging from 000 to 999 is very likely to be a credit card verification code if it is found next to a credit card number, but a field with exactly the same data is very unlikely to be a credit card verification code if found in a table where all the other tags refer to medical procedure properties.

Finally, the analysts can accept or reject these inferred tags, as illustrated in Figure 8-4, thereby training Waterline Data's AI engine.

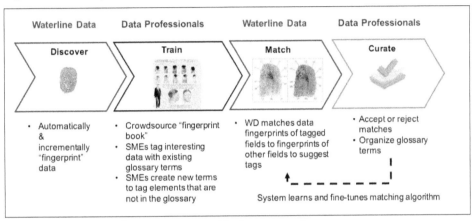

Figure 8-4. Automated tagging, approved by human analyst

This process greatly reduces the need to manually tag data sets, so new data sets become findable as soon as they are cataloged.

Logical Data Management

While tags are a great way for analysts to find data using familiar business terms, they also provide a consistent "logical" view of the enterprise data. Data stewards and analysts can now create consistent policies for all the data assets without having to keep track of what different fields are called in different data sets and systems. From data protection to data quality, modern data management tools are embracing tag-based policies as a way to automate what has traditionally been manual, error-prone, labor-intensive, and fragile technology that slowed down data projects and impeded self-service.

Sensitive Data Management and Access Control

One of the great worries of data governance teams is how to manage sensitive data. There are numerous industry-specific and country-specific regulations that govern usage and protection of personal or sensitive information, such as the GDPR in Europe, HIPAA in the US, and PCI internationally. In addition, companies often maintain their own lists of internal "secret" information that must be protected. We refer to any data that is subject to regulatory compliance and access restrictions as *sensitive*. To manage sensitive data, enterprises have to first catalog it (i.e., find out where it is stored) and then protect it, through either restricting access or masking the data.

Traditionally, security administrators had to manually protect each field. For example, if a database had a table with a column that contained Social Security numbers (SSNs), the administrator had to figure that out and manually create a rule that allowed access to that field only to authorized users. If for some reason users started putting SSNs in a different field (say, the Notes field), that field would stay unprotected until someone noticed it and created a new rule to protect it. Instead, modern security systems such as Apache Ranger and Cloudera Sentry rely on what's called *tag-based security*. Rather than defining data access and data masking policies for specific data sets and fields, these systems define policies for specific tags and then apply these policies to any data sets or fields with those tags. (For a detailed discussion of managing access, please refer to Chapter 9.)

Automated and manual vetting

Without an automated approach to sensitive data management, new data sets ingested into the data lake cannot be released for use until a human has reviewed them and figured out whether they contain anything sensitive. To drive this process, some companies have tried creating a "quarantine zone" where all new data sets go and stay until they've been manually reviewed and blessed for general use. Although the quarantine zone approach makes sense, these companies report significant backups in working their way through quarantined data sets. This is because the process is time-consuming and error prone—a problem that's often exacerbated by a lack of budget for doing this type of work, because most of the data sets are not immediately being used for any projects. This neglect, unfortunately, leads to a vicious circle. Since the files in the quarantine zone are not accessible to anyone, they are not findable and cannot be used by the analysts, nor can the analysts influence the order of curation.

A much more elegant solution can be achieved by using automated sensitive data detection. Data sets in the quarantine zone can be automatically scanned by the cataloging software and automatically tagged with the type of sensitive data that they contain. Tag-based security can then be applied to automatically restrict access to those files or deidentify sensitive data.

As an additional precaution, instead of making the data sets automatically available, manual vetting can be done on demand. Such a system applies automated tagging and adds the metadata for the data sets to the catalog to make the data sets findable.

Once an analyst finds a data set that they would like to use, this data set is manually curated to verify the correctness of the tags, and any sensitive data can be deidentified. This way, while all the data sets are findable and available, the limited resources of the data steward group doing curation are spent on useful files and funded projects.

Finally, as data sets are provisioned, data sovereignty laws and other regulations can be respected. For example, if an analyst in the UK asks for access to German data, instead of shipping the data over to the UK, they may be granted permission to access the local German data lake.

Data Quality

Data quality is a broad topic covered elsewhere in this book. In this chapter, we will focus on using the catalog to capture and communicate information about the quality of data. A couple of important innovations that a catalog brings to the table in this regard are the ability to apply tag-based data quality rules and to measure the annotation quality and curation quality of a data set.

Tag-based data quality rules

Less sophisticated cataloging techniques hardcode the rules for data quality and sensitivity for each physical field in each physical table or file. More modern catalogs—especially catalogs with automated tagging—allow data quality specialists and data stewards to define and apply data quality rules for a specific tag. The idea is to define the rules and then apply these rules to any field tagged with that tag. For example, if we create data quality rules for Age that specify that it should be a number between 0 and 125, we can then apply it to any field tagged with Age and count the number of rows that do not contain a number between 0 and 125. The quality score can then be captured as a percentage of rows that do not conform to the quality rule. In Figure 8-5, out of the five rows, only three conform to the data quality rule; therefore, the quality level is 60%.

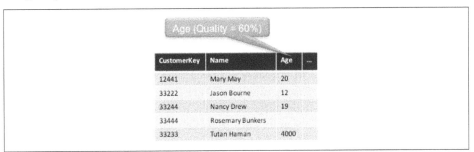

Figure 8-5. Data quality level

The following sections cover some other ways data quality can be measured.

Annotation quality

Annotation quality refers to how much of a data set is annotated. For example, if each field has a tag the annotation quality is 100%, if only half of the fields have a tag it's 50%, and so on. Note that annotation quality can take into account both manual and automatically suggested tags. In addition to the tags, it can include such information as whether a data set has a description, whether it has lineage (imported, manually specified, or automatically suggested), and whether required properties (such as sovereignty) are populated.

Curation quality

Curation quality refers to how many of the tags have been approved or curated by humans. The ultimate concern is trustworthiness, and a manually curated data set is usually more trustworthy than an automatically annotated one.

Unlike annotation quality, which simply checks whether tags are present, curation quality does not count an automatically suggested tag as "valid" unless a data steward or other authorized user has approved it. Curation quality can also reflect whether the data set has a description and lineage (imported, manually specified, or automatically suggested), and, if the lineage was automatically suggested, whether a curator has approved it.

Data set quality

Data set quality can summarize the other three types of quality: tag-based data quality, annotation quality, and curation quality. Again, the central issue is trustworthiness; the trick is to blend all the measurements into a single one with a meaningful value. There is no best practice or formula for this. The approaches range from only considering the quality of curated tags to trying to reflect every aspect of data quality.

For example, if we consider only the quality of curated tags, if every field has a curated tag with a quality level of 100%, the data set's quality level can be said to be 100%. If only half the fields have curated tags and the average quality of those fields is 80%, the data set quality level is 40%, and so on.

However, even if a data set has perfectly formed fields with corresponding tags, can we really trust it if we do not know where it came from? If the answer is no, how do we normalize quality of data with quality of lineage in a single measurement? This is a difficult problem, and most companies punt (take the easy way out) and simply use different properties to reflect the different aspects of data quality or trustworthiness. In fact, this is the solution I recommend: aggregate the tag-based quality of all the fields to produce one value at the data set level, and keep annotation and curation quality separate. Don't try to come up with a formula that can reflect all three.

Relating Disparate Data

One of the challenges of data science work is that it often requires data scientists and data engineers to bring together data that has never been combined before. The challenge of finding data then becomes not only to find the data sets that contain the data you need, but to be able to tell if these data sets can be combined. This has two aspects:

- Can these data sets be joined? In other words, is there a way to correctly relate data in one data set to the data in another data set? For example, suppose a data scientist finds a great data set containing personal demographics with people's names, but wants to correlate it to people's incomes. A search for income data may return a number of data sets, but can any of these be correlated to the demographic data? If any of the income data sets contain name and address information, that would be a great start. If none of them have that data but some contain SSNs, the data scientist may then be able to search for a data set containing both SSNs and names and addresses and use that data set to join the income and demographic data sets together.

- Will joins produce meaningful results? Even if the data scientist in the previous example finds some data sets that can be joined, what if these data sets contain nonoverlapping data? For example, what if they hold demographic information for US customers and income information for EU customers? Even if they both contain names and addresses, there will be very little overlap.

In order to be useful, catalogs should assist users in finding related data and estimating the usefulness of combining it. There are several ways that can be achieved:

Field names
    In many well-designed systems, fields with the same name are assumed to contain the same data, so analysts often look for columns with the same names in tables that need to be joined. This, unfortunately, is often not the case in larger systems, and relying on field names may lead to incorrect results across different systems with different naming conventions. It also does not help ascertain the usefulness of a join without actually running it.

Primary and foreign keys
    In relational databases, tables are related to each other using keys. These are called primary key–foreign key (PKFK) or referential integrity relationships. To use the example from earlier in this chapter, suppose you have a table containing customer information. This table will have a primary key to uniquely identify each customer, and all other tables will refer to that customer using this key. The columns in other tables that reference the primary key in the customer table are called foreign keys. PKFK relationships are often captured in entity relationship

(ER) diagrams created using data modeling tools such as Erwin Data Modeler from ERwin or ER/Studio from Idera. PKFK relationships are also sometimes declared as referential integrity constraints in relational databases, although most production systems avoid these constraints because of the overhead they introduce. PKFK relationships are a great way to guarantee that joins will return good results. Unfortunately, these relationships are typically only available inside a single system and do not help with relating data across systems.

Usage

Useful joins can be gleaned from data usage—for example, by looking at existing artifacts that join the data, such as database views, ETL jobs, and reports. They can also be inferred by scanning database SQL logs to see what queries are being used to join the data. While the artifacts typically provide some context for the joins through names and descriptions and usually guarantee that joins will produce useful results, SQL queries may not provide information on why the data was joined or whether the join was successful.

Tags

The most difficult joins are the ones that have never been done before—especially joins across disparate systems and different data formats. Catalogs can greatly help with this effort by helping users identify related data by finding data sets with the same tags. An estimate of a join's usefulness can sometimes be deduced from the technical metadata obtained during profiling, or it may be necessary to actually execute the join and profile the result.

Establishing Lineage

One of the critical questions a catalog needs to answer is whether the analyst can trust the data, and knowing where the data came from is a big part of that. This is called the data's *lineage* or *provenance* (a detailed discussion of lineage can be found in Chapter 6). One of the jobs of a catalog is to show lineage for the data assets and to fill in the gaps where the lineage is missing.

Most BI tools, like Tableau and Qlik, capture lineage information indicating how visualizations and reports are created. Similarly, most ETL tools, like Informatica, IBM InfoSphere, and Talend, capture lineage information automatically as they move and transform data. However, a lot of advanced analytics are done using R and Python scripts, and a lot of the data transformation and movement is done using FTP, scripts written in Pig or Python, and open source Hadoop tools such as Sqoop and Flume. These tools do not capture or expose the lineage of data. Since lineage is useful only if you can trace it all the way back to the source, it's critical to fill these gaps. Some tools try to fill in missing lineage information by scraping system logs (Cloudera Navigator), instrumenting open source systems to report lineage (Apache Atlas), requiring users to manually provide lineage information for every job they write (Apache

Falcon), or trying to deduce it by examining the content of the files (IBM InfoSphere Discovery and Waterline Data) or SQL logs (Manta and Alation).

As you can see, there really isn't one single way to get all the lineage, but the catalog is responsible for importing this information from wherever possible and stitching it all together. "Stitching" refers to the process of connecting different lineage segments. For example, a table may have been ingested from an Oracle data warehouse using Informatica's ETL tool into a data lake file in Parquet format, then joined with a JSON file generated from a Twitter feed using a Python script to create a new Hive table, which then was used by a data prep tool to create a CSV file that was loaded into a table in a data mart, which in turn was used by a BI tool to generate a report. To get a complete picture of where the data in the report came from, all these steps need to be connected or stitched together. If any of the steps is missing, there will be no way for the analyst to tie the report back to the original sources—the Oracle data warehouse and Twitter feed.

As this hypothetical example illustrates, data often undergoes many changes by many tools. Another issue is that even if lineage is available, it is often expressed in the language of the tool that generated the data—and not all analysts are well versed in all tools. To be able to interpret what's been done to the data, the analyst needs the steps to be documented in business terms. This is called *business lineage*. Unfortunately, most enterprises today do not have a place to capture and track business lineage. Each job and step may be documented, but this is often done inside the tool (for example, as comments in a script), or in the developers' notebooks, Excel files, or wikis. Catalogs present an attractive place to gather such lineage documentation together and make it available to the users of the data.

Data Provisioning

Once the right data set or sets are identified, the user will want to use those in other tools. To support this, catalogs often provide data provisioning options. Data provisioning may be as simple as opening the data set with a specific tool—for example, if an analyst finds a data set containing sales information, they may wish to open it in their favorite BI tool to visualize and analyze the data. Similarly, if a data scientist or a data engineer has found an interesting raw data set, they may want to open it in their favorite data prep tool. This is similar to using the Mac Finder or Microsoft Explorer to find a file, right-clicking on it, and getting an "Open with" menu that lists all the programs that the file can be used in. Since there is a great variety of tools that can be used with data, you should make sure that the provisioning capability is extensible and can be configured for any tools that users may wish to use.

Another provisioning operation involves getting access to the data. One of the great advantages of using a data catalog is that it makes data findable without having to give users access to it. That means that when users find the data they need, they must request access before they can use it. An access request may be as simple as sending an email to the data owner with a request to add the user to the access control group so they can access the data in place, or as complex as creating a ticket and starting a lengthy approval workflow that will bring the data into the data lake. Access management and ingestion are covered in more detail in Chapter 9.

Tools for Building a Catalog

Several vendors provide data catalog tools, including Waterline Smart Data Catalog, Informatica Enterprise Data Catalog, Alation, IBM Watson Knowledge Catalog, AWS Glue, and Apache Atlas (developed by Hortonworks and its partners). When choosing a vendor, you should consider several important capabilities:

- Native big data processing for performance and scalability
- Automated data discovery and classification
- Integration with other enterprise metadata repositories and single-platform catalogs
- User-friendliness

The first consideration is support for native big data processing tools such as Hadoop or Spark. A data lake is the largest data system in the enterprise, and the combined power of a large cluster of nodes is required to process and catalog the data it contains. The whole point of Hadoop is not just to provide a cost-effective place to store data—we've had that for years—but also a cost-effective place to *process* data. Trying to catalog Hadoop-scale data without leveraging Hadoop's processing capabilities simply won't work. While some of the available tools were designed natively for Hadoop, others, like Alation and Collibra, were designed to work with relational databases and either require data to be loaded into an RDBMS or have proprietary engines that run outside Hadoop and won't be able to scale to handle a data lake.

Another issue is that the sheer scope and complexity of data in the data lake makes it impossible for humans to manually classify or tag all the data with business metadata. Therefore, an automated approach is required to complete this classification. While all the tools mentioned here allow analysts to tag data in some fashion, some, like Waterline Data, provide an automated discovery engine that learns from analyst tagging and automatically classifies other data sets.

Of course, a Hadoop data lake is only part of the enterprise data ecosystem, and as such has to integrate with the rest of the governance infrastructure. Many enterprises will have extensive metadata investments already that need to be incorporated into the new data lake. There are several tools that provide enterprise data repositories. While Hadoop may be the most scalable and cost-effective platform to process both data inside Hadoop and data from other sources, single-platform solutions like

Cloudera Navigator or AWS Glue are limiting and will not address enterprise requirements.

Finally, a lot of metadata solutions are designed for IT and governance specialists. To be widely adopted, the inventory solution must be intuitive and usable by non-technical analysts, usually without much, if any, training. A business analyst–focused UI helps by providing an uncluttered view with business terms and descriptions instead of cramming in a lot of technical details. Technical details are certainly necessary for some of the users, and should be easily accessible, but should not be forced onto the business users. Some catalogs achieve this by having different role-based views, while others present a business view and provide a way for technical users to drill in to see technical details.

Tool Comparison

Table 8-4 summarizes the capabilities of a selection of data cataloging products. There are basically three groups of tools:

- Enterprise cataloging tools that try to catalog all the data in the enterprise.
- Single-platform cataloging tools that focus on a particular platform.
- Legacy/relational cataloging tools that do not provide native big data support. These tools do not run natively in Hadoop or other big data environments and require a relational interface, such as Hive, to be able to catalog big data meaningfully. They are sometimes put in place as part of a data pond (a data warehouse built on a big data platform, as described in Chapter 5, where the only access to data is through Hive), but will not be able to support a data lake with lots of raw data in native Hadoop file formats.

Table 8-4. Catalog tool comparison

	Big data support	Tagging	Enterprise	Business analyst–focused UI
Enterprise				
Waterline Data	Native	Automated	Y	Y
Informatica Enterprise Data Catalog	Native	Manual	Y	Y
Single platform				
Cloudera Navigator	Native	Manual		
Apache Atlas	Native	Manual		
AWS Glue	Native	Manual		
IBM Watson Catalog	Native	Automated		Y
Legacy/relational				
Alation	Hive only	Manual	Y	Y
Collibra	Hive only	Manual	Y	Y

The Data Ocean

If catalogs provide location transparency, the question arises of whether we even need a data lake. Why not catalog *all* the data and make it available, in a so-called "data ocean"? Some enterprises are embarking on such ambitious projects, but the scope and complexity of these undertakings is quite staggering and will likely require years of dedicated effort. Nevertheless, it is such an attractive alternative to shuffling and copying data around that some early adapters are willing to embark on this journey. In addition, the current regulatory climate that requires data transparency, mandates data privacy, and specifies appropriate uses of data is a strong driver forcing enterprises to work on creating a single point of visibility, governance, and audit centered on data catalogs. The regulatory compliance and data ocean efforts are synergistic and often work hand in hand.

Conclusion

Data catalogs are an integral part of data lakes and the enterprise data ecosystem. As data grows exponentially and data use pervades all aspects of business, having an automated way of cataloging the data and enabling users to find, understand, and trust it is a necessary first step on the road to data-driven decision making.

CHAPTER 9

Governing Data Access

This chapter describes the challenges of providing analysts access to the data in a data lake and presents several best practices for doing so. Data lakes differ from more traditional data storage in several ways:

Load
The numbers of data sets, users, and changes are extremely high.

Frictionless ingestion
Because a data lake stores data for future, yet-to-be-determined analytics, it usually ingests the data with minimal, if any, processing.

Encryption
There are often government or internal regulations that require sensitive or personal information to be protected, yet that data is needed for analysis.

Exploratory nature of work
A lot of data science work cannot be anticipated by IT staff. Data scientists often do not know what's available in the huge and diverse data store. This creates a catch-22 situation for traditional approaches: if analysts cannot find data that they don't have access to, they can't ask for access to it.

The easiest access model is to provide all analysts access to all data. Unfortunately, this cannot be done if the data is subject to government regulations (as is the case, for example, with personally identifiable information or credit card information), is copyrighted with restricted access (e.g., if it has been purchased or obtained from external sources for very specific or limited use), or is considered critical and sensitive by the company for competitive or other reasons. Most companies have data they consider sensitive—anything from trade secrets to customer lists to engineering designs and financial information. Therefore, except for a limited set of projects mostly dealing with public data, research data, and non-sensitive internal data, it's typically impossible to give full access to all data in data lakes to everyone.

Authorization or Access Control

Authorization is the common way of managing data access. It involves explicitly assigning permissions to perform specific *actions*, such as reading or updating, on specific *data assets*, such as files and tables, to specific *analysts*. To streamline this process, security admins usually create *roles* (collections of permissions) and assign those roles to groups of analysts.

Most legacy systems provide their own internal authorization mechanisms. Since more and more companies are opting to use more and more applications, often in the cloud, instead of using a single integrated application from a single vendor, single sign-on (SSO) systems have become very popular. With single sign-on, users log in once and their credentials are supported by all the applications and systems.

Unfortunately, there are several challenges with this approach. Notably:

- It is very difficult to predict in advance what data analysts will need for their projects.
- Unless the analysts have access to data, they cannot tell whether they need that data.
- There is a high cost to maintaining authorizations, which may be spread out over many time periods and activities:
  - Whenever a new employee is hired, the security admins need to provide appropriate authorizations.
  - As an employee changes roles or projects, the security admins need to provide new privileges and revoke old privileges.
  - When a new data set shows up, the security admins need to figure out all the users who may need access to this data set.
  - When an analyst needs a data set that contains sensitive data, a version of that data set needs to be created that either removes or deidentifies the sensitive data.

The challenges are so formidable that some enterprises are resorting to monitoring the access logs to make sure that the analysts are accessing appropriate data. Unfortunately, this approach only catches people after the fact and does not prevent them from intentionally using the wrong data, or help them avoid using it unintentionally. Enterprises that want to be more proactive take various approaches to address these challenges, including:

- Using tag-based data access policies
- Deidentifying sensitive data by removing, encrypting, or replacing it with generated random data, and granting access to these deidentified data sets to everyone
- Implementing self-service access management by creating a metadata-only catalog that allows the analysts to find all available data sets and then request access to the relevant ones from data set owners or security admins

We'll explore these different approaches to controlling access in the following sections.

Tag-Based Data Access Policies

Traditional access control is based on physical files and folders. For example, the Hadoop File System (HDFS) supports typical Linux access control lists (ACLs). A "set file access control list" (-setfacl) command allows an administrator or file owner to specify which users and groups of users can have what access to a specific file or folder. For example, if a file contains salaries, the administrator may make it readable by users in the human resources (HR) department using the following command:

```
hdfs dfs -setfacl -m group:human_resources:r-- /salaries.csv
```

This command basically says that any user in the group *human_resources* can read the *salaries.csv* file.

Obviously, if a data lake contains millions of files, setting permissions for each one manually would not be very practical. Instead, administrators usually set up folders and grant access permissions to groups for all the files in those folders or folder trees. For example, they might create an *hr_sensitive* folder and allow any user in the *hr* group to read any file in that folder. Often this approach is sufficient, but it presents some big challenges, including:

- Having to support complex permission schemes that reflect organizational reality
- Having to determine and set permissions for every file
- Having to detect and address schema changes

Organizational realities in large enterprises are usually very complex. For example, if we decide that instead of giving all HR users permission to see all the data in the *hr_sensitive* folder we want only HR users from a particular division to see the data for that division, we would need to create multiple subfolders—one for each department (e.g., *human_resources/engineering*, *human_resources/sales*, etc.)—and create a separate group for each department (e.g., *hr _engineering*, *hr _sales*, etc.).

Every new file ingested into the data lake has to be examined to determine who should have access to it. One approach is to quarantine all new data until a data steward or security analyst can review it by, for example, keeping it in a separate folder—a quarantine zone, as illustrated in Figure 9-1. Sometimes, companies can take shortcuts and assume that, say, any data coming from an HR application should be accessed only by HR. But in general, with millions of files, this is an impossible task to accomplish manually. And yet, companies cannot risk opening up the data to everyone until someone determines what it contains and who should have access to it.

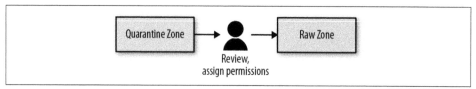

Figure 9-1. Manual review in quarantine zone

While this has some chance of working for ingested data, especially if new types of data are rarely added to the set, it is not practical for the data created in a data lake. If any new file created in the data lake had to be quarantined until someone manually examined it and decided on access control policies, the work in the lake would grind to a screeching halt.

A much more elegant solution implemented in some Hadoop distributions is tag-based security. For example, Cloudera Navigator and Apache Ranger (shipped as part of the Hortonworks Hadoop distribution) support tag-based policies. Instead of specifying ACLs for each file and folder, with these tools security administrators can set up policies using tags. While you still need a quarantine zone, the analysts can simply tag files and folders instead of manually creating ACLs for each one, as illustrated in Figure 9-2.

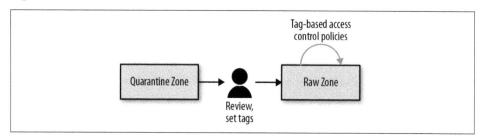

Figure 9-2. Quarantine process with tag-based policies

These tags can be set in local catalog tools like Cloudera Navigator and Apache Atlas and get automatically picked up by policy-based access control tools like Apache Ranger. For instance, the Hortonworks Ranger tutorial (*http://bit.ly/2MTK809*) shows how to set a policy for any file tagged with the PII (personally identifiable information) tag, regardless of where it may be located.

This tag-based access control policy approach also addresses the challenges of reflecting complex organizational reality, since you are no longer trying to reflect it in the folder structure. Instead, files and folders can live where they like and policies can be arbitrarily complex and rely on multiple tags. For example, to refine an access control policy to take department into consideration, you just need to add tags with the department names (Engineering, Sales, etc.) to the files and create separate policies for each combination of tags (e.g., HR and Engineering, HR and Sales). You do not have to create new folders, move data, or rewrite applications that relied on the old folder structure.

Tags provide a powerful way of managing and organizing data. In fact, with tags, you do not even need a separate quarantine area. Instead, newly ingested files can be tagged as "quarantined" as part of the ingestion process, and a policy can be created to restrict access to such files by anyone but the data stewards. Data stewards can then review the files, tag them with appropriate sensitive data tags, and finally remove the quarantine tag, as illustrated in Figure 9-3.

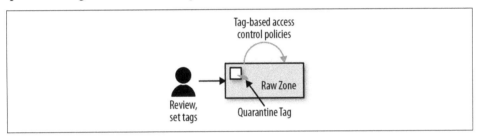

Figure 9-3. Using tags to quarantine files

Although tag-based security solves the organizational challenges around data and expedites manual review processes, tags stand in direct conflict with the premise of data lakes, where data is stored for an undetermined future and loaded using frictionless ingestion without any processing. Frictionless ingestion makes loading data fast and puts minimal stress on source systems, but it also makes it very difficult to figure out what sort of data you have just received and whether it is sensitive, in either a traditional or company-specific sense.

Furthermore, analysts can easily get overwhelmed by the amount of new data and lose the ability to work through the quarantined items in a timely manner. Detecting sensitive data is a challenging exercise. How does the analyst really know that a million-row file does not happen to have some Social Security numbers or other sensitive identifiers in some (maybe tens of thousands!) of its rows that just happen to be stored in a field called Notes? Looking at the first few hundred rows may not reveal anything—in fact, some columns might be entirely empty—and doing large queries against the entire data set will take time and may require scripting or development of specialized tools.

Even if the analyst is able to write and run the scripts required to detect sensitive data, schema and data changes present an additional challenge. If a new file comes in and the analyst does not find any sensitive information in it, it's possible that subsequent changes to that file (new partitions) will contain additional fields that do hold sensitive data, or that such data might be added to fields that were not originally sensitive.

The only practical solution to handling sensitive data and access control management is automation. Tools like Informatica, Waterline Data, and Dataguise scan all new files—newly ingested files, new partitions to previously ingested files, and new files created in the data lake—and automatically detect sensitive data and tag the files, as illustrated in Figure 9-4. They then export those tags to the local catalog tools, like Apache Atlas, to be used for enforcing tag-based policies.

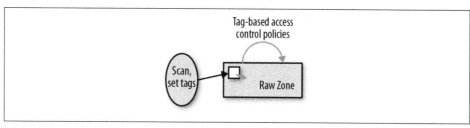

Figure 9-4. Automatic tagging of sensitive data

Deidentifying Sensitive Data

Once you identify sensitive data, you can restrict access to it. Unfortunately, that means that this data cannot be used for analytics. Instead, enterprises often encrypt sensitive data and give everyone access to the encrypted data sets. There are different forms of encryption that can be applied, including:

- Transparent encryption
- Explicit encryption
- Deidentification

To describe these, let's say we have a data set—for simplicity, let's make it tabular—that contains some patient information at a healthcare provider (see Figure 9-5).

Name	Address	City	State	Weight
Guido Sarducci	1212 Main St	Menlo Park	CA	189
Yoko Okamoto	322 Bryant St	Palo Alto	CA	112
Jorge Rodriquez	19 Cowper Ave	Palo Alto	CA	150

Figure 9-5. A sample of the patient information data set

Transparent encryption (like that provided by Cloudera Navigator) automatically encrypts data on disk when it is written and automatically decrypts it when it is read, as illustrated in Figure 9-6. This is done to prevent someone from accessing or copying raw disk volumes and reading them one byte at a time to recreate the data file, thereby avoiding all access controls.

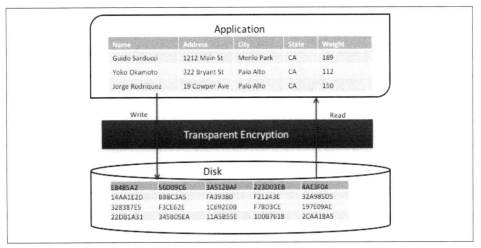

Figure 9-6. Transparent encryption

However, transparent encryption does not prevent analysts with read privileges on the file from seeing sensitive data. For that, enterprises usually deploy *explicit encryption* and encrypt each value separately, as illustrated in Figure 9-7. While this may seem straightforward—there are many open source encryption functions available and a range of tools providing encryption, from vendors such as Dataguise, Informatica, IBM, Privitar, Vormetric, and many others—it makes the sensitive data completely unusable, as the figure illustrates.

That creates real problems for data scientists trying to use the data sets. As mentioned in Chapter 1, one data scientist I interviewed told me how at his company all data in the data lake is encrypted unless someone can prove that the attributes are not sensitive. The data scientist did not care for that approach. As he rhetorically put it, "How am I expected to prove that an attribute is not sensitive if I can't find or view it?"

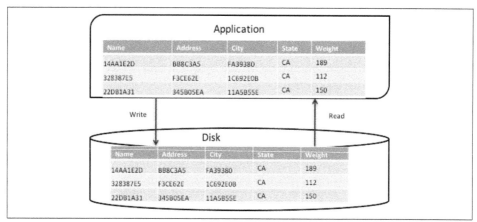

Figure 9-7. Explicit encryption makes the data unusable

Even if only truly sensitive attributes are encrypted, often these attributes encode important information that data scientists use to derive variables for their models. For example, in a data set where people's names are included but gender information is missing, it is often possible to infer the gender from the first name. It is sometimes also possible to figure out ethnicity from the first and last names. If the first name is encrypted, none of this information can be derived. Similarly, while encrypting address information is necessary, it prevents geographical analysis. To enable these kinds of analysis while protecting individuals' privacy, a class of "deidentification" or "anonymization" techniques have been developed. These techniques replace sensitive information with randomly generated values that preserve the important characteristics of the original data values. For example, an ethnic name might be replaced with a random name reflecting the same ethnicity and an address might be replaced with some other valid address within a 10-mile radius, as illustrated in Figure 9-8.

Clear Data

Name	Address	City	State	Weight
Guido Sarducci	1212 Main St	Menlo Park	CA	189
Yoko Okamoto	322 Bryant St	Palo Alto	CA	112
Jorge Rodriquez	19 Cowper Ave	Palo Alto	CA	150

Deidentification
Deidentified Data

Name	Address	City	State	Weight
Paolo Babeno	223 Oak St	Menlo Park	CA	189
Aoki Ito	12 El Padre Ct	Los Altos	CA	112
Miguel Hernandez	211 Green St	Palo Alto	CA	150

Figure 9-8. Data deidentification

Again, several tools, including Dataguise, Privitar, IBM InfoSphere Optim, and Informatica, provide these capabilities.

While deidentification or encryption of sensitive data is an effective solution in many cases, sometimes analysts will need access to the real data. Furthermore, even when there is no sensitive data, most enterprises compartmentalize data access and provide it on an as-needed basis only. Since data science is by its nature exploratory, it is difficult to predict what data the analyst is going to need. Even for simple analytics, a lot of power comes from understanding what data is available and getting access to it. As a compromise between very high-maintenance tightly managed privileges and a free-for-all approach that requires no management, companies are turning to self-service access management.

Data Sovereignty and Regulatory Compliance

In order to comply with regional, country, and industry data protection regulations, more and more information needs to be collected about a data set and stored in its metadata. For example, to comply with data sovereignty laws, it is important to know what country the data set came from and, more importantly, which country's citizens' data it contains. Instead of hardcoding policies for each physical data set, policies can be developed that, for example, specify that German data cannot be copied outside of the European Union.

Data lineage, discussed in detail in Chapter 6, can also be used to track down the country of origin of a data source. Figure 9-9 illustrates how this might work. For each data set, we create a Provenance property that captures where the data set came from. For example, for a data set that originated in the US, this property would be set to USA. If a data set is created by combining data from multiple other data sets, the provenance of each source that data came from is added to the Provenance property. So, if data from a CRM system in the US and an ERP system in Germany was loaded into a data warehouse in the UK and then into a data lake in France, the Provenance property of the final data set would contain the values USA, Germany, UK, and France. The policy can then specify that if the Provenance property contains Germany, certain rules will apply.

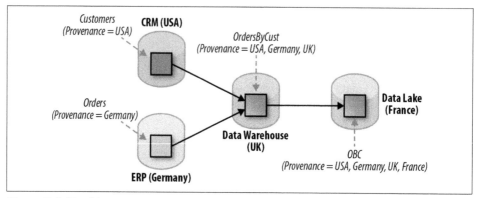

Figure 9-9. Tracking provenance

Similarly, the profiling described in "Technical Metadata" in Chapter 8 can be used to identify where any addresses in the data set are from. Consider the tables in Figures 9-10 and 9-11. The first is a `Customers` table that contains customers' names and addresses, whereas the second table contains the number of rows in the `Customers` table that contain a specific value in the `Country` field, as determined by profiling.

Customers				
(Referenced Countries= USA, Brazil, France, Spain, Israel, Germany, UK, ...)				
Name	Address	City	Province	Country
Mark Jones	W 1st St	San Jose	California	USA
Lisa Fernandez	12 Plaza Del Madre	Madrid	Madrid	Spain
Moishe Hogan	12 Golda St	Tel Aviv		Israel
Johan Hoffmann	5 12 Strasse	Munchen	Bavaria	Germany

Figure 9-10. Assigning a property with country provenance

Country	Count
USA	1,233,221
Brazil	90,120
France	15,200
Spain	12,033
Israel	10,232
Germany	9,233
UK	6,233
...	...

Figure 9-11. Count of rows for each country

A `Referenced Countries` property can then be created and populated (ideally, programmatically) by the values in the `Country` column's profile, and a policy can be developed that states, for example, that if a data set has a `Referenced Countries` property and it contains `Germany` as an entry, certain rules should apply. This approach would enable compliance with the data sovereignty laws of countries like Germany and China that prohibit moving data about their citizens out of the country.

In addition to concerns about data provenance, many regulations mandate usage restrictions for specific data sets. For example, the GDPR mandates that customer data can be used only for the business purpose for which it was collected, and any additional use requires explicit customer consent. All this information needs to be captured and stored somewhere so it can be considered when granting access to data, and a data catalog is the perfect place to store and manage it.

Self-Service Access Management

While proactively and automatically protecting sensitive data makes sense and is often required by government regulations, access control often extends beyond sensitive data and requires consideration of who in the organization should have access to what data. For example, many companies do not share the prices that customers pay for their products beyond the sales teams and management, do not share engineering designs of upcoming products outside the project teams, and so on. As we've seen, managing this access can be done proactively as new files are created and as users are added to the data lake, change projects, or change responsibilities. Alternatively, it can be done in an on-demand manner using self-service access management.

The premise of the data lake is to keep data for future, yet-to-be-determined uses. An obvious issue is that it will of course be difficult to determine who will need access to which data in the future, and why. On the other hand, if the analysts don't have access to the data and do not know that it exists, they will never be able to find and use it. Self-service access management coupled with a data catalog addresses this problem by making all the data findable. This system moves access control and data masking decisions to the time when someone actually needs the data for their project. The system offers several distinct characteristics and benefits:

- Analysts can explore (search and browse) metadata for all the data sets that may be made available to them.
- Analysts can request access to a data set from the data set owner.
- The owner of the data set decides who can access it, in what way, and for how long.
- All the requests, justifications, and permissions are tracked for security audit purposes.

Figures 9-12 through 9-15 illustrate a self-service access management and data provisioning system. The steps are as follows:

1. The data owner publishes data assets to the catalog (Figure 9-12). At this point, analysts are able to find the data, but don't have permission to read or change it.

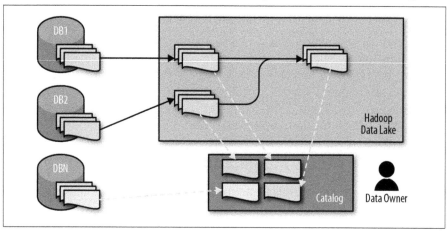

Figure 9-12. Publishing data

2. A data analyst finds data sets in the catalog (Figure 9-13). Since the analyst does not have access to the data, the search has to be done on metadata. That's why it is so important to have good metadata and business-level descriptions, as described in the preceding chapter.

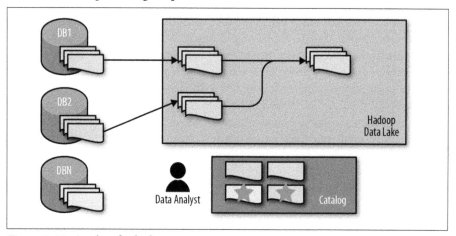

Figure 9-13. Analyst finds data

3. The analyst requests access from the data owner (Figure 9-14). Analysts can use the catalog to find data but not to access it; they have to ask the data owner for

permission to use it. This way, the data owner is in full control of who is using the data and why.

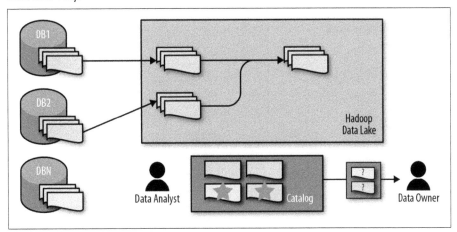

Figure 9-14. Analyst requests access

4. The data owner approves the request (Figure 9-15).

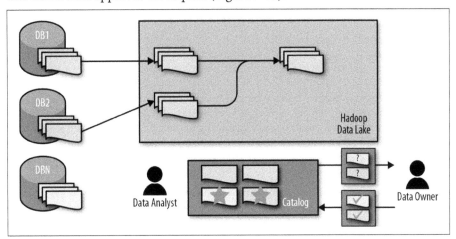

Figure 9-15. Access request approved

5. The data sets are provided (provisioned) to the analyst (Figure 9-16). This can be accomplished in a variety of ways, ranging from giving the analyst access to the source system to copying the data over to the analyst's personal work area. The process may also include a deidentification step to mask sensitive data. The key here is that the work is done only if and when the data set is requested and there is a real business reason to do it.

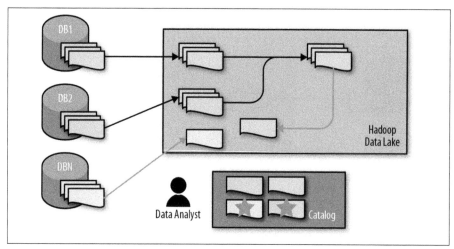

Figure 9-16. Requested data sets are provisioned to the data lake and provided to the data analyst

There are many advantages to this approach. As an IT executive at a large enterprise that I interviewed for this book explained:

> People are afraid to share data unless they can make sure it is used appropriately. By giving them the power to decide who can use it and how, we created an environment where they feel safe sharing data. Before we implemented this self-service approach, obtaining data required months of negotiations up and down the management chain. Everyone always asked for everything they could think of to make sure they did not have to go through the pain and delays of negotiations again. This made data owners distrustful of the true needs of the requesters and forced them to institute strict review processes where the requesters had to provide very detailed requirements and justifications, causing ever more work and more delays. It was virtually impossible to explore data in such an environment.

> With the self-service access management, requesters can study the data sets in the catalog and figure out what they need before they even place access requests, so there are many fewer requests, and a lot less data is being requested even when the requests are made, since the analysts have done pretty extensive exploration with the catalog and found what data is fit for purpose. Finally, because access requests are pretty automated, making additional requests is quick and straightforward.

In short, this self-service process gives data owners control over who uses their data and gives analysts the ability to explore the data sets and obtain access quickly. In addition, by granting access to data for a specific period of time, this approach eliminates both the maintenance associated with managing permissions to all possible data sets and the inevitable legacy access that the analysts retain after the project is over, just in case they may need it. With the self-service approach, they can just place another request for the access to be quickly reinstated.

Once the authorization has been obtained, physical access to the data can be provided to analysts in a variety of ways, depending on the nature of the data sets and the needs of the projects. A popular way of granting access is to create an external Hive table for the data set. External Hive tables do not copy or change the data sets and can be created or deleted with negligible compute costs (since they are just metadata definitions). The analysts are then granted access to the Hive tables.

For some projects, analysts may want to make copies of the files or create their own Hive tables (for example, with different input formats that tell Hive to parse and interpret data). In such cases, they can be given a copy of the data set or granted read access to the data set itself.

Provisioning Data

The previous section covered the benefits and gave an overview of self-service data access. Data provisioning is an important part of building a data lake and deserves a deeper discussion. It consists of four steps, as illustrated in Figure 9-17.

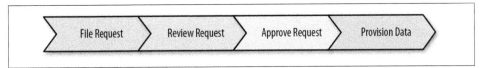

Figure 9-17. Data provisioning steps

The first step is done by an analyst who wants access to a data set. The request usually describes:

- What data is needed (which data set and whether the entire data set or part of the data set is needed)
- Who needs the access (a list of users or groups that need to access the data)
- The project (what project the data is needed for)
- The business justification for access (why the data is needed)
- How long the data is needed (the duration of time after which access can be rescinded)
- How to provision it (if users should get access to the data in place, or if it should be copied to the specified database or data lake)

If the data is to be copied, the request should additionally specify:

- Where the data should be placed
- Whether it should be a private copy or can be shared
- Whether it should be a one-time snapshot or should be kept up to date

- Whether after access expires it should be kept up to date or removed

The request is usually filed via a standard case tracking system like ServiceNow or Jira, or using a BPM/workflow/case management system like Pegasystems or Eccentex. The tracking system routes the request to the data owners or stewards. In some cases, automated approval rules may be implemented—for example, if the requester is in a certain group, the approval can be given automatically. If the data needs to be copied somewhere, the administrator of the target system may need to sign off on the request.

The logic may also get more sophisticated. For example, if the requester has access to the data at the source but wants it copied somewhere, only the target admin may need to approve the request. Conversely, if the requester is asking for a shared copy and the data already exists in the target system, only the source data steward may need to approve it since no additional storage is being used at the target.

The tracking system also provides a single point of access and audit, so the company has a record of who was using what, and for what purpose. This is not just good data security hygiene, but often a regulatory requirement for external regulations like the GDPR.

Since the data is copied from elsewhere, most of the time the requested data will not be modified, but rather will be used to create a new data set. Therefore, it is very attractive to share this data between multiple requesters. The data is copied to a predefined place (usually in the landing or raw zone) and kept up to date as long as there are any outstanding requesters.

Let's work through a provisioning scenario. Imagine that we have a data warehouse with a table called Customers, shown as a small rectangle in Figure 9-18. A user named Fred requests access to that table through a shared copy in the data lake from June 1 to August 5.

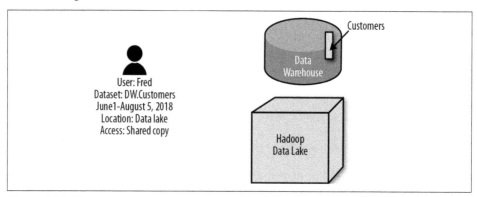

Figure 9-18. User requests access to a data set in the data warehouse

Assuming the request is approved, the table will be copied to a standard path in the staging area, as illustrated in Figure 9-19, on June 1. All the data in the table will be copied to a directory whose name matches the date when it was copied.

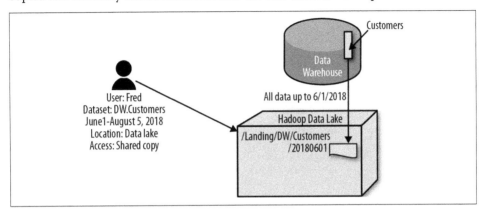

Figure 9-19. Data set is provisioned to the data lake

The next day, only the changes that occurred since the initial copy was made will be copied to a new directory. Its name will reflect that date (in this case June 2), as illustrated in Figure 9-20.

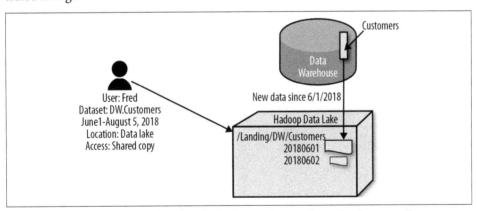

Figure 9-20. Data lake is updated with the latest changes from the data warehouse

This will continue until the request expires on August 5, 2018.

Now imagine that another user, Mandy, requests the same table from June 15 to July 15, as illustrated in Figure 9-21.

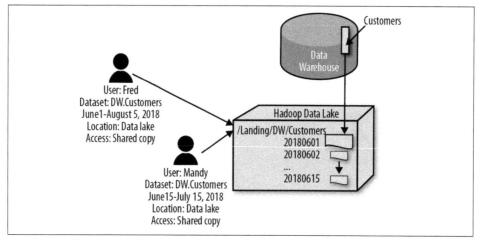

Figure 9-21. Another user requests the same data set

Provided her request is approved, on June 15 Mandy will get access to */Landing/DW/ Customers*—a shared copy of the `Customers` table—as illustrated in Figure 9-22. Mandy will continue to have access through July 14.

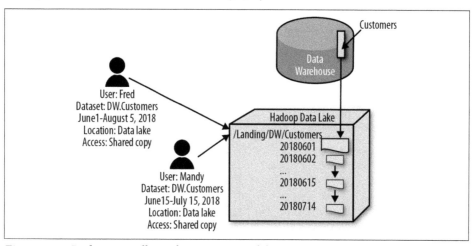

Figure 9-22. Both users will use the same copy of the provisioned table

On July 15, Mandy's access will expire and Fred will once again be the only user of this data set, as illustrated in Figure 9-23.

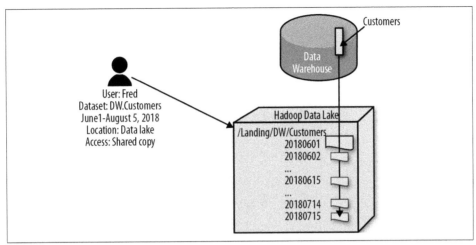

Figure 9-23. Once the second user's access has expired, there will again be only one user with access to the data set

Fred will continue using this data set until August 4 and the data set will continue getting updated, as illustrated in Figure 9-24.

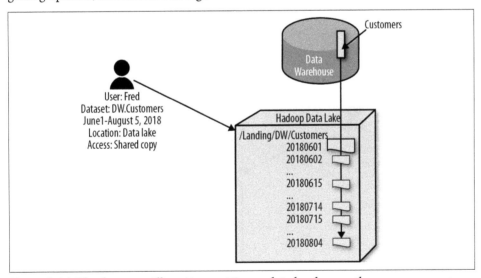

Figure 9-24. The data set will continue getting updated as long as there are any users using it

Then, on August 5, Fred's access will expire and there will be no users for this data set. The updates will stop until a new user requests it, as illustrated in Figure 9-25, or the system may continue updating it on a less frequent (say, monthly) basis.

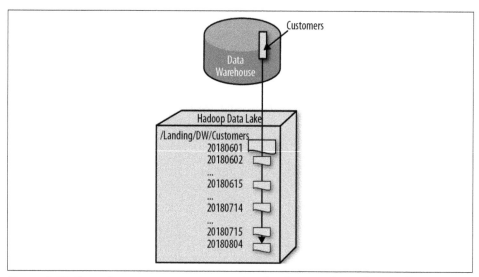

Figure 9-25. Once there are no more users using the data set, the updates will stop

If a new user puts in a request for this table, it will be updated with any data that was added between August 5 (when the updates stopped) and the access request date—in the following example, August 15. This way, the folder for August 15 will have all the updates made between August 5 and 15, as illustrated in Figure 9-26.

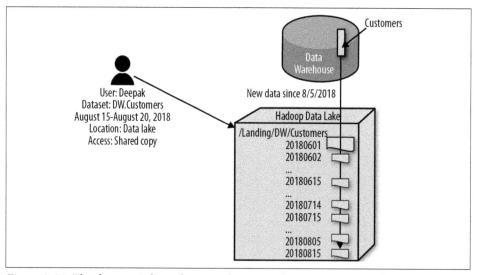

Figure 9-26. The data set is brought up to date once there is a new user for it

Sometimes, it is desirable to keep each day's batch in a separate folder named for that date. This helps tools such as Hive (SQL on Hadoop) decide which queries to execute against which partitions. In such cases, the data can still all be loaded on August 15, but for each day's changes a separate partition can be created, as illustrated in Figure 9-27. Even though all the changes are extracted on August 15, each day's changes (based, for example, on the change timestamp) are stored in a separate folder—August 6 changes go into the *20180806* folder, August 7 changes go in *20180807*, and so on.

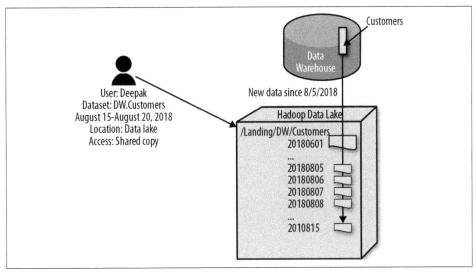

Figure 9-27. Each day's updates can be kept in a separate partition

Conclusion

Access control is one of the most critical aspects of the data lake to get right. By combining automation, on-demand self-service authorization techniques, and proactive sensitive data management, your organization can govern access to enormous and fast-changing collections of data efficiently and effectively.

CHAPTER 10

Industry-Specific Perspectives

This chapter contains a collection of essays about the implementation of data lakes by data experts from various industries. One essay had to be published anonymously because the writer could not get permission to reveal their affiliation, while the others are fully attributed. While the rest of the book is focused on best practices and characteristics of successful data lakes gleaned through numerous discussions with practitioners, this chapter is focused on industry specifics. Each essay is by a different industry expert and addresses some or all of the following questions:

Why?
> The essays provide an overview of some of the main initiatives driving big data lake adoption for different industries.

Why now?
> What has changed to enable these solutions? How have Hadoop, big data, data science, or data lakes changed the equation?

What's next?
> Where does the author see the industry going in adopting big data and analytics? How is data going to change their industry?

First you will hear from Jari Koister, who does advanced analytics in the financial services industry for FICO and teaches data science at Berkeley. Jari's essay focuses on improving business outcomes. The next essay, from Simeon Schwartz, focuses on using big data for governance and compliance at Schwab and other large financial services organizations.

Next, you will hear from a big data lead from a major insurance company, followed by an essay on smart cities from Brett Goldstein, who led analytics for the City of Chicago and the Chicago Police Department.

Finally, you'll hear from Opinder Bawa, the CIO of the University of San Francisco, and former CIO of the University of California, San Francisco School of Medicine and CTO of Boston City Hospital, on using analytics in medical research.

There are many, many more examples and stories that I could share, but I felt that these give a broad and comprehensive perspective of what's possible.

Big Data in Financial Services

Jari Koister is currently VP for the FICO Decision Management Suite (DMS), a platform for a variety of analytics- and optimization-driven solutions in the finance industry and beyond. Jari leads product strategy, planning, execution, and research; he also oversees research into advanced analytics and AI and the incorporation of these into DMS. The objective is to provide capabilities that make FICO's and FICO customers' solutions successful and increasingly competitive. Previously Jari has led product and engineering teams at Salesforce.com, Twitter, and Oracle. He has also led research teams at Ericsson and HP Laboratories. Jari holds a PhD in distributed systems from the Royal Institute of Technology, Sweden, and is a professor in the data science program at UC Berkeley, California.

Consumers, Digitization, and Data Are Changing Finance as We Know It

A wave of disruption is hitting the financial and banking sector. Consumers expect new ways of interacting, digital banking is disrupting many subsegments, there is an increased exposure to fraud, there is pressure to grow business outside traditional markets...and the list of changes goes on. Meanwhile, risk management is becoming a central and increasingly strategic area of concern for financial institutions, and there is an increased level of regulation to protect consumers from indiscriminate decisions and exposure. All of this contributes to massive changes for established companies and creates opportunities for new entrants.

Consumers expect more, have more choices, and are heard more clearly than ever before. They are more informed than in the past, and they trust their peers. Consumers can more easily find and be approved for new products, such as credit cards. They interact with banks over multiple channels, and they expect broad functionality and timely answers regardless of the channel they use. They travel the world and expect their banks to keep up and support them rather than creating obstacles. They are informed and compare products and services. Customer segments such as millennials and the so-called "under-banked" are not attached to the big banks but open to new alternatives.

At the same time, banking is going digital. Users expect to be able to perform most business online, without ever entering a physical branch. That said, they expect a responsiveness using digital media that matches or exceeds that of working directly with bank service personnel. They expect to be able to go online to apply for credit and trade stocks, deposit checks, and withdraw or transfer money. Customers want the experience to be simple and without friction—or they take their business elsewhere. Going digital also changes how a bank does marketing and reaches consumers. Digital marketing and word of mouth become more critical, while branches play a lesser role.

The wave of new user expectations and digital banking requires banks to rethink how they offer services. It also forces them to rethink how to reduce overheads and remove friction from consumer interactions. These changes also expose the banks to increased opportunities for fraud, due both to the nature of the services and how these services are offered to customers. For example, online loan approvals require new ways of identifying a customer. Retina scans, online fingerprints, or images are needed to make sure that an online loan recipient is in fact who they claim to be.

Access to banking services, and even their provision, are also affected by new technologies, such as mobile phone payments, blockchains, and national initiatives in rapidly developing countries such as India. Indian initiatives meant to reduce fraud include a universal national ID card called the Aadhaar card (*https:// en.wikipedia.org/wiki/Aadhaar*) and an API for building financial services called the IndiaStack.

New and expanded sets of data allow more efficient analyses of markets and customer characteristics and needs. This analysis allows banks to provide consumers with more attractive offers while keeping their own risk levels low.

Competition for new business also drives financial services to make offers to consumers and demographics previously not served. However, they may be missing background data traditionally considered necessary to onboard customers. Historically, people who did not present the "right" data, such as for calculating credit scores, would be dismissed as unacceptable risks for credit or lending. With new sources of data and new predictive models, banks can calculate new scores that allow them to make offers to these customers with acceptable risk and profitability.

These examples illustrate why risk analytics are becoming increasingly important and strategic to financial institutions. They are essential for managing risk related to portfolio management, credit risk, currency risk, operational risk, and more. Financial institutions are managing their risks more aggressively by using new risk assessment models and new sources of data. By creating new models, they can increase their income, lower costs, reduce risks, and improve efficiency.

This new era in banking and finance calls for broader and better data sources and is enabled by the emergence of new data sources in an era of big data and analytics. It drives the breakdown of data silos and a democratization of data access within organizations. The concept of data lakes plays a central role in this evolution, and the value of data lakes is coupled to the organization's ability to convert data and insights into better decisions.

Saving the Bank

The changes just outlined create many threats to established banks, but also opportunities for newcomers and disruptors. Digital banking has both external and internal implications, as illustrated in Figure 10-1.

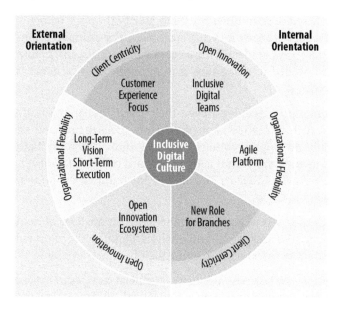

Figure 10-1. Two sides of digital culture

The external factors require drastic changes to the consumer experience. All aspects of the customer lifecycle must become increasingly customer-centric, including how customers are acquired, onboarded, and retained. Banks must maintain an open attitude toward external factors, designing and executing flexible strategies to nimbly adapt to changes in technology and customer needs.

These external factors in turn drive internal needs. Changing the external view of a bank requires a data-savvy culture of innovation that relies on a robust, scalable architecture and sophisticated technology. It requires a more agile and adaptive approach to developing concepts, products, and services. As markets change, banks must change, and new products must be launched in months or quarters, not years.

As the interactions with customers change, so do the role of branches. In extreme cases, branches become obsolete because customers interact using digital devices, such as depositing checks by scanning them with their mobile phone cameras. In other models, branches remain important for marketing, support, and high-end services such as private banking.

Data, of course, plays a pivotal role in enabling internal factors and eventually leading to change in external factors. A data lake is a mechanism for enabling many of the required changes, so data lakes can greatly impact a bank's business strategy.

By automating processes and using data to identify the best offers for a customer, digital banks can reduce operating costs by an order of magnitude compared to a traditional bank. Such dramatic reductions in cost can enable institutions to offer new products to traditionally less profitable customers at a profit, with increased customer satisfaction. They can also translate lower costs into new benefits for existing customers, helping to retain these customers. Another approach is to apply new and more nuanced risk models to investments to make a healthy profit. Regardless of which of these strategies are adopted, data plays an intrinsic role in identifying, assessing, and operationalizing these products.

The breadth of a data lake strategy can vary. It can be limited to a few central data sets and grow gradually, or it can involve a broad integration of data from day one. Some financial institutions may be more conservative in their approach, while others include any data they can get their hands on. Some may introduce changes in a more deliberate, stepwise, and careful manner, while others boldly disrupt how the organization operates. The reasons for differing paces and strategies may range from difficulties in changing culture rapidly to a desire to protect current core businesses while taking advantage of new opportunities. Some financial institutions, such as Santander with its wholly owned online Openbank subsidiary, apply a gradual approach to their existing business but enable a disruptive approach through an upstart division.

Figure 10-2 illustrates various stages of digital transformation.

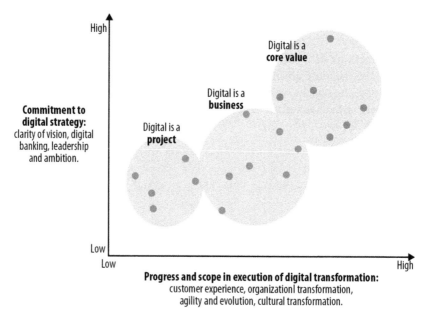

Figure 10-2. Maturity of digital strategy and execution

Meanwhile, fraud is increasing, along with the number and sophistication of fraudsters. Although transaction fraud in general declines due to technological advances such as chipped cards, other types of fraud are on the upswing. Identity fraud is growing along with the prevalence of online commerce. Anti-money-laundering campaigns are getting increased attention as new ways of transferring money are being rolled out. New types of fraud are being created at a rapid pace. They require speedy development of new fraud detection and prevention methods. More data and new techniques need to be leveraged in the development of these methods.

At the same time, fraud detection needs to get friendlier to consumers. False positives in identifying credit card or identity fraud are highly detrimental to good customer experience. Who wants to be told they can't pay for the meal they just had in a foreign country because their credit card was rejected? Similarly, a customer being denied an operation by a digital bank due to suspicion of identity fraud can lead to very bad publicity.

The use of data creates the risk of inappropriate use, which can be intentional or completely unintentional, due to errors or mistakes in the data. New regulations such as the GDPR are intended to protect consumers. While financial institutions want to leverage the data available to them to optimize their products and make automated decisions, they also need to comply with these new regulations.

The fundamental point is that the shift to digital banking leads to new types of services, representing both threats and opportunities to banks or any organization providing financial services. Data is critical to efficiently creating and managing all aspects of financial products. This spans digital marketing, risk analytics, product risk optimization, efficient payment collection, and fraud.

New Opportunities Offered by New Data

The availability of new data allows banks to create new products that are more tailored to customers from both a customer need and a risk perspective. Sophisticated solutions fueled by this data trade off multiple attributes such as risk, customer desires, profitability, and market share. This is a win-win, because consumers get access to valuable services and banks have new sources of revenue.

By adopting new ways to deal with identification and fraud, banks can offer a digital way of applying for loans and credit that improves speed of delivery and customer satisfaction. Customers can complete online applications with no need to visit a branch. An application meeting the right financial criteria is approved within minutes and money is often deposited instantaneously.

Credit scoring is the go-to method for determining whether a consumer will pay back their debt. Historically, credit score calculations required payment history, a statement of outstanding debts, history of recent credit enquiries, and so on. Bank staff would analyze the results thoroughly to determine risk and profitability levels. The risks of a consumer having specific credit scores such as 550 or 710 are well understood. But now, banks want to expand the applications of a score to a wider population that lacks adequate data for a traditional credit score. This is called the "financial inclusion problem," and it's not just an issue in developing nations; it also exists in the United States. As illustrated by Figure 10-3, 55 million of a 325-million US population cannot be scored and face barriers to being considered bankable. They end up overpaying for basic, everyday financial services such as check cashing or buying large consumer items on credit.

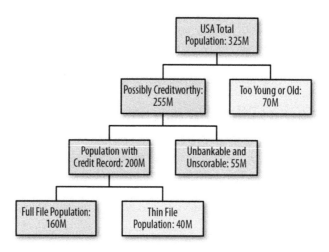

Figure 10-3. Classification of bankable population

In other countries such as India, the portion of the population whose creditworthiness cannot be scored using traditional methods is even larger. The percentage in the US is roughly 17%. In India, it is roughly 19%, or 250 million people. Another large portion of the population in India, some 700 million, are also considered non-credit seekers. Aadhaar, which I mentioned earlier, is targeted to enable a more significant portion of this population to participate in the financial system. To be able to extend credit to these large groups of people, banks are considering additional data sources such as bill payment data, along with non-financial data such as social networks, mobile data, retail purchases, education, and public records, to establish creditworthiness. Such calculations require synthesis and analysis of a wide variety of data sources, and ultimately consumer delivery mechanisms to operationalize results from the data analysis. There are also significant privacy implications in the collection, centralized storage, and use of these diverse sorts of data.

More data, and more diverse data, enables analysts to significantly improve these risk models. In general, many of the improvements and strategies hinge on the availability and use of many data sources, some of which may be new while others were previously unused or underused. Data lakes are an important component in any architecture that allows the widening of the data used for providing financial services to broader segments of populations across the globe.

Some major benefits of risk analytics include:[1]

- Improved interest income through the introduction of risk-differentiated offers and targeted campaigns. These can often increase revenue by 5–15%.

- Lower sales and operating costs, due to more efficient prescreening from risk and policy perspectives. This may increase productivity by 15–50%.

- Risk reduction through risk clustering and early warning systems. These tend to decrease loan losses by 10–30%.

- Improved capital efficiency through better calibration and refinement of models. These typically decrease risk-weighted assets by 10–15%.

Financial institutions want to understand more of what their customers are doing, across all the services they provide and beyond. They want what industry observers like to call a *360-degree view* of the customer (Figure 10-4). This may include financial transactions, financial status, purchases, email messages, support calls, social media postings, and any other interactions that are tracked. By having a more complete view of customer activity, companies can provide better marketing, better service, and better customer experiences. This view naturally involves many data sources and requires that banks and financial institutions break down the data silos that exist today. Data lakes are the technological foundation for enabling this data sharing while managing the data efficiently and adhering to applicable regulations.

Figure 10-4. Customer 360-degree view

However, these services can be vulnerable to new types of application fraud. The availability of data and algorithms allows banks to deploy fraud techniques that

---

1 See also "Risk Analytics Enters Its Prime" by Rajdeep Dash et al., McKinsey & Company, June 2017.

use face recognition, fingerprints, or even voice recognition. Without new anti-fraud measures, the level of fraud may cancel out the revenues from such services.

Key Processes in Making Use of the Data Lake

I've outlined some of the key directions, opportunities, and risks for banking and financial services. There are some common themes behind both saving the bank and addressing new opportunities. Both rely on the availability and sophisticated use of data, as well as on sources of data that financial institutions have not traditionally used. While banks have been excellent at efficiently using data from individual silos, they now need to bring the data together and use multiple data sources to efficiently reach their goals. Whether they acknowledge it or not, many banks are in fact creating data lakes, or at least moving along the path toward data lakes by creating large data puddles.

Many financial institutions have large numbers of siloed data sources. Combining these silos is a monumental task, which could engender substantial investments without corresponding benefits. The financial industry is very well acquainted with the concept of "decisioning." Decisions determine the outcomes for customers, such as credit line increases, loan approvals, and collection actions. Decisions generally have a large impact on revenue and risk. But they can be optimized, A/B tested, tracked, and governed. The challenge is to efficiently make decisions by processing the disparate data from a data lake.

Banks take many different approaches to this. Some explicitly create data lakes with the intent to deal with the complexity of the data problems. Others organically grow data puddles with the intent to organize them into a lake at some later point. Finally, there are those who just recognize that they need data, but may not have an explicit strategy for how to get from a collection of siloed data to better decisions with impacts on the bottom line.

I am proposing that there are three main components that bring a data lake from an unusable state to something that can be decisioned on. This proposal is nothing revolutionary; rather, it is to move from a set of unorganized, often poorly understood data to a state where it is cataloged, consolidated, and made ready for data science, data wrangling, and ultimately operationalized decisions. The data science and wrangling help prepare the data for decisions in an iterative cycle. The key is the integration of cataloging and decision development so that data is easily accessible, identifiable, detected, and traced.

Figure 10-5 emphasizes the central architecture for such a data lake solution. Obviously, the organization needs to ingest and retrieve the data from all the numerous data sources in use. The three components I believe are necessary for successfully preparing data for decisions are data inventory and cataloging, entity resolution and fuzzy matching, and analytics and modeling.

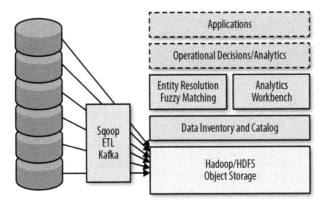

Figure 10-5. Data lake underpinning for analytics and decisioning in digital banking

Data inventory and cataloging

This first step identifies data, discovers schemas automatically, matches fields, determines and tracks lineage, and so on. It provides an overview of all the data that is created in the data lake. It also helps organize and understand the data so that it can be discovered and handled efficiently.

Joining disparate data sources is one of the important steps in extracting value from a data lake. However, it is not by any means guaranteed that the data sets possess a common key on which they can be joined. Rather, it is quite likely that there is no such key and that we'll need to find other ways of resolving entities (identifying the same entity—e.g., the same customer—across all the data sources). That's the task of the next process: entity resolution and fuzzy matching.

Entity resolution and fuzzy matching

Let's consider an example of three data sources that don't share a common key for data records. Each data source records some user behavior. One could be web activity, another email activity, and the third one point-of-sales transactions. Users may use different means of identifying themselves in each of the data sources. They may even have different addresses or misspelled addresses, use nicknames or deliberately obfuscated names, provide different email addresses, and so on.

Figure 10-6 illustrates these data sources as three separate timelines of events that may or may not at some point result in a purchase. The goal is to create a combined timeline by identifying which events belong to the same consumer, even if the data is different, incomplete, or wrong. This merged timeline will allow us to create more accurate predictive models since we have more relevant data that can help improve the models.

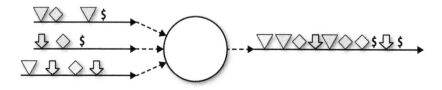

Figure 10-6. From disparate multi-channel data to a 360-degree view

Entity resolution and fuzzy matching can perform this kind of mapping across data sources. I believe that this mapping is key for extracting value from a data lake.

Analytics and modeling

A powerful analytics workbench with capabilities for data wrangling, exploration of structured and unstructured data, querying over big data sets, and machine learning is, of course, a key component in taking advantage of a data lake. Ultimately, you are not extracting real value until you turn the insights from the data into operational decisions for bank customers. Architectures for modeling and implementing decisions are outside the scope of this essay, but the foundation outlined here is a way for financial organizations to set themselves up for operational decisions.

Value Added by Data Lakes in Financial Services

 **Simeon Schwarz** *is Director of Data and Analytics for OMS National Insurance and former Managing Director of Distributed Data Services at Charles Schwab, where he supported data and database technology across relational, semi-structured (NoSQL), and big data product areas. Prior to Schwab, Simeon served as VP of Operations at Centerpost Communication, and started a data management solution consulting practice.*

The financial industry can use data lakes in numerous ways to improve its services and earnings, while dealing with the many challenges of the current era. Compliance, marketing, and efficiency can all take leaps forward through use of a data lake.

Compliance is the most obvious area to benefit from the automation and standardization enabled by a data lake. A company in the extensively regulated industry of financial services undergoes audits on a frequent and regular basis, based on regulatory requirements and the number of product and business lines carried. Compliance and risk administration require massive, enterprise-wide efforts. A virtual data lake that spans all enterprise data assets, across all existing technology, is required to support these initiatives.

A related example of compliance is access attestation and certification, a common process documenting that no unauthorized access exists to systems and data, and tracking all existing and changing access entitlements. To ensure that all access is indeed authorized, and that the company has a validated record of such authorizations, relevant parties have to review and sign off on each and every credential type, technology, and vendor offering for every piece of existing managed data, and do such sign-offs on a regular basis (the attestation process). Each application vendor may have a specialized point solution for their product, and the platform vendors may offer solutions for the technology platform stacks behind multiple-application offerings, so a single enterprise-wide approach requires a unified view of all information—basically, a virtual data lake offering a consistent approach to collecting and comparing server, data asset type, and access level information. Although this is a massive undertaking, a number of factors are contributing to its increasing feasibility, among them:

- Cheap compute power
- The speed and ease of deploying modern infrastructure through use of virtualization, instrumentation, and automation
- Tremendous increases in the velocity of software development

Once data lake technology is in place, coupled with modern advances in analytics, numerous other benefits for financial services emerge. These include the ability to rapidly create, use, and manage solutions that provide fast insight based on enterprise information. Data lakes also enable better tracking of information usage, such as resource utilization oversight and technology asset management.

Marketing may benefit from a data lake that contains significant insight (internal and external) about the customers and their interaction with company offerings to understand and influence customer behavior. For example, in websites, marketing can measure when, why, and where (on the site and page) a customer is placing a trade; they can track activity prior to trade placement, number of clicks, percentage of trades aborted, the path a customer takes to the point of making a decision, activity within the browser, and more. Another example may be completion of a new account application: it's possible to investigate where potential customers stop, why, and for how long, as well as where and when they quit the process, and at what rate. This can help the company improve the application experience, increase revenue, and decrease direct costs involved in acquiring qualified leads that might have been lost in the account creation process. An example of the technology experience involves decisions about when to "time out" the customer: waiting too long can impair security, whereas timing out too soon can force the bad user experience of a re-login. By instrumenting the website and analyzing user behavior, the company can answer these and other questions using data instead of guesswork, allow the experience to be tailored, see the results, and make a significant impact on operational results and customer satisfaction.

In short, as the enterprise is becoming ever more instrumented, tracked, and measured, data lakes are making it possible to achieve higher levels of efficiency and effectiveness for business, IT, and regulatory compliance.

Data Lakes in the Insurance Industry

The author of the next piece is a big data visionary at a major insurance company. They shared their perspective but were unable to reveal their affiliation.

The foundational core for any insurance organization is its assessment of risk. Analysis and underwriting principles are based on assessing risks when issuing policies to customers and ensuring liquidity to honor claims. This kind of assessment is beneficial to the insurance policy requester as well. If individuals can assess their exposure to risk better, they can make the right decisions on the kind of coverage they need.

Efficiency for an insurance company is usually defined by its ability to suggest the right amount of coverage with an affordable premium based on an individual's financial background, along with issuing the policy in a timely fashion. I don't mention customer service since I consider it to be the backbone of any business: be it selling coffee or life insurance policies, you can't survive in today's competitive marketing environment if customers aren't happy with the services you provide.

Over a number of decades, the underwriting process has evolved at a much slower pace due to the lack of valuable varied data points in digital format, alongside the lack of inexpensive platforms for analysis. This has changed significantly in the past five years, with the advent of big data technologies running on cheap commodity hardware. Some industry players are curiously exploring new ways to rewrite underwriting rules using advanced predictive modeling techniques with capabilities to analyze massive amounts of disparate data elements. This latest set of technologies are helping to improve efficiency, reduce costs, provide a better framework for claims management, and detect fraud. The technologies are driving product innovation by presenting personalized products to consumers.

The other revolutionary piece of technology that is catching up and is being used as a vehicle for strategic change is the Internet of Things (IoT), with some of the insurance players embracing it and seeing its value. One key factor for this rapid adoption of big data analytics is the direct link it offers with connected devices, gathering data points and translating them to actionable analytical information.

The IoT, for instance, can benefit insurance providers as well as insured people in the areas of health. By monitoring one's health, vital signs, and general well-being, devices can satisfy an individual's desire for health-related metrics while providing valuable data to insurance companies to better analyze morbidity and mortality. This provides an opportunity to come up with innovative products catering to varied risk classes that may have previously been out of scope.

As exciting as these developments are, I personally believe that technology does not have a cataclysmic impact on an industry; instead, there is always a ripple effect. Once again, health provides a major example. There is a considerable focus (with billions of dollars of US government subsidies) on the digitization of healthcare and biometric records. Projects such as the Precision Medicine Initiative (*https://ghr.nlm.nih.gov/primer/precisionmedicine/initiative*) seek to build a unified, global platform of services between public and private companies to share customer medical records in a secure and efficient manner. This in itself in the near future will help bridge the gap between consumers, the healthcare industries, and insurance companies. The broader impact would be the introduction of products and services for the uninsured and those outside of the explored risk classes.

The sky is the limit here, and it would be amazing to look at the kind of trends this combined data set would provide for an entire city, community, state, country, or even whole continents—all in the quest to address the well-being of the human race.

Smart Cities

Brett Goldstein *is cofounder and managing partner of Ekistic Ventures, a group of urban problem solvers who are cultivating a portfolio of disruptive companies that bring new solutions to critical urban problems. He has served as CDO and CIO of the City of Chicago, and previously worked as a police officer and the head of analytics at the Chicago Police Department. In 2013, Brett curated and edited* Beyond Transparency: Open Data and the Future of Civic Innovation *(Code for America Press), an anthology on the potential of open data to reshape the relationship between residents and government.*

In addition to his work with Ekistic Ventures, Brett serves as a Senior Fellow and Special Advisor for Urban Science at the University of Chicago. He advises governments, universities, and major corporations around the globe on how to use data to better understand urban ecosystems.

We have heard for years that big data has the potential to usher in an era of "smart cities," where technology helps improve quality of life, reduce crime, and optimize spending and resources. However, the first step in building smart cities requires us to gather data into a data lake, optimizing this information for predictive analytics.

As CDO and, later, CIO of the City of Chicago, I drove the effort to "liberate" data across thousands of silos into a single data lake. Traditionally, data was backed up to tape and eventually deleted. By using inexpensive big data technology that supports flexible schemas—specifically, in our case, the MongoDB data store—the city was able to easily load raw data from all the different systems. It then scanned data sets for geospatial information and created a location index. The goal was to understand where data is and to have documented metadata, so that data can be used someday when the appropriate project presents itself.

Loading data from different systems into one system presented challenges ranging from getting access to the data to mapping different coordinate systems. Most city problems are hyperlocal, so it was critical to create the location index so that the data lake could answer questions such as:

- Where is a police car?
- Where are the potholes in a neighborhood?
- What is the exact location of a problematic building?

While knowing the locations of things is critical, data lakes can also be used for predictive analytics, such as predicting where riots are most likely to take place, which garbage cans will need repair, and how soon streets will develop potholes. The biggest win for Chicago's data lake came when it was used to create the situational awareness platform WindyGrid for the NATO operation—one of the biggest events in the history of Chicago.

The problems that cities face are not new, but practical solutions were hard to come by until the current generation of big data technology. Excel is a great tool, but it couldn't scale to handle the myriad information flowing in real time to today's smart cities. Relational systems could scale enough, but combining and harmonizing data from different systems was too difficult and expensive. With big data technology that provides inexpensive storage and flexible schemas, it is now possible to combine data across many different systems, in many different formats, and invest in extracting, harmonizing, and cleaning only the parts that are required for a specific project. The scalability of big data makes it possible to implement IoT projects with billions of GPS events, while the ability to store and process massive amounts of data affordably is a big deal for cities where budgets are strained. For example, the ability to reuse old machines and use disparate hardware to build Hadoop clusters inexpensively is an important cost-saving advance.

While we are still conquering the problem of storing and managing data, we are beginning to move from reactive to proactive analytics and responses. Preventive maintenance is one example: instead of repairing potholes after they form, we can prevent them by repairing the roads before potholes appear. Smart cities are becoming a reality with the rapid influx of sensor data—data on local climates, air pollution, service delivery, and more—and effective use of this data requires a hyperlocal approach to data and decisions. By starting with smarter data architecture, particularly data lakes, we can move into more sophisticated analytics and machine learning.

At the same time, cities must respect transparency and explainability, avoiding the allure of the black-box algorithm. It is important to not just trust data-driven results, but understand why they are being made. Only then can we move into the era of the truly smart city.

Big Data in Medicine

Opinder Bawa *is the Vice President for Information Technology and CIO at the University of San Francisco (USF), where he is responsible for institution-wide technology deployment and innovation. Previously, he was CTO at the University of California, San Francisco (UCSF), and CIO of the UCSF School of Medicine. In these roles he provided leadership in the planning and delivery of innovative technology solutions across research, education, and patient care. Opinder has also served as CTO at the Boston Medical Center and Senior Vice President at The SCO Group, where he led their worldwide software product lines and customer services. He holds a BCS from City University of New York and an MBA from the University of Phoenix.*

The process of transformation, in any industry, typically takes 30 to 50 years to complete, and so it will be for the life sciences. Each of these transformation periods is initiated by a catalyst. The 2010 Patient Protection and Affordable Care Act was the catalyst for the life sciences industry's most recent period of transformation. As proven repeatedly over the past half-century, technology will remain steadfast as the nucleus that enables such industry transformations, and such will be the case for our country's healthcare system.

Arguably one of the most important aspects of healthcare today and tomorrow will be clinical trials that identify promising new therapies, validate treatment protocols, and inform decisions to discontinue development efforts for less-promising drugs as quickly as possible. As the life sciences industry approaches the second decade of this metamorphosis and examines the impending landscape, it is clear that the successful conduct of future clinical trials and their outcomes will require technology that disrupts the industry or substantially increases the efficiency of its supply chain, in areas ranging from identifying and recruiting (and retaining) patients to collecting data, core analysis, and early interventions with potential subjects.

Cutting-edge data analytic solutions are enabling life sciences companies to automate the most critical part of the clinical trial supply-chain and thus achieve vital results in ways previously unimaginable. Data analysis can create the finely tuned engine needed to advance the collection, curation, analysis, and reporting of data generated by patients.

It's not a stretch to locate data collection and analytics at the heart of this transformative experience. If you review the work of Dr. William Bosl at USF, who has been able to identify autism (*http://bit.ly/2tbNT8c*) in infants as young as three months old, or research into identifying player concussions on the football field in real time, you have a front-row seat on the potential of data and analytics to change the world. Another research study (*https://www.health-eheartstudy.org/*) that reflects this potential is being led by Dr. Jeff Olgin at UCSF. It seeks to substantially improve the famed Framingham Heart Study by enrolling an unprecedented 100,000 patients, and is centered on the use of state-of-the-art technology to collect data and analytics.

As the life sciences industry moves into the second phase of its current technological transition, leading clinical trial companies striving for growth and success will further embrace the clinical trial supply chain solutions offered by data analytics industry leaders. These solutions will begin to put a spotlight on early interventions resulting from highly efficient clinical trials, and ultimately change the way healthcare is practiced overall.

Index

A

access control
  data provisioning using catalogs, 153
  for sensitive data, 148
  governing data access, 157-177
    authorization or access control, 158
    data sovereignty and regulatory compli-
      ance, 165-167
    deidentifying sensitive data, 162-165
    tag-based access policies, 159-162
  newer, more agile approach to, 111
  self-service management, 167-177
  traditional approaches to, 110
access control lists (ACLs), 159
Adtech, data science-driven projects for, 68
alerts and notifications, 94
Amazon Web Services (AWS), elastic cloud
  data lake offerings, 130
Amazon.com-style interface, 10
analysis
  and visualization of data, 19
  stages of, 15
    finding and understanding data, 16
analyst crowdsourcing tools, 17
analysts
  need for processed data, 10
  self-service data prep tools, use of, 99
analytics
  as IT service, 98
  birth of data warehousing, 28
  challenges of data warehouses, 76
  data preparation for exploratory analytics,
    115
  dimensional data modeling for, 77

limitations of data warehouse as historical
  repository, 79
new workflow in business intelligence analysis, 117
self-service, 99
tools for, in data warehousing, 46
annotation quality, 150
Apache projects (see listings throughout with
  Apache omitted in names)
artificial intelligence (AI), 1
  use in automated data discovery, 103
Atlas, 160, 162
authorization, 158
automation
  automated actions, 94
  automated data discovery, 103
  automated processing, moving to data lakes,
    71
  automated sensitive data detection, 148
  automated tagging and annotation of ele-
    ments in data sets, 146
  automatic tagging of sensitive data, 162
availability in cloud data lakes, 131

B

banking industry, 180
  (see also financial services industry)
  consumers, digitization, and data, changes
    from, 180
  shift to digital banking, 182-185
big data, 1
  data science, 55-59
  Hadoop, 50-55
  MapReduce, 49

using to further adoption of data lakes, 67-74
virtualization, 132
bimodal data governance, 121
bimodal IT, 73
blending data, 19
business analysts, 100-116
    establishing trust for data, 103
    finding and understanding data, 101-103
    provisioning data, 110-111
    workflow, 100
business intelligence (BI)
    as IT service vs. self-service, 98
    capture of lineage information, 152
    self-service trends, 116-120
        governance, 119
        IT moving from gatekeepers to shop-keepers, 118
        new analytic workflow, 117
business lineage (of data), 105, 153
    example, 107
business metadata, 143-145
    automated tagging of elements in data sets, 154
    folksonomies, 145
    glossaries, taxonomies, and ontologies, 143
    industry ontologies, 145

C

cardinality
    calculating in data profiling, 140
    in data quality rules, 104
cataloging data lakes, 137-156
    comparison of catalog tools, 155
    data inventory and cataloging in financial services, 189
    data provisioning, 153
    logical data management, 147-150
        data quality, 149
        sensitive data management and access control, 147-149
    organizing the data, 137
        business metadata, 143-145
        technical metadata, 138-143
    relating disparate data, 151-152
    tagging, 145-147
        automated, 146
    tools for building a catalog, 154
catalogs

challenges in building and maintaining, 101
self-service tools for, 99
using to identify redundant and unused data, 135
virtual data lakes and, 133
virtualization vs. catalog-based logical data lake, 22
cleaning data, 19
cloud data lakes, 20, 129-131
    limitations of, 130
Cloudera Navigator, 160
Cloudera, on-premises tool for Hadoop and HDFS, 53
columnar databases, 36
completeness
    challenges in a physical data lake, 134
    in logical data lakes, 21
complex event processing (CEP), 94
compute resources
    in AWS EC2 cloud data lakes, 130
    in on-premises data lakes, 129
conforming data, 78
conforming dimension, 37
consistency
    effects of a virtual data lake on, 134
    maintaining in deidentification of data, 126
contextual search, 11
cost-effectiveness
    advantages of merging multiple data lakes, 128
    cloud data lakes and, 131
    of big data technologies, 7, 70
    of Hadoop, 65
credit scoring, 185
critical data elements (CDEs), 101
crowdsourcing
    analyst crowdsourcing tools, 17
    of tribal knowledge from data analysts, 101
curation quality, 150
customers in financial services industry, learning about, 187

D

dashboards, 46, 93
data blending, 118
data federation (see federation)
data formats, 104
    format frequencies, 141
data integration tools (data warehouse), 37-41

data interpolation, 84
data lakes
    about, 2
    architecting, 121-136
        cloud data lakes, 129-131
        organizing the data lake, 121-127
        using multiple data lakes, 127-129
        virtual data lakes, 131-136
    architectures, 20-24
        in the public cloud, 20
        logical data lakes, 21-24
    creating, prerequisites for, 7-12
        platforms, 7
        right interface, 9
        saving data in native format, 8
    differences from traditional data storage,
        157
    loading data not in data warehouse, 83-89
        external data, 84-89
        IoT and other streaming data, 86
        raw data, 83
    roadmap to success, 12-20
        organizing the data lake, 14
        setting up for self-service, 15
        standing up the infrastructure, 13
    stages of maturity, 3
    starting, 63-74
        Hadoop, 63-66
        preventing data puddle proliferation, 66
        strategies using big data, 67-74
    target systems consuming data from, 92-95
        data warehouses, 93
        operational data stores, 93
        real-time applications and data products,
            93
data modeling
    change management for models in machine
        learning, 61
    in machine learning, 59
    tools used in data warehousing, 43
    tools, creating entity relationship diagrams,
        152
data oceans, 3
    cataloging data and making it available in,
        156
data ponds, 3
    defined, 6
    growing into a data lake, 83-89
    limitations of, 6

moving from data warehouse to, 79-83
    implementing slowly changing dimen-
        sions, 81
    resulting from creation of data warehouse
        schemas, 77
data preparation, 19
    preparing for analysis, 112
    situating in Hadoop, 113
    use cases, 114-116
        exploratory analytics and machine learn-
            ing, 115
        preparation for IT operationalization,
            115
        self-service automation for analytics or
            business applications, 115
data preparation tools, 19, 112
    self-service, 99
data profiling, 30, 104
    (see also data quality)
    hierarchical data, 141
    profiling tools, 42
    using to bridge gap between data and meta-
        data, 140
data puddles, 3
    defined, 5
    preventing proliferation of, 66
data quality (DQ), 104, 149
    and metadata flow in data warehouse eco-
        system, 30
    annotation quality, 150
    curation quality, 150
    data set quality, 150
    tag-based rules for, 149
    tools used for in data warehousing, 41
data science, 55-59
    exploratory nature of work, 157
    identifying high-visibility initiative in, 67
    using to further adoption of data lakes, 69
data scientists
    data lake as primary data source, 3
    need for raw data, 10
data sets, 94
    automating annotation of, 102
    data-set level granularity in technical lineage
        of data, 106
        example, 107
    quality of, 150
data silos, 9
data sovereignty, 20, 149

compliance with, 165-167
data swamps, 11
data transformations (see transformations)
data types, 104
data warehouse (DW) appliances, 36
data warehouse offloading, 6
data warehouses
    as historical storage for enterprise data, 75
    birth of, 28
    consuming data from data lakes, 93
    ecosystem, 29-47
        consuming data, 46
        data flow in, 30
        loading data, data integration tools,
            37-41
        metadata flow in, 30
        organizing and managing data, 41-46
        storing and querying data, 31-37
    essential functions, 76-79
        challenges in historical analysis, 77
        dimensional modeling for analytics, 77
        integrating data from different sources,
            78
        limitations as historical repository, 78
        preserving history using slowly changing
            dimensions, 78
    tools for creation and management of, 29
data wrangling, 113, 118
    (see also data preparation)
    in analytical workflow, 113
data, history of, 25
data-driven decision making, 2
database management systems (DBMSs), 26
databases
    birth of, 25-28
    columnar, 36
    consolidating and eliminating unnecessary
        ones, 135
    in-memory, 37
    NoSQL, 50
    virtual, 131
deidentifying sensitive data, 18, 126, 148,
    162-165
    access control and, 159
    deidentification or anonymization techni-
        ques, 164
    using explicit encryption, 163
    using transparent encryption, 163
denormalization of data

denormalized data models in data ware-
    houses, 32, 37
denormalizing attributes to preserve state,
    81
density (of data), 141
dev zone, 14
    (see also work zone)
dimensional data modeling, 76, 77
    dimension tables in star schemas, 32
    slowly changing dimensions, 33, 78
        implementing in a data pond, 81
    with ETL tools, 37
distributed joins, 23

E

education, data science-driven projects for, 68
Elastic Compute Cloud (EC2), 130
elastic computing, 129
Elastic MapReduce (EMR), 130
ELT (extract, load, transform), 38, 91
encryption
    explicit encryption of sensitive data, 163
    in data lakes, 157
    of data in sensitive zone, 126
    transparent encryption of sensitive data, 162
enterprise information integration (EII), 39
entity resolution and reconciliation, 90, 189
ETL (extract, transform, load)
    and data flow in data warehouse systems, 30
    and metadata flow in data warehouse eco-
        system, 30
    offloading, 5, 77
        expansion into a data lake, 91
        transforms, 70
    use in data warehouses to integrate data, 78
    vs. ELT, 38
ETL tools
    and data lineage, 105
    capture of lineage information, 152
    in data warehousing, 37
Excel, 19, 112
external data, 84-86

F

faceted search, 11
fact tables (star schema), 32
features (in machine learning), 60
federation, 39, 131
field names, 151

field-level granularity in technical lineage of data, 106, 108
files, variety handled by data lake platforms, 7
financial services industry, 180-192
    consumers, digitization, and data changing finance, 180
    data science-driven projects for, 68
    key processes in making use of the data lake, 188-190
        analytics and modeling, 190
        data inventory and cataloging, 189
        entity resolution and fuzzy matching, 189
        new opportunities offered by new data, 185-188
        saving the bank, 182-185
        value added by data lakes, 190
finding and understanding data, 16
fingerprinting, 17
folksonomies, 102, 145
foreign key, 27
    primary key-foreign key relationships, 141, 151
formats (see data formats)
fraud
    development of new detection and prevention in digital banking, 184
    increased exposure to in digital banking, 180
    new anti-fraud measures in financial services, 187
frictionless ingestion, 7, 65, 157
    tag-based data access policies and, 161
future-proofing with data lake platforms, 8
fuzzy matching and entity resolution, 189

G

glossaries (business), 143
gold (or production) zone, 14, 123
    division of data into folders and files, 124
governance
    bimodal data governance in self-service era, 121
    data governance tools in data warehousing, 45
    establishing central point of, 72
    governing data access, 157-177
        authorization or access control, 158

data sovereignty and regulatory compliance, 165-167
    deidentifying sensitive data, 162-167
    self-service access management, 167-177
    tag-based access policies, 159-162
in old days of data warehousing, 121
IT governing data for self-service business intelligence, 119
providing through a catalog, 23
reflecting data usage and user requirements, 14
sensitive data management and access control, 147-149

H

Hadoop, 50-55, 63-66
    benefits for long-term data storage and management, 65
    benefits for storage and analysis of historical data, 79
    cataloging data lakes, 154
    ecosystem of projects, 53
    ETL jobs, 91
    Hadoop File System (HDFS), 50
        and schema on read, 53
        support for Linux ACLs, 159
    MapReduce job and file storage, 51
    moving processing of non-tabular data to, 70
    on-premises fixed-size cluster, 129
    performing transformations, 90
    platform and ecosystem, sample architecture, 64
    situating data preparation in, 113
    Sqoop and Flume, 152
    tag-based security, 160
    using for ETL offloading, 92
harmonization of data, 90
HCatalog, 125
healthcare, data science-driven projects for, 68
hierarchical data, profiling, 141
historical data
    keeping in a data pond, 79-81
    limitations of data warehouse as repository for, 78
    preserving in data warehouses with slowly changing dimensions, 78
Hive, 64, 107-109
    partitioned tables, 80

Hortonworks
　Apache Ranger in Hadoop distribution, 160
　popular on-premises tools related to
　　Hadoop and HDFS, 53

I

in-memory databases, 37
industry ontologies, 145
industry-specific perspectives on data lakes,
　179-196
　big data in medicine, 195
　financial services industry, 180-192
　insurance industry, 192-193
　smart cities, 193-195
interfaces, choosing right interface for a data
　lake, 9
Internet of Things (IoT), 1
　data lakes for data from, 87
　insurance industry and, 193
IT
　analytics as IT service, 98
　and new trends in business intelligence, 116
　governing data for self-service business
　　intelligence, 119
　reducing load on with self-service analytics,
　　99
　role in new self-service business intelligence
　　analytics, 118
IT operationalization, data preparation for, 115

J

joins, 28
JSON files, profiling, 141

K

Kafka, 70
kappa architecture, 88

L

lambda architecture, 88, 89
landing zone, 14, 123
　(see also raw zone)
lineage (or provenance) of data, 105
　data set quality and, 150
　establishing, 152
　tracking down country of origin of data
　　sources, 165
log files, storing using Hadoop, 71

logical data lakes, 13, 21-24
　catalog-based, virtualization vs., 22
logical data management, 147-150
　data quality, 149
　sensitive data management and access con-
　　trol, 147-149

M

machine learning, 1, 56, 59-62
　change management for data models, 61
　data preparation for, 115
　explainability, 60
　in analyst crowdsourcing tools, 17
　in data preparation tools, 19
　use in automated data discovery, 103
manufacturing, data science-driven projects
　for, 68
MapR, 53
MapReduce, 49
　Amazon Elastic MapReduce (EMR), 130
　Spark and, 54
　using with Hadoop, 51, 64
massively parallel processing (MPP) systems,
　35
master data management (MDM) systems, 43
medicine, big data in, 195
metadata
　about data sets, providing through a catalog,
　　23
　business, 143-145
　　folksonomies, 145
　　glossaries, taxonomies, and ontologies,
　　　143
　　industry ontologies, 145
　catalog tools and, 154
　flow in data warehouse ecosystem, 30
　repositories in data warehousing, 44
　technical, 138-143
　　profiling hierarchical data, 141
　　profiling the data, 140
Microsoft Excel (see Excel)
model drift, 61
modeling and implementing decisions, 190
modeling data (see data modeling)
modularity (Hadoop), 65
multi-modal IT, 14
multiple data lakes, 127-129
　advantages of keeping data lakes separate,
　　127

advantages of merging the data lakes, 128

N
non-tabular data, storage in a data lake, 84
normalization, 26
    information lost in process, 83
normalized data models, 37
NoSQL databases, 50
notifications, 94

O
OLAP tools, 46
online analytical processing (OLAP) cubes, 99
ontologies, 143
    industry, 145
Oozie, 64
operational data stores, 93

P
partitions, use in data ponds, 79
performance optimization in data transformations, 90
permissions for files in data lakes, 159
platforms for data lakes, 7
predictive analytics, 59
    (see also machine learning)
preparation of data (see data preparation)
primary key, 27
    primary key-foreign key relationships, 141, 151
product information management (PIM) systems, 43
production zone, 14
    (see also gold zone)
profiling (see data profiling)
projects
    enterprise projects, advantages of merging data lakes for, 129
    project folders in work zone, 125
projects zone, 125
    (see also work zone)
provenance of data, 105
    establishing, 152
    tagging for, 165
provisioning data, 18, 110-111, 171-177
    in virtual data lakes, 133
    using catalogs, 23, 153

Q
quarantine zone, 148, 159
    using tags to quarantine files, 161

R
range (data), 104, 141
Ranger, 160
ranking and sorting data, 11
raw (or landing) zone, 14, 123
raw data, 2
    frictionless ingestion into a data lake, 9
    storing in a data lake, 83
real-time applications and data products, 93
real-time data lakes, 87
    best practices, 87
real-time or streaming processing, moving to big data system, 70
redundancy
    challenges in a physical data lake, 134
    elimination of, in virtual data lakes, 134
    in logical data lakes, 21
    reduction of data redundancy in merging data lakes, 128
referential integrity, 27, 42, 44, 104
    primary key-foreign key relationships, 151
regulatory requirements
    cloud data lakes and, 131
    compliance in financial services industry, value of data lakes, 190
    data ocean and, 156
    data sovereignty and regulatory compliance, 165-167
    keeping data lakes separate because of, 127
    respecting for sensitive data, 149
related data, finding and estimating usefulness of combining, 151
relational database management systems (RDBMSs), 26
    normalization of data, 27
relational databases
    big data platforms vs., 6
    catalog tools, 154
    relations, primary and foreign keys, and normalization, 26
reports, 46
Resilient Distributed Dataset (RDD), 54
retail, data science-driven projects for, 68
risk analytics in financial services industry, 187

S

sandboxes, 5
scalability
    enabled by big data technology, 1, 7
    Hadoop, 65
schema on read, 7
    in Hadoop File System (HDFS), 53
schema on write, 7
schemas
    creation for data warehouses, 77
    design for operational databases, 43
    in relational database management systems,
      26
    loose coupling or schema on read in
      Hadoop, 65
    maintenance problems in virtual databases,
      132
    virtual schema in data warehousing, 39
searches
    contextual search, 11
    faceted search, 11
selectivity (of data), 104, 140
self-service
    analytics with raw data, 2
    beginnings of, 98-100
    data access management, 159, 167-177
    drive for self-service data and birth of data-
      bases, 25-28
    for business analysts, 100-116
    setting up the data lake for, 15
    trends in business intelligence, 116-120
    value of, 97
sensitive data
    and authorization or access control for, 158
    automatic tagging of, 162
    deidentifying, 162
    detection of, challenges posed to analysts,
      161
    management and access control, 148-149
sensitive zone, 14, 125-127
    best practices in structuring, 126
    deidentification of data in, 126
service-level agreements (SLAs), 14
shaping data, 19
shredding, 142
single sign-on (SSO), 158
smart cities, 193-195
snapshots, using to preserve state, 82
Spark, 54, 64

SQL (Structured Query Language), 26
    Hive interface to Hadoop data, 80, 107
    view of each file in gold zone of data lake,
      124
staging zone, 123
    (see also landing zone; raw zone)
standard deviation, 141
star schemas, 32, 77
    slowly changing dimensions, 33
    tables in simple star schema, 32
state information
    denormalizing attributes to preserve state,
      81
    preserving state using snapshots, 82
stewardship of data, 102, 110
stitching (lineage), 153
storage
    in cloud data lake with AWS Simple Storage
      Service (S3), 130
    in on-premises data lakes, 129
streaming data
    best practices for real-time data lakes, 87
    loading into a data lake, 86
streaming processing, moving to big data sys-
    tem, 70
subject matter experts (SMEs), 98
    crowdsourcing knowledge of, 102
supervised learning, 59
system engineering, 57

T

tag-based data quality rules, 149
tag-based security, 148
tagging, 145-147
    automated tagging in sensitive data detec-
      tion, 148
    for provenance of data, 165
tags
    annotation quality, 150
    curation quality, 150
    data set quality and, 150
    tag-based data access policies, 159-162
    using in determining usefulness of joining
      data sets, 152
target systems, consuming data from data lake,
    92-95
    data warehouses, 93
    operational data stores, 93
    real-time applications and data products, 93

---

taxonomies, 143
technical lineage (of data), 106
    example, 107
    field-level technical lineage, example of, 108
    granularity, 106
    transformation representations, 106
technical metadata, 138-143
    profiling hierarchical data, 141
    profiling the data, 140
Teradata, 70
transformations, 90-92, 105
    adding detail to data set-level transforma-
        tion nodes, 108
    normalized representation, 106
    original representation, 106
transparent encryption, 163
tribal knowledge, 17, 101
trust, establishing for data, 103-110
    data quality, 104
    lineage or provenance, 105
    stewardship, 110
trustworthiness, 150

U

understanding the data, 17
unsupervised learning, 60
usage (of data), determining useful joins from,
    152
user folders in work zone, 125

V

virtual data lakes, 131-136

big data virtualization, 132
    eliminating redundancy, 134
    using data federation, 131
virtualization
    data virtualization tools, 39
    vs. catalog-based logical data lake, 22
visualization of data, 19
visualization tools, self-service, 99
Vs of big data (volume, variety, velocity, and
    veracity), 1

W

work zone, 14, 125
    project and user folders, 125

X

Xerox PARC model, 69
XPATH expressions, 142

Y

Yarn, 64

Z

zones, 10
    organization of data lake into, 14, 122
        gold (or production) zone, 123
        landing or raw zone, 123
        sensitive zone, 125-127
        quarantine zone, 159

About the Author

Alex Gorelik has spent the last 30 years developing and deploying leading-edge data-related technologies and helping large companies like BAE (Eurofighter), Unilever, IBM, Royal Caribbean, Kaiser, Goldman Sachs, and dozens of others to solve their thorniest data-related problems.

As one of the founders and CTO of an ETL company (Acta, designated a visionary by Gartner and acquired by Business Objects/SAP), and having done several years of hands-on consulting on large analytic and data warehousing projects, Alex has firsthand experience with the development of data warehouses. His second company, Exeros (acquired by IBM), focused on helping large enterprises understand and rationalize their data. As a Distinguished Engineer at IBM and as SVP and GM at Informatica, he led the development and adoption of Hadoop technology. Finally, as Entrepreneur in Residence at Menlo Ventures and later, founder and CTO of Waterline, he has worked with some of the leading experts in managing big data lakes and doing data science at companies such as Google and LinkedIn, large banks, government agencies, and other large enterprises. Alex holds a BSCS from Columbia and an MSCS from Stanford, and lives in San Francisco with his wife and four kids.

Colophon

The animal on the cover of *The Enterprise Big Data Lake* is a red-breasted merganser (*Mergus serrator*), a sawbilled duck found throughout North America, Europe, and Asia. It is migratory, traveling north to freshwater lakes and rivers for spring breeding season and south to coastal areas for the winter. The name *serrator* refers to the serrated edge of the bird's beak, which helps it grip the fish, frogs, aquatic insects, and crustaceans that make up its diet. It is adept at diving and swimming underwater to hunt for food.

Red-breasted mergansers are sexually dimorphic: males have the aforementioned red chest, as well as a white neck, dark green head, black back, and a white belly. Females (pictured on the cover of this book) have more subdued coloring with a reddish head and grey body. Both sexes have a spiky crest of feathers. These ducks grow to be about 20–24 inches long. In breeding season, males compete by holding courtship displays in front of multiple females, and females build nests on the ground near the water.

A red-breasted merganser holds the record for the fastest flight speed of any duck species: 100 miles per hour (while trying to evade an airplane).

Many of the animals on O'Reilly covers are endangered; all of them are important to the world. To learn more about how you can help, go to *animals.oreilly.com*.

The cover illustration is by Karen Montgomery, based on a black and white engraving from *Meyers Kleines Lexicon*. The cover fonts are Gilroy Semibold and Guardian Sans. The text font is Adobe Minion Pro; the heading font is Adobe Myriad Condensed; and the code font is Dalton Maag's Ubuntu Mono.

O'REILLY®

There's much more
where this came from.

Experience books, videos, live online
training courses, and more from O'Reilly
and our 200+ partners—all in one place.

Learn more at oreilly.com/online-learning